Combating London's Criminal Class

Combating London's Criminal Class

A State Divided, 1869–95

Matthew Bach

BLOOMSBURY ACADEMIC
LONDON • NEW YORK • OXFORD • NEW DELHI • SYDNEY

BLOOMSBURY ACADEMIC
Bloomsbury Publishing Plc
50 Bedford Square, London, WC1B 3DP, UK
1385 Broadway, New York, NY 10018, USA
29 Earlsfort Terrace, Dublin 2, Ireland

BLOOMSBURY, BLOOMSBURY ACADEMIC and the Diana logo
are trademarks of Bloomsbury Publishing Plc

First published in Great Britain 2020
This paperback edition published in 2022

Copyright © Matthew Bach, 2020

Matthew Bach has asserted his right under the Copyright, Designs
and Patents Act, 1988, to be identified as Author of this work.

Cover image:
Criminal Types London 1867 (© Chronicle / Alamy Stock Photo)

All rights reserved. No part of this publication may be reproduced or transmitted in any form or by any means, electronic or mechanical, including photocopying, recording, or any information storage or retrieval system, without prior permission in writing from the publishers.

Bloomsbury Publishing Plc does not have any control over, or responsibility for, any third-party websites referred to or in this book. All internet addresses given in this book were correct at the time of going to press. The author and publisher regret any inconvenience caused if addresses have changed or sites have ceased to exist, but can accept no responsibility for any such changes.

Every effort has been made to trace copyright holders and to obtain their permissions for the use of copyright material. The publisher apologizes for any errors or omissions and would be grateful if notified of any corrections that should be incorporated in future reprints or editions of this book.

A catalogue record for this book is available from the British Library.

A catalog record for this book is available from the Library of Congress.

Library of Congress Cataloging-in-Publication Data
Names: Bach, Matthew, author.
Title: Combating London's criminal class : a state divided, 1869-1895 / Matthew Bach.
Description: London, UK ; New York, NY : Bloomsbury Academic, 2020. |
Series: History of crime, deviance and punishment |
Includes bibliographical references and index.
Identifiers: LCCN 2020015227 (print) | LCCN 2020015228 (ebook) | ISBN 9781350156210 (hardback) | ISBN 9781350156227 (ebook) | ISBN 9781350156234 (epub)
Subjects: LCSH: Crime prevention–England–London–History–19th century. | Criminals--England–London–History–19th century.
Classification: LCC HV7434.G72 L6633 2020 (print) | LCC HV7434.G72 (ebook) | DDC 364.409421/09034--dc23
LC record available at https://lccn.loc.gov/2020015227
LC ebook record available at https://lccn.loc.gov/2020015228

ISBN:	HB:	978-1-3501-5621-0
	PB:	978-1-3501-9717-6
	ePDF:	978-1-3501-5622-7
	eBook:	978-1-3501-5623-4

Series: History of Crime, Deviance and Punishment

Typeset by Integra Software Services Pvt. Ltd.

To find out more about our authors and books visit www.bloomsbury.com
and sign up for our newsletters.

For Phoebe, who is such a joy

Contents

List of Tables	viii
Acknowledgements	ix
Introduction	1
1 The Origins of the *Habitual Criminals Act 1869*: 'Our Wretched Little Bill'	29
2 Repeal and Reintroduction: Parliamentary Debate and the Question of Liberty	61
3 Registering Habitual Criminals: A 'Salutary Control'?	87
4 Police Supervision of the Criminal Class: A Spy System	115
5 Sentencing Repeat Offenders: Leniency and Severity in the Late Nineteenth Century	139
Conclusion	167
Bibliography	176
Index	188

Tables

3.1	The use and success of the registry in London, 1870–3	94
3.2	Attendances at the Convict Supervision Office, 1890–4	100
3.3	Search forms filed at the Convict Supervision Office, 1891–4	100
3.4	Identifications made at the Convict Supervision Office, 1890–4	101
3.5	Prisoners identified in Holloway by Criminal Investigations Officers and Warders as having been previously convicted, 1883–93	106
3.6	The rate of prosecution of habitual criminals in various English cities, 1871–90	112
4.1	People convicted within the Metropolitan Police District and sentenced to a period of police supervision, 1870–3	123
4.2	Habitual criminals apprehended in the Metropolitan Police District for failure to report, 1888–94	132
4.3	Licence-holders, supervisees and expirees apprehended for fresh offences, 1888–94	133
5.1	Persons convicted within the Metropolitan and City of London Police Districts of crime, with sentences and proportion of all convictions, 1870–3	147
5.2	Sentences of penal servitude in London, including as a percentage of all those convicted, 1870–3 and 1893–5	157

Acknowledgements

While writing this book I have received outstanding support from numerous staff at the University of Melbourne. First and foremost, my thanks must go to the incomparable Professor Elizabeth Malcolm. This book is based upon research I carried out for my PhD thesis, of which Elizabeth was the principal supervisor. Her wise counsel and expertise have been of more worth to me than I can say. In addition, Dr Una McIlvenna provided me with much help. As one of my assistant supervisors, Una read late drafts of my PhD and provided me with invaluable advice. She was also incredibly helpful as I sought publication of this work. Associate Professor Michael Arnold read many early drafts of my work and gave me considerable encouragement and guidance.

I should thank staff at various other institutions. On my many visits to the National Archives I was aided immensely by knowledgeable and passionate staff members. The same was true of my time spent at the British Library. Meanwhile, the interlibrary loan staff of the Bodleian Library, Oxford, rendered me vital aid. Back at the University of Melbourne, I received excellent support from the team at the Baillieu Library. At Bloomsbury, Maddie Holder and Abigail Lane have been ever encouraging and helpful. At this point is it customary for authors to thank their partners. Oftentimes this is done (by male authors in particular), apologetically, for a partner's sufferance during the author's period of research and writing. The impression I normally get is that of the little wife keeping the home fires burning. Well, the painting of such a picture would do a great injustice to my wonderful wife, Amy, who is caring, strong and smart. So I will thank her, instead, for her unfailing love and constant encouragement, and for choosing me all those years ago, much to my surprise and glee.

Introduction

The criminal classes … is [sic], in fact, a great army – an army making war on society, and it is necessary that society should for its own defence make war upon them … Now, the question that presents itself is this – How are we to deal with this vast mass of criminals – with this great army of crime with which we have to contend?[1]

(The Earl of Kimberley, Liberal peer, 26 Feb. 1869)

In 1869 the new Liberal government of the United Kingdom, led by William Gladstone, responded to this question with an extraordinary set of measures. The *Habitual Criminals Act 1869* introduced a system of police supervision in the community for specified repeat offenders and a central registry containing information regarding all so-called habitual criminals. Surveillance, the government hoped, would lead to a decrease in crime. The registry was intended to aid police supervision and to ensure magistrates and judges had all relevant information about offenders before them at the point of sentencing, leading to longer prison terms. The legislation, which was re-enacted in 1871 with numerous alterations, was remarkable for its repressive potential. It also represented a stunning reversal of the parliament's long-held position on police supervision, which it had found to be a repugnant French innovation. The threat posed by repeat offenders was apparently so great that individual liberty, a long-cherished British value, was now relegated to a position of secondary importance. Historians have offered differing views about the motivation for and effects of mid- and late Victorian efforts to control elements of the working class that were deemed a threat to law and order. However, the genesis and impact of the only two pieces of legislation that were specifically designed to combat the so-called criminal class are little, and incorrectly, understood. This book is an attempt to right this wrong. It analyses why the legislation was put in place and then re-enacted so soon after.

---

[1] The Earl of Kimberley (Liberal), 194 *Parl. Deb.*, HC (3rd ser.), col. 338 (26 Feb. 1869).

Then, it seeks to explore the extent to which the key aims of the government were achieved in London's Metropolitan Police District in the period up to 1895.

The legislation applied throughout the UK. Yet London was the focal point of many anxieties regarding crime and the activities of a criminal class.[2] Thus this work focuses solely on the capital. Concerns about a criminal class were fostered by published statistics estimating its size and because of the gradual ending of transportation to Australia, which occurred between 1840 and 1868. These concerns centred on London because of the opportunities to hide criminal activity presented by a city of its size and character, its great wealth, and a major media-inspired panic regarding crime in the capital in 1862. The 1851 census revealed that London's population was 2,362,236. This figure grew significantly over the coming decades, reaching 4,231,431 in 1891. The commissioner of the Metropolitan Police Force consistently noted that such a large, and growing, population centre presented great opportunities for criminals to evade the police.[3] Anonymity was made easier by the physical layout of the city. In 1869 the journalist James Greenwood listed various 'vile nests' – often called rookeries – that appeared almost to have been designed for the concealment of crime.[4] Other contemporary sources also noted that London appeared to be a 'maze'.[5] The capital, in addition, was the seat of much wealth. According to the social commentator Henry Solly, this made it a magnet for what he labelled 'the rough'.[6] In short, evidence reveals significant concern that London was, in Gareth Stedman Jones's words, 'the Mecca of the dissolute'.[7] The impact of the 1869 and 1871 legislation in the City of London, which was policed by a small and separate force, is not considered here. This is because there is limited data for London's financial and business centre, which covers only slightly more than one square mile.

[2] S. J. Stevenson, 'The "Habitual Criminal" in Nineteenth-Century England: Some Observations on the Figures', *Urban History*, vol. 13 (May 1986), pp. 37–60; Donald Thomas, *The Victorian Underworld*, London: Hodder and Stoughton, 1998, p. 3; Lynda Nead, *Victorian Babylon: People, Streets and Images in Nineteenth-Century London*, New Haven and London: Yale University Press, 2000, pp. 3–10, 71–2.
[3] For representative comments see the *Report of the Commissioner of Police of the Metropolis*, [C 150] HC 1870, xxxvi, p. 2; *Report of the Commissioner of Police of the Metropolis*, [C 358] HC 1871, xxviii, p. 3; *Report of the Commissioner of Police of the Metropolis*, [C 652] HC 1872, xxx, p. 3; *Report of the Commissioner of Police of the Metropolis*, [C 839] HC 1873, xxxi, p. 1.
[4] James Greenwood, *The Seven Curses of London*, London: Stanley Rivers and Co., 1869, p. 68.
[5] Nead, *Victorian Babylon*, p. 4; Jon Mee, *The Cambridge Introduction to Charles Dickens*, Cambridge: Cambridge University Press, 2010, p. 56.
[6] Henry Solly, *A Few Thoughts on How to Deal with the Unemployed Poor of London, and with Its 'Roughs' and Criminal Classes*, n.p.: Society of Arts, 1868.
[7] Gareth Stedman Jones, *Outcast London: A Study in the Relationship between the Classes in Victorian Society*, Oxford: Clarendon Press, 1971, p. 12. Also see Henry Mayhew and John Binny, *The Criminal Prisons of London: And Scenes of Prison Life*, London: Griffin, Bohn, and Co., 1862, pp. 3–7; *Times*, 8 Nov. 1866, p. 7.

A significant press-inspired panic regarding violent crime in London by repeat offenders in 1862 heightened these anxieties.[8] Between midnight and one o'clock on the morning of 17 July 1862 James Pilkington, MP for Blackburn, was attacked by two men while en route to the Reform Club following a late sitting of the House of Commons. This attack was widely reported as an example of garotting, in which the victim is attacked from behind and incapacitated by pressure from the assailant's arm upon the throat. For the remainder of 1862 many allegedly similar attacks were reported in London's press, supposedly perpetrated by repeat offenders. *The Times*, for example, argued in a leading article on 14 August 1862 that such attacks were being carried out by members of the 'criminal class' who were building up in London due to the cessation of transportation to Australia.[9] *The Times*, a three-penny morning newspaper, was widely read among the middle and upper classes and especially politicians. As Richard Shannon has said, it was London's 'heavyweight' newspaper.[10] These 'brutal ruffians', argued the liberal *Daily News* in another leading article on 4 December 1862, were determined to 'attack society'.[11] The published statistics of crime seemed to support the idea that violent crime was increasing in London. In the Metropolitan Police District the recorded number of offences against the person accompanied by violence, other than sexual assaults, rose from 191 in the year up to 29 September 1861 to 345 over the next twelve months, which took in the first two and a half months following the attack on Pilkington.[12] However, as Rob Sindall has noted, such figures 'are open to the interpretation that they were influenced by the reporting of the initial deviance and the subsequent escalation of police activity'.[13] It is also possible that people felt encouraged to report violent crimes due to the very significant attention given to such

---

[8] Barry Godfrey, David Cox and Stephen Farrall, *Serious Offenders: An Historical Study of Habitual Criminals*, London: Oxford University Press, 2010, p. 12; Peter Bartrip, 'Public Opinion and Law Enforcement: The Ticket-of-Leave Scares in Mid-Victorian Britain', in Victor Bailey (ed.), *Policing and Punishment in Nineteenth Century Britain*, London: Croom Helm, 1981, pp. 150–81; Jennifer Davis, 'The London Garotting Panic of 1862: A Moral Panic and the Creation of a Criminal Class in Mid-Victorian England', in V. A. C. Gatrell, Bruce Lenman and G. Parker (eds.), *Crime and the Law: The Social History of Crime in Western Europe since 1500*, London: Europa Publications, 1980, pp. 190–213.

[9] *Times*, 14 Aug. 1862, p. 8.

[10] Richard Shannon, *The Age of Disraeli, 1868–1881: The Rise of Tory Democracy*, London and New York: Longman, 1992, p. 128.

[11] *Daily News*, 2 Dec. 1862, p. 4.

[12] *Judicial Statistics. 1862. England and Wales. Part 1. Police-Criminal Proceedings-Prisons*, [C 3025] HC 1863, lvi, p. 16; *Judicial Statistics. 1863. England and Wales. Part 1. Police-Criminal Proceedings-Prisons*, [C 3370] HC 1864, lvii, p. 16.

[13] Rob Sindall, *Street Violence in the Nineteenth Century: Media Panic or Real Danger?* Leicester: Leicester University Press, 1990, p. 53.

offences in the press. Moreover, the statistics provided 'no link' between the apparent increase in crime and repeat offenders.[14] Nonetheless, it seems clear that press reports caused a significant panic about crime in London, perpetrated by a so-called criminal class.[15]

Given the evidence that many mid-Victorians saw London as the centre of recidivist crime, it has been chosen as the site of this study. Among mid- and late Victorians, as S. J. Stevenson has claimed, there was a 'popular and enduring image of a "criminal class" largely concentrated in London'.[16] I have selected the time span because of the significant changes to the mechanisms for the identification of repeat offenders that occurred in 1895 as new approaches, including fingerprinting, were embraced.[17] Up until that time the key measures of the 1871 legislation were in force, albeit having undergone several alterations. Now, what of the relevant historical literature?

What do other scholars have to say about the habitual criminals' legislation of 1869 and 1871, which very significantly altered the manner in which recidivists were to be dealt with? In short, not much. This point has been made most recently by Barry Godfrey, David Cox and Steve Farrall. Specifically regarding the acts of 1869 and 1871 they ask, 'What was the impact of these on the lives of "habitual" offenders?' And what were the 'eventual outcomes'?[18] They conclude that as yet these questions cannot be adequately answered. Seventeen years earlier Martin Wiener also highlighted the need to look more closely at these two pieces of legislation, saying that they bring 'into sharp relief a coercively activist face of Victorian liberalism long ignored by historians'.[19] Histories of crime in Victorian England have been criticized for not containing 'discussion of the impact of the habitual criminals' legislation of 1869 and 1871'. Thus, one historian has called for 'additional ... tests' of the legislation's effect.[20] This book is an effort to provide one.

---

[14] Bartrip, 'Public Opinion and Law Enforcement', p. 162.
[15] Godfrey, Cox and Farrall, *Serious Offenders*, p. 12; Bartrip, 'Public Opinion and Law Enforcement', pp. 150–81; Davis, 'The London Garotting Panic of 1862', pp. 190–213.
[16] Stevenson, 'The "Habitual Criminal" in Nineteenth-Century England', p. 38. Also see Thomas, *The Victorian Underworld*, p. 3.
[17] Stefan Petrow, *Policing Morals: The Metropolitan Police and the Home Office 1870–1914*, Oxford: Clarendon Press, 1995, p. 91.
[18] Barry Godfrey, David Cox and Stephen Farrall, 'Persistent Offenders in the North West of England, 1880–1940: Some Critical Research Questions', *Crimes and Misdemeanours*, vol. 1, no. 1 (2007), p. 85.
[19] Martin Wiener, *Reconstructing the Criminal: Culture, Law and Policy in England, 1830–1914*, Cambridge: Cambridge University Press, 1990, p. 151.
[20] Victor Bailey, 'Review of V. A. C. Gatrell, Bruce Lehman and Geoffrey Parker' (eds.), *Crime and the Law: The Social History of Crime in Western Europe since 1500*, London: Europa Publications, 1980, *Social History*, vol. 7, no. 3 (Oct. 1982), p. 349.

Yet there is a small body of literature directly relevant to the suite of measures introduced in 1869 and 1871 to combat the criminal class. Some work has been carried out concerning the reasons for the implementation of the Liberal government's habitual criminals' legislation. The consensus regarding the genesis of the *Habitual Criminals Act 1869*, it appears, is that the legislation was brought about by a media-inspired panic, similar to that which occurred in 1862, regarding violent crime and garotting in particular.[21] For example, in reference to the parliamentary debate on the *Habitual Criminals Bill 1869*, in which the government denied the existence of panic, W. G. Runciman has argued that 'this could be interpreted, without undue cynicism, as disavowal of the kind that gives the game away'.[22] Pete King, in agreement that the government was responding to public sentiment, has said that it rode 'on the back of a media-created crime wave'.[23] And Drew D. Gray has said, even more explicitly, that 'as a result of the garotting panic the government passed the Habitual Criminals Act in 1869'.[24] These historians all use Stanley Cohen's framework of moral panic, which he defines as a period when public anxiety serves to amplify deviance and promote new measures for its control.[25] In this case anxiety was apparently caused by an increase in the reporting of violent crime, especially in *The Times*.[26] In keeping with Cohen's model, it is argued that the government responded with repressive legislation.

However, there is scant evidence to support the notion that fear of crime increased in the period directly before the introduction of the *Habitual Criminals Bill* in February 1869. Why, then, was the legislation introduced? One factor that demands close examination was the advocacy of a pressure group, the Social Science Association (SSA). The association, a forum for the discussion of social questions, held its first congress in Birmingham in July 1857. The president, Lord Brougham, explained that the purpose of the association was 'to aid legislation by preparing measures' and 'stimulating the legislature to adopt them'.[27] Since

---

[21] W. G. Runciman, *Very Different, but Much the Same: The Evolution of English Society since 1714*, Oxford: Oxford University Press, 2015, p. 69; Pete King, 'Moral Panics and Violent Street Crime 1750–2000: A Comparative Perspective', in Barry Godfrey, Clive Emsley and Graeme Dunstall (eds.), *Comparative Histories of Crime*, Cullompton: Willan, 2003, p. 57; Drew D. Gray, *London's Shadows: The Dark Side of the Victorian City*, London: Continuum, 2010, p. 57.
[22] Runciman, *Very Different, but Much the Same*, p. 69.
[23] King, 'Moral Panics and Violent Street Crime', p. 57.
[24] Gray, *London's Shadows*, p. 57.
[25] Stanley Cohen, *Folk Devils and Moral Panics: The Creation of the Mods and Rockers*, 3rd ed., London: Routledge, 2002 (first published in 1972), p. 7.
[26] King, 'Moral Panics and Violent Street Crime', p. 57.
[27] Lord Brougham, 'Inaugural Address', in *Transactions of the National Association for the Advancement of Social Science, 1857*, London: John W. Parker and Son, 1858, p. 23.

its inception the SSA had consistently, and with much success, advocated penal reform, including the key provisions contained in the *Habitual Criminals Bill 1869*: police supervision and registration of repeat offenders. Consequently, and due to its strong relationship with the new home secretary, Lawrence Goldman and Michael Melling argue that the SSA played a role in the introduction of the *Habitual Criminals Bill 1869*.[28] Their work invites serious questions about the adequacy of the framework of moral panic in explaining the genesis of the Gladstone government's habitual criminals' legislation. In answering these questions this book makes a significant and original contribution to our understanding of the driving forces behind nineteenth-century penal policy.

A fascinating re-evaluation has recently taken place regarding the role of the Metropolitan Police Force as an instrument of social control.[29] A central finding of this work is that the Metropolitan Police Force was both unwilling and unable, largely due to the actions of magistrates, to fully implement legislation that targeted elements of the working class, such as the *Habitual Criminals Act 1869* and the *Prevention of Crime Act 1871*. However, the literature concerning the impacts of this legislation is dominated by scholars who utilize social control interpretations to determine its impacts. Key to these interpretations is the belief that social order is maintained through various means, which include legal systems, police forces and prisons, and social institutions such as the family and religion.[30] Notwithstanding differences of approach and emphasis, numerous historians have used social control interpretations to argue that the legislation, while flawed, was an oppressive tool that was part of a broader apparatus of control.[31] But others have argued that British police forces cannot be seen as

---

[28] Lawrence Goldman, *Science, Reform and Politics in Victorian Britain: The Social Science Association 1857-1886*, Cambridge: Cambridge University Press, 2002, p. 3; Michael Melling, 'Cleaning House in a Suddenly Closed Society: The Genesis, Brief Life and Ultimate Death of the Habitual Criminals Act, 1869', *Osgoode Hall Law Journal*, vol. 21, no. 2 (Sept. 1983), p. 318.

[29] Terence Stanford, *The Metropolitan Police 1850-1914: Targeting, Harassment and the Creation of a Criminal Class*, unpublished doctoral thesis, University of Huddersfield, 2007, pp. 91-198, 240-72; Stephen Inwood, 'Policing London's Morals: The Metropolitan Police and Popular Culture, 1829-1850', *London Journal*, vol. 15, no. 2 (1990), p. 129.

[30] A. P. Donajgrodzki (ed.), *Social Control in Nineteenth Century Britain*, London: Croom Helm, 1977, p. 9.

[31] Martin Wiener, 'The March of Penal Progress?' *Journal of British Studies*, vol. 26, no. 1 (Jan. 1887), pp. 84, 95; Petrow, *Policing Morals*, pp. 51, 82; Godfrey, Cox and Farrall, *Serious Offenders*, p. xii; Douglas Hay, 'Crime and Justice in Eighteenth and Nineteenth Century England', *Crime and Justice*, vol. 2 (1980), p. 66; Clive Emsley, *Crime and Society in England: 1750-1900*, 2nd ed., London: Longman, 1996, pp. 172-4.

willing and able elements of such an apparatus.[32] Concerning the Gladstone government's habitual criminals' legislation in London, both positions cannot be correct.

The effectiveness of this legislation was first investigated in any detail by Leon Radzinowicz and Roger Hood, who utilized a 'whiggish' interpretation to determine its impact.[33] The 1869 and 1871 legislation, they claim, went against the grain of criminal legislation that was increasingly mitigating the severity of the legal code. For example, in 1810 there were 222 capital offences, yet following a gradual process that culminated in the six criminal law consolation acts of 1861, this number had been reduced to just four. Radzinowicz and Hood mount a convincing case that, in very large measure, the acts of 1869 and 1871 failed in their efforts to ensure that so-called habitual criminals were always identified as such and closely supervised in the community by the police. This failure was, predominantly, due to flaws in the drafting of the legislation and the incapacity of police forces to effectively monitor such a large group of people.[34] Indeed, repressive legislation that went against the march of progress, they claim, was always likely to fail.[35] They point, for example, to the failure to include any mechanism to force those under supervision to report themselves to police in the initial legislation. They also argue that once monthly reporting was introduced by the 1871 act for male offenders, London's magistrates interpreted the relevant clause in such a way as to make it inoperative until legislative change in 1879. Under section 20 of the *Prevention of Crime Act 1871* the chief officer of police, to whom a supervisee was to report, was interpreted by London's magistrates to mean the commissioner himself. This meant that London's magistrates would only convict a defendant for failure to report on the sworn testimony of the commissioner. Supervision was, as a result, a 'dead letter' in London.[36] Women were excused from reporting as the government presumably believed they did not pose as great a risk to society as male offenders.[37] Instead, female criminals

---

[32] A. L. Beier, 'Identity, Language, and Resistance in the Making of the Victorian "Criminal Class": Mayhew's Convict Revisited', *Journal of British Studies*, vol. 44, no. 3 (Jul. 2005), p. 515; Howard Taylor, 'Rationing Crime: The Political Economy of Criminal Statistics since the 1850s', *Economic History Review*, vol. 51, no. 3 (Aug. 1998), pp. 578–9; Stanford, *The Metropolitan Police*, pp. 91–198, 240–72; Inwood, 'Policing London's Morals', p. 129.
[33] Leon Radzinowicz and Roger Hood, 'Incapacitating the Habitual Criminal: The English Experience', *Michigan Law Review*, vol. 78, no. 8 (Aug. 1980), pp. 1305–89; Wiener, 'The March of Penal Progress?' pp. 84, 95.
[34] Radzinowicz and Hood, 'Incapacitating the Habitual Criminal', pp. 1343, 1345–52.
[35] Ibid., pp. 1344–9.
[36] Ibid., p. 1345.
[37] For the greater threat that male criminals were believed to represent see Martin Wiener, *Men of Blood: Violence, Manliness and Criminal Justice in Victorian England*, Cambridge: Cambridge University Press, 2004, pp. 123–69.

in London were often referred to one of the city's women's refuges on their release from prison. These institutions, such as the Elizabeth Fry Refuge for the Reception of Female Prisoners, attempted to assist prisoners in their efforts to re-enter respectable society through a variety of means, including the learning of skills that could aid employment.[38]

The measures included in the 1869 and 1871 legislation to aid the identification of repeat offenders were also flawed. Initially, the compilation of the habitual criminals' register was carried out in strict accordance with the wording of the act. Consequently, all those convicted 'of crime' were listed.[39] By 1874 a huge number of criminals, 117,568 in all, had been registered. In 1876 Benjamin Disraeli's Conservative government introduced the *Prevention of Crimes Amendment Act*, which gave discretionary powers to the home secretary in order to stipulate parameters regarding who should appear in the register. As a result, from 1877 only repeat offenders were included in the register.[40] Radzinowicz and Hood found that this change meant the register enabled more positive identifications and that, consequently, 'the only tangible success to emerge from the Habitual Criminals legislation was the system of registration and identification', which could function as a means of control.[41] These scholars' thorough work remains the most fulsome assessment of the working of these acts. Yet Martin Wiener has justifiably levelled criticism at the work of Radzinowicz and Hood on the basis that it fails to situate criminal legislation within broader mid- and late Victorian efforts to control the working class and is overly accepting of the notion that reforms were part of a process characterized by progress. As Wiener notes, in their 1980 article they make no mention of Michel Foucault, whose significant work, *Discipline and Punish: The Birth of the Prison*, in which he argued powerfully that penal changes in this period were not animated by a desire to decrease the harshness of punishment, but rather in order to punish more effectively, had been published in an English translation three years before.[42] Radzinowicz and Hood's failure to even consider such '"social control" interpretations' is therefore a serious defect in their work.[43]

Other scholars have considered such interpretations and argued that mid- and late Victorian police forces were in fact increasingly capable of exerting control

[38] Sean McConville, *English Local Prisons 1860–1900: Next Only to Death*, London: Routledge, 1995, p. 325.
[39] *Habitual Criminals Act*, 32 & 33 Vict., c. 99, 1869, s. 6.
[40] Metropolitan Police Orders, 15 Mar. 1877, TNA, MEPO 3/88.
[41] Radzinowicz and Hood, 'Incapacitating the Habitual Criminal', p. 1348.
[42] Michel Foucault, *Discipline and Punish: The Birth of the Prison*, Alan Sheridan (trans.), London: Allen Lane, 1977 (first published 1975), pp. 135–69.
[43] Wiener, 'The March of Penal Progress?' p. 87.

over those deemed to be part of a 'criminal class'.⁴⁴ In a frequently cited 1980 book chapter, V. A. C. Gatrell claimed that criminals were not able to adapt to the increasing efficiency of the police, leading, in England, to a real decrease in crime over the latter half of the nineteenth century.⁴⁵ Criminals, according to Gatrell, had not managed to learn the new 'rules of the game'.⁴⁶ The newly formed and well-resourced Metropolitan Police Force replaced an amateurish system and managed to 'cut into the criminal world' due, largely, to its competence.⁴⁷ Gatrell asserted that London's gangs, described by Dickens in *Oliver Twist*, had arisen and thrived before the establishment of the Metropolitan Police Force. But, after the introduction of this force in 1829, gang structures were broken up and nothing meaningful took their place. Various scholars have embraced Gatrell's position. For example, Lynn McDonald has written that 'crime rate decreases proved the effectiveness of the police' and Victor Bailey accepts Gatrell's thesis that the police gained 'mastery over the unsophisticated world of casual and professional crime'.⁴⁸ Wiener, Douglas Hay and Stefan Petrow have all argued that the police were increasingly capable of controlling criminals, contextualizing this change within broader efforts to control the working class.⁴⁹ While this explanation is plausible, there were other factors at work. The whig view that decreasing crime during a period of industrialization was due to an 'ever deepening consensus between classes' has been discredited by authors who point to clear examples of ongoing class antagonism.⁵⁰ Petrow, for instance, cites statistics demonstrating significant levels of working-class violence against members of the Metropolitan Police Force throughout the nineteenth century and 'at least into the 1920s'.⁵¹ But the contention that the crime rate declined in line with economic and social advances is convincing. As Yue-Chim Richard Wong has argued, 'the declining crime rate observed in this period is explained primarily by the rising economic prosperity and educational standards of the population'.⁵² Nonetheless, contrary

---

⁴⁴ Petrow, *Policing Morals*, p. 80.
⁴⁵ V. A. C. Gatrell, 'The Decline of Theft and Violence in Victorian and Edwardian England', in V. A. C. Gatrell, Bruce Lehman and Geoffrey Parker (eds.), *Crime and the Law: The Social History of Crime in Western Europe since 1500*, London: Europa Publications, 1980, pp. 238–337.
⁴⁶ Ibid., p. 261.
⁴⁷ Ibid.
⁴⁸ Lynn McDonald, 'Theory and Evidence of Rising Crime in the Nineteenth Century', *British Journal of Sociology*, vol. 33, no. 3 (Sept. 1982), p. 408; Bailey, *Review*, p. 349.
⁴⁹ Wiener, *Reconstructing the Criminal*, p. 258; Hay, 'Crime and Justice in Eighteenth and Nineteenth Century England', p. 64; Petrow, *Policing Morals*, pp. 294–6.
⁵⁰ Harold Perkin, *The Origins of Modern English Society, 1780–1880*, London: Routledge, 1969, p. 340.
⁵¹ Petrow, *Policing Morals*, p. 41.
⁵² Yue-Chim Richard Wong, 'An Economic Analysis of the Crime Rate in England and Wales, 1857–1892', *Economica*, vol. 62, no. 246 (May 1995), p. 245.

to Radzinowicz and Hood's sunny whiggism, the increased power of the state, manifested through the new police forces, certainly shifted the balance of power away from criminals.

However, in the context of this discussion, several historians have justifiably argued, as Radzinowicz and Hood had earlier done, that the key provisions of the acts of 1869 and 1871 were initially ineffective in London. One of the most vocal critics of the legislation has been Petrow, who studied under Gatrell. Petrow has argued that the Metropolitan Police was a powerful force for the imposition of middle-class norms on working-class communities. Yet in a brief analysis of two key elements of the Gladstone government's habitual criminals' acts, he asserts that they were deeply flawed. Police supervision, for example, was initially 'practically useless' due to various errors in the drafting of the legislation.[53] He cites similar evidence to that used by Radzinowicz and Hood. In particular, he notes that within the Metropolitan Police District mandated monthly reports had to be made to the commissioner himself due to the interpretation of London's magistracy, which was unique throughout the UK. As a result, Petrow's criticism of the legislation's implementation is valid for London at least. Furthermore, the numerous registers of repeat offenders were 'far from infallible'.[54] This was predominantly the case, Petrow argues, due to the bulk of the habitual criminals' register, which made searches very time-consuming and, consequently, the number of positive identifications 'meagre'.[55] In addition, the Metropolitan Police Force kept its own registers at the Convict Supervision Office (CSO), which was created in 1880 in order to better facilitate the work of police supervision, primarily through the provision of officers in plain clothes who were specifically trained to carry out surveillance.[56] However, there was 'little intercommunication' between the CSO and those who managed the habitual criminals' register, further decreasing the usefulness of the various documents that were intended to enable the identification of repeat offenders.[57] Petrow's short discussion of the habitual criminals' legislation presents strong evidence of the ineffectiveness of two of its key elements.

Similar criticisms of police supervision have been levelled by numerous others. Weiner has criticized supervision, especially in London, where, as discussed, those under supervision could not be prosecuted for failing to report themselves

---

[53] Petrow, *Policing Morals*, p. 82.
[54] Ibid., p. 83.
[55] Ibid., p. 84.
[56] Ibid.
[57] Ibid., p. 86.

to the police until 1879. Consequently, he has claimed that the 'protective power of police supervision came to exist more as a useful myth than an ever present reality'.[58] And Godfrey, Cox and Farrall have said that supervision under the 1869 act was 'inoperative'.[59] They stress the great number of those under supervision at any one time, with 5,638 repeat offenders subjected to the punishment between 11 August 1869 and 31 December 1869.[60] A like assessment of supervision has also been made by Radzinowicz and Hood.[61]

So the legislation of 1869 and 1871 was far from perfect. But the police, according to several of these same scholars and some others, made the utmost of their new powers as they were refined throughout the period of this study.[62] It is argued that the tools given to the police in order to combat recidivists increasingly helped them to focus their attentions on those they suspected to be repeat offenders. D. J. V. Jones, David Garland, Donald Thomas and Petrow – notwithstanding his strong criticisms of the legislation – all claim that changes to the way identification was carried out aided the police to monitor repeat offenders.[63] The registers were a more efficient way of identifying known offenders than the informal mechanisms that had previously existed. Petrow, for example, has argued in a manner that contradicts the bulk of his evidence that while the systems of registration and identification were most imperfect when first introduced, ongoing refinements, including those of 1877, represented 'essential steps towards singling out for special punishment habitual offenders'.[64] Godfrey, Cox and Farrall have said that the other key measure of the legislation, police supervision, also helped the police to monitor repeat offenders following the improvements that have already been discussed.[65] Therefore, while these scholars acknowledge the defects of the 1869 and 1871 legislation, they nonetheless argue that it broke 'significant new ground in the

---

[58] Wiener, *Reconstructing the Criminal*, pp. 303–7.
[59] Melling, 'Cleaning House in a Suddenly Closed Society', pp. 315–62; Godfrey, Cox and Farrall, *Serious Offenders*, p. 67. While Godfrey, Cox and Farrall have largely focused on the north of England in their research, they also refer to, and use examples from, London. See ibid., pp. 16, 23, 40, 55, 125, 126, 133, 180.
[60] Ibid., p. 67.
[61] Radzinowicz and Hood, 'Incapacitating the Habitual Criminal', p. 1345.
[62] D. J. V. Jones, 'The New Police: Crime and People in England and Wales, 1829–1888', *Transactions of the Royal Historical Society*, Fifth Series, vol. 33 (1983), p. 162; David Garland, *Punishment and Welfare*, London: Gower, 1985, p. 62; Thomas, *The Victorian Underworld*, p. 285; Petrow, *Policing Morals*, p. 101.
[63] Jones, 'The New Police', p. 162; Garland, *Punishment and Welfare*, p. 62; Thomas, *The Victorian Underworld*, p. 285; Petrow, *Policing Morals*, p. 101.
[64] Petrow, *Policing Morals*, p. 101.
[65] Godfrey, Cox and Farrall, *Serious Offenders*, p. 205.

extension and intensification of state power'[66] and that various changes to the way identification and supervision were carried out enabled the police to 'beset' the 'every move' of those deemed to be habitual criminals.[67] This contradiction compels a re-examination of the impacts of the Gladstone government's habitual criminals' legislation.

Various scholars have taken this position further, arguing that the legislation of 1869 and 1871 actually aided in the creation of a criminal class.[68] A greater police focus on the identification and supervision of repeat offenders, it is claimed, led to a higher arrest rate than would have otherwise been the case and, consequently, further convictions. After one conviction as a habitual criminal, coupled with time in prison, 'another conviction was sure to follow'.[69] Petrow has therefore found that the legislation 'helped the police manufacture a criminal class'.[70] Increased police attention and the difficulty of finding employment once stigmatized by being branded a habitual criminal made this the case. Godfrey, Cox and Farrall, Clive Emsley and Helen Johnston have made similar arguments.[71] Johnston, for instance, whose work was published in 2015, has said that the habitual criminals' legislation was 'stigmatising' and, as a result, could 'reproduce' criminality.[72] According to these scholars, the legislation actually contributed to the creation of what it was intended to destroy: a criminal class.

But the evidence in support of such claims is very limited. Petrow provides none and indeed focuses predominantly on the defects of the legislation. He nonetheless claims that detectives could 'probably' prove to magistrates that a person under supervision had breached the conditions of the 1869 and 1871 acts, whether in fact they had or not.[73] As will be discussed later, such a bias among magistrates, especially in London, cannot be so easily assumed. Godfrey, Cox and Farrall also produce little evidence to prove their assertion that the acts of 1869 and 1871 contributed to the 'production' of their 'objects'.[74] The authors only give one example of supervision being 'overbearing for some'. Notes of an

---

[66] Wiener, *Reconstructing the Criminal*, p. 149.
[67] Ibid., 149; Petrow, *Policing Morals*, p. 51.
[68] Petrow, *Policing Morals*, pp. 51, 82; Stanford, *The Metropolitan Police*, p. 5; Godfrey, Cox and Farrall, *Serious Offenders*, p. xii; Hay, 'Crime and Justice in Eighteenth and Nineteenth Century England', p. 66; Emsley, *Crime and Society in England*, pp. 172–4.
[69] Petrow, *Policing Morals*, p. 51.
[70] Ibid., p. 82.
[71] Godfrey, Cox and Farrall, *Serious Offenders*, p. xii; Emsley, *Crime and Society in England*, pp. 172–4; Helen Johnston, *Crime in England 1815–1880: Experiencing the Criminal Justice System*, Abingdon: Routledge, 2015, p. 36.
[72] Johnston, *Crime in England*, p. 36.
[73] Petrow, *Policing Morals*, p. 51.
[74] Godfrey, Cox and Farrall, *Serious Offenders*, p. xii.

Exeter detective show that in 1908 a suspected person, who may or may not have been under police supervision, was kept under observation following some earlier robberies.[75] More evidence than this, along with the approving comments of one former police officer regarding the efficacy of supervision, is needed to justify the assertion that police 'attention must have fallen heavily on ... those who were thought dangerous enough to be sentenced to police supervision'.[76] Emsley also offers no evidence to support his argument that habitual criminals' legislation 'probably contributed' to repeat offenders being treated like their own 'property' by the police, who subjected them to 'harassment'.[77] And finally, Johnston's remarks, quoted in the paragraph above, seem odd given that she cites no evidence to support them and the majority of her comments regarding the 1869 and 1871 legislation focus upon its flaws.[78] Scholars who make the significant claim that the Gladstone government's habitual criminals' legislation was an important factor in the creation of a criminal class have not provided the evidence required to prove its veracity.

Other evidence suggests that in London the police may not have acted in the manner that these scholars claim. From the inception of the force in 1829, the need to maintain workable relations with working-class communities meant that many policemen were unwilling to play the role of spy. Evidence suggests that working-class communities deeply resented the insertion of state power, through police forces, into spaces such as the street and the public house.[79] In particular, the notion that the police would surreptitiously monitor working-class activity met with fierce animosity from the working class and many within the middle and upper classes also. According to Bernard Porter, a strong tradition of limited government and individual liberty meant that 'the slightest hint' of spying by agencies of the state was 'resisted vociferously' by 'nearly every section of British society' in mid-Victorian Britain.[80] There were, as

---

[75] 'Investigation following the burglary of a shop', 24 Dec. 1908, detective enquiry books, Exeter constabulary, *Devon Archives*, reproduced in Godfrey, Cox and Farrall, *Serious Offenders*, p. 186.
[76] Ibid.
[77] Emsley, *Crime and Society in England*, pp. 173–4.
[78] Johnston, *Crime in England*, p. 36.
[79] Robert D. Storch, 'The Plague of Blue Locusts', *International Review of Social History*, vol. 20, no. 1 (Apr. 1975), pp. 67, 77; A. P. Donajgrodzki, '"Social Police" and the Bureaucratic Elite: A Vision of Order in the Age of Reform', in Donajgrodzki (ed.), *Social Control in Nineteenth Century Britain*, London: Croom Helm, 1977, pp. 54–5; Robert D. Storch, 'The Policeman as Domestic Missionary: Urban Discipline and Popular Culture in Northern England, 1850–1880, *Journal of Social History*, vol. 9, no. 4 (1976), pp. 481–2.
[80] Bernard Porter, *The Origins of the Vigilant State: The Metropolitan Police Special Branch before the First World War*, London: Weidenfeld and Nicolson, 1987, pp. 1, 4.

The Times observed in 1870, 'deep rooted prejudices against police supervision'.[81] The Metropolitan Police Force was aware of public unease and, as a result, took significant steps to mitigate such sentiment. Stephen Inwood, Howard Taylor and A. L. Beier have argued strongly that the Metropolitan Police Force resisted pressure to vigorously enforce legislation that would have harmed their relationship with the working class.[82] Given the considerable literature concerning the significant impact of popular attitudes on policing, such a thesis is plausible.[83] Inwood, for example, uses 'orders', which were sent from the commissioner to each station, to demonstrate that constables were actively encouraged to develop a 'practical compromise' with poor communities in order to enhance relationships that had been greatly strained by the introduction of the force in the first place.[84] The notion that the Metropolitan Police Force was a compliant cog in a broader machine of mid- and late Victorian social control requires further analysis.

The work that has most directly questioned the willingness of the Metropolitan Police Force to utilize the measures contained in the acts of 1869 and 1871 has been carried out by Terence Stanford. He has argued, similarly to those above, that 'public opinion' played a major role in ensuring that the monitoring of working-class suspects by the Metropolitan Police Force did not amount to 'improper targeting' or 'harassment'.[85] 'Public opinion', he says, was strongly against such actions.[86] Like Inwood, Stanford links these sentiments to the instructions given to policemen. Correspondence from the commissioner shows that members of the Metropolitan Police Force were 'continually being warned' about the care needed in dealing with repeat offenders.[87] If they did not heed such warnings they were 'disciplined', as the record shows a small number were.[88] Consequently, he argues convincingly that the monitoring of criminals occurred to a limited degree in the Metropolitan Police District.

Compelling as this argument is, Stevenson has put forward other evidence to support his argument that the habitual criminals' legislation was largely

---

[81] *Times*, 16 Apr. 1870, p. 9.
[82] Inwood, 'Policing London's Morals', p. 134; Beier, 'Identity, Language, and Resistance in the Making of the Victorian "Criminal Class"', p. 515; Taylor, 'Rationing Crime', pp. 578–90.
[83] R. H. Peters, 'Political Interference with Police: Is It Something New?' *Police Journal*, vol. 64, no. 2 (Apr. 1991), pp. 96–103; David Ascoli, *The Queen's Peace: The Origins and Development of the Metropolitan Police, 1829–1979*, London: Hamish Hamilton, 1979, pp. 96–7, 120, 124–5; Porter, *The Origins of the Vigilant State*, p. 17.
[84] Inwood, 'Policing London's Morals', pp. 134, 144.
[85] Stanford, *The Metropolitan Police*, pp. 183, 26.
[86] Ibid., p. 183.
[87] Ibid., p. 221.
[88] Ibid., p. 187.

Introduction

ineffective in London. Stevenson has brought together data on the number of repeat offenders who were registered and prosecuted in London and the nineteen other largest towns and cities in England. Under both of these categories the figures for London, in proportion to population, are among the lowest. Given the image of London as the centre of criminality, such evidence means London is 'an enigma', an 'exceptional case'.[89] The key explanation given, which has been largely ignored by historians since Stevenson wrote in 1986, is that London's magistrates opposed, and sought to undermine, the legislation. Stevenson points to the view of London's magistrates that those reporting themselves monthly to the police must be received by the commissioner of the Metropolitan Police. This interpretation was distinctive to London. Stevenson claims that London's magistrates expressed a kind of 'liberal paternalism' that was unique among the magistracy. This was the case because London's magistrates were well paid, unlike many counterparts elsewhere, and were highly qualified in the law. They therefore, Stevenson appears to argue, lacked the conservative impulses of many other magistrates who were drawn from the upper classes and the clergy.[90] This conclusion is bolstered by the work of Jennifer Davis, which Stevenson cites, in which she argues that London's magistrates viewed their role as 'a working class resource', settling disputes and providing advice. Consequently, they often pushed back against statutes that they believed unreasonably targeted the poor.[91] Stevenson's work, which focuses predominantly on the period from 1869 to 1880, provides further cause to question the thesis that this legislation helped create a criminal class, particularly in London. In doing so it shows that, along with the Metropolitan Police Force, London's magistrates did not unquestioningly implement the government's agenda, while leaving significant scope for further analysis of their role in interpreting the acts of 1869 and 1871, which has been largely overlooked.[92] In carrying out this analysis I will argue that much scholarly work concerning the unity of the nineteenth-century state is wrong.

Within the literature regarding Victorian efforts to combat criminality there is much agreement that police forces were able to closely monitor elements of the working class that they deemed a threat to public order and private property and, in doing so, were part of a broader system of social control. Most historians

---

[89] Stevenson, 'The "Habitual Criminal" in Nineteenth-Century England', pp. 47, 46.
[90] Ibid., p. 47.
[91] Jennifer Davis, 'A Poor Man's System of Justice: The London Police Courts in the Second Half of the Nineteenth Century', *Historical Journal*, vol. 27, no. 2 (Jun. 1984), p. 310.
[92] See Emsley, *Crime and Society in England*, pp. 173–4 for a brief and rare example of a discussion regarding the role of magistrates in implementing the habitual criminals' legislation of 1869 and 1871.

who have examined the habitual criminals' legislation of 1869 and 1871 believe that, despite its flaws, it aided the police in this endeavour. In doing so, it is argued, the legislation actually helped to create a criminal class. However, some scholars have sought to re-evaluate the extent to which police forces monitored and targeted for arrest those known to have been previously convicted. Some work on the attitudes of London's magistrates further undermines the dominant view, at least in the capital. So, in short, the literature regarding the *Habitual Criminals Act 1869* and the *Prevention of Crime Act 1871* is limited. It is also dominated by scholars, the foundations of whose work is shaky at best. Thus the legislation is ripe for further analysis.

Current debates about the most effective means of punishing repeat offenders, now often called career criminals, will also benefit from a reassessment of Victorian measures to combat a criminal class. Calls for the strict supervision and registration of certain offenders are a common feature of contemporary discussions about penal policy – across the Western world in particular. The imposition of longer sentences, likewise, has many supporters in pressure groups, parliaments and, if polling data is anything to go by, the public.[93] For instance, in criticizing the sentencing of repeat offenders in the UK the Conservative MP and home secretary Priti Patel has said that 'dangerous career criminals' were 'laughing in the face of a justice system that should be removing them from our streets'. The courts, she has said, are 'soft' on 'repeat offenders'.[94] Registers of criminals also remain very much in vogue. The Royal Society for the Protection of Animals is currently calling for an animal welfare offender register in addition to the Violent and Sexual Offender Register that already operates throughout the UK.[95] Numerous other countries have similar registers. Indeed, in recent years governments have heeded many of these types of calls. Once again in the UK, the former justice minister, Damian Green, has boasted, 'We have made the toughest sentencing options available to the courts.' And in 2013 the Conservative government introduced 'mandatory supervision for all offenders leaving prison' as a further measure specifically designed to reduce recidivism. Supervision would, Green said, 'allow us to track the whereabouts

---

[93] Karen Gelb, *Myths and Misconceptions: Public Opinion versus Public Judgment about Sentencing*, Melbourne: Sentencing Advisory Council, 2016, pp. 20–71.

[94] Matthew Davis, 'Repeat Offenders Are Escaping Jail', *Express*, 25 Aug. 2013, online ed., https://www.express.co.uk/news/uk/424449/Repeat-offenders-are-escaping-jail (accessed 10 Jul. 2019); 'Courts Go "Soft" on Supervillains', *Daily Star*, 28 Oct. 2012, online ed., https://www.dailystar.co.uk/news/latest-news/279379/Courts-go-soft-on-supervillians (accessed 10 Jul. 2019).

[95] 'Animal Offender Register for Wales', Dec. 2017, https://www.rspca.org.uk/getinvolved/campaign/penalties/offenders (accessed 10 Jul. 2019).

of repeat offenders'.⁹⁶ Coming to a greater understanding of the effectiveness of registration, supervision and measures to ensure longer sentences – when introduced through the *Habitual Criminals Act 1869* and the *Prevention of Crime Act 1871* – will, I trust, also illuminate some factors that will impact their chances of achieving their stated objectives today.

*

In enacting this legislation the parliament sought to suppress a criminal class that it believed was most prevalent and dangerous in London. What was the genesis of this idea of a criminal class? Was such a class really believed to exist?

As early as the sixteenth century, concern was being expressed in England regarding the existence of a criminal class which made its living from crime.⁹⁷ Print references to the notion of a distinct body of repeat offenders continued throughout the seventeenth and eighteenth centuries.⁹⁸ However, such references increased significantly from the 1830s, and the use of the term was most prevalent in the 1850s and 1860s.⁹⁹ Recorded statistics concerning the number of repeat offenders in England and Wales, while highly problematic as a gauge of recidivist offending, help to explain why this was the case. Firstly, these statistics were consistently brought to the attention of the public and appeared to suggest that persistent offenders, labelled in these official documents as a criminal class, were the cohort responsible for most crime. Police estimates of the number of 'habitual depredators' or people of 'known bad character' were tabled annually in parliament from 1839, one year before the end of transportation to New South Wales sparked significant concern regarding the release of known criminals in Britain. In that year the constabulary force commissioners believed there were 10,444 such offenders living wholly by crime, including prostitutes and vagrants, in London.¹⁰⁰ A lesser number, albeit representing a greater proportion of the overall population, were reported to reside in various other locations.¹⁰¹ These statistics provided a most inaccurate indication of the number of Londoners whose criminality was in any way habitual. Prior to 1861 the returns for 'known thieves and depredators' included

---

[96] Davis, 'Repeat Offenders Are Escaping Jail'.
[97] Godfrey, Cox and Farrall, *Serious Offenders*, pp. 2–4.
[98] A. Bell, *Literature and Crime in Augustan England*, London: Routledge, 1991, p. 15.
[99] Johnston, *Crime in England*, p. 26.
[100] *First Report of the Commissioners Appointed to Inquire as to the Best Means of Establishing an Efficient Constabulary Force in the Counties of England and Wales*, [C 169] HC 1839, xix, p. 8.
[101] Ibid., p. 8. The locations reported upon were the Borough of Liverpool, the City and County of Bristol, the City of Bath, the Town and County of Kingston-on-Hull and the Town and County of Newcastle-on-Tyne.

anyone who had ever been convicted of an offence. After 1861 those who were no longer thought to be active were excluded and after 1864 those who had not committed a crime for at least one year were omitted.[102] Furthermore, until a significant overhaul of the method of compiling the criminal statistics was undertaken in 1892, regional police forces also interpreted the definition of 'habitual depredators' in different ways.[103] The different methods of 'definition, collection and presentation', as Sindall has noted, 'made the statistics unreliable as evidence'.[104] At least partly as a result of the changes made after 1861, the statistics showed a significant reduction in the number of the 'criminal classes' prior to the introduction of the 1869 legislation, both in London and throughout England and Wales.[105] For instance, from 1867–8 to 1868–9 the total number of the 'criminal classes' in England and Wales declined from 56,584 to 54,249 and in London from 5,772 to 4,336.[106] Yet from 1839, as transportation was being curtailed, annual statistics purported to show that thousands of repeat offenders resided in London.

The capital's many influential newspapers regularly reported the recorded crime figures to their eager readership. Since the advent of official statistics in 1839, all major London papers frequently reported on the size of the criminal class, and the figures were often accompanied by commentary that stressed the threat from this group. Despite the limitations of these data in 1858 the *Standard*, a penny daily conservative paper, believed they were 'a reliable measure of the vices of the community'.[107] Sometimes the problems inherent in attempts to judge the size of the criminal class were acknowledged. But, when this was done, it was usually argued that the statistics underestimated the size of the problem.[108] Far more often they were simply accepted. In 1863, for instance, a leading article in the liberal *Daily News* reproduced data from the annual judicial statistics and argued that 'the real source of danger' is 'the habitual offender'.[109] An analysis of *The Times* shows that every year through various means, including leading articles, court reports, reports of parliamentary debates and letters to the editor, its readers were made aware of the new annual data concerning the size of the

---

[102] Sindall, *Street Violence in the Nineteenth Century*, p. 20.
[103] Ibid., p. 24.
[104] Ibid., p. 20.
[105] *Judicial Statistics. 1869. England and Wales. Part 1. Police-Criminal Proceedings-Prisons*, [C 195] HC 1870, lxiii, p. x.
[106] Ibid.
[107] *Standard*, 26 Jul. 1858, p. 4.
[108] *Pall Mall Gazette*, 25 Oct. 1867, pp. 4–5.
[109] *Daily News*, 14 Jan. 1863, p. 4.

so-called criminal class.¹¹⁰ Taking 1868, the year before the introduction of the *Habitual Criminal Bill 1869*, as an example, *The Times* published two lengthy leading articles on the 'Criminal Classes at Large', which cited the judicial statistics, and a letter to the editor by a 'Chairman of Quarter Sessions' that once again referred to the published data and argued Britain's major cities were 'infested by old offenders'.¹¹¹ London's newspapers therefore ensured that their readers were well aware of statistics that suggested a significant mass of dangerous repeat offenders lived in the city.

Reports such as these shaped perceptions of the significance of the criminal threat in the capital. London's press in the second half of the nineteenth century had a huge readership. Between 1850 and 1870 a dramatic growth in newspaper circulation occurred. This was partly due to a fall in the price of paper per ream from 55 shillings in 1845 to 40 shillings in 1855. Furthermore, the abolition of the advertisement tax in 1853 and then of stamp duty in 1855 made publishing newspapers a more attractive financial prospect.¹¹² In addition, from the second quarter of the nineteenth century technical improvements in printing presses allowed the hourly production rate of newspapers to rise. In London 4,000 copies of newspapers could be produced per hour in 1827. This rose to 20,000 in 1847 and then 168,000 after 1870. Finally, this trend was hastened by the abolition of paper duty in 1860. These various factors meant that by 1860 most daily newspapers in London sold for a penny. Consequently, their circulation trebled between 1855 and 1860 and doubled again between 1860 and 1870.¹¹³ By the middle of the nineteenth century newspapers had become the major medium for the dissemination of news and opinion. In 1851, a select committee was informed, albeit with obvious exaggeration, that 'newspapers are the only thing that people will ever read' and 'all the information they get is through that means'.¹¹⁴

So from the 1840s onwards an increasingly large London readership was exposed to reports of a substantial criminal class. However, this does not necessarily mean that these readers believed such reports. To what extent did newspapers in the second half of the nineteenth century shape the views of their readership? Hannah Barker has correctly said that in mid-Victorian Britain

---

[110] For the 1860s see *The Times*, 27 Jan. 1860, p. 5; 24 Oct. 1861, p. 11; 14 Aug. 1862, p. 8; 20 Feb. 1863, p. 6; 4 Apr. 1864, p. 11; 29 Jul. 1865, p. 12; 16 Jan. 1866, p. 10; 16 Aug. 1867, p. 9; 11 Jul. 1868, p. 12; 27 Jan. 1869, p. 7.

[111] *Times*, 11 Jul. 1868, p. 12; 26 Oct. 1868, p. 4; 4 Nov. p. 5.

[112] Hannah Barker, *Newspapers, Politics, and English Society, 1695–1855*, New York: Routledge, 2000, p. 1.

[113] Sindall, *Street Violence in the Nineteenth Century*, pp. 30–1.

[114] *Report from the Select Committee on Newspaper Stamps: Together with the Proceedings of the Committee, Minutes of Evidence, Appendix, and Index*, [C 558] HC 1851, xvii, p. 227.

the press 'was widely perceived to be the most crucial factor in forming and articulating public opinion'.[115] Numerous contemporary sources, including Whig foreign secretary Viscount Castlereagh, believed that public support for various social reforms following the end of the Napoleonic wars in 1815 was the result of agitation in the press.[116] As the century wore on similar views concerning the impact of newspaper reporting were often expressed. Journalist Henry Reeve, writing in 1855, believed 'newspapers are just as truly representative of the people as legal senators'. It was 'scarcely possible to exaggerate' their influence.[117] Then in 1871, James Grant, the editor of the trade journal of licensed victuallers, the *Morning Advertiser*, wrote that 'within the last few years the appellation of "The Fourth Estate" given to our newspaper journalism, has acquired an appropriateness to which it was never entitled at any previous period of history'.[118] London's numerous and popular newspapers therefore surely influenced the opinions of their readers.

Various social commentators also produced statistics concerning the number of repeat offenders and stressed the existence of a discrete cohort, most noticeable in London, that seemingly committed crime with impunity. The social investigator Henry Mayhew made estimates of London's 'criminal class' in 1862 in the widely read fourth volume in his series on *London Labour and the London Poor*. He argued that 80,000 prostitutes worked in London, part of a 'hostile army' of repeat offenders.[119] Prostitutes were widely feared due to their perceived capacity to spread both venereal disease and, worse, immorality.[120] Thus, an apparent force of tens of thousands of prostitutes was a terrifying prospect. In 1869 the journalist James Greenwood said that London's criminal class represented an 'army' of thieves that was 20,000 strong.[121] The Reverend H. W. Holland, who claimed to have lived among London's thieves for two years, was more circumspect regarding the number of repeat offenders. Nonetheless, in an article in the *Cornhill Magazine* in 1862, he said they 'count by many

---

[115] Barker, *Newspapers, Politics, and English Society*, p. 1.
[116] See Kevin Gilmartin, *Print Politics: The Press and Radical Opposition in Early Nineteenth-Century England*, Cambridge: Cambridge University Press, 1996, pp. 65, 74.
[117] H. Reeve, 'The Newspaper Press', *Edinburgh Review*, vol. 102 (Oct. 1855), p. 479.
[118] J. Grant, *The Newspaper Press*, vol. 2, London: Tinsley Brothers, 1871, p. 459.
[119] Peter Quennell (ed.), *London's Underworld: Being Selections from 'Those That Will Not Work', the Fourth Volume of 'London Labour and the London Poor'* by Henry Mayhew, vol. 7, London: Hamlyn, 1969, p. 32.
[120] For a detailed discussion of contemporary attitudes towards prostitution see Judith R. Walkowitz, *Prostitution and Victorian Society: Women, Class, and the State*, Cambridge and New York: Cambridge University Press, 1988 (first published 1980), pp. 11–48.
[121] Greenwood, *The Seven Curses of London*, p. 57.

thousands'.¹²² These figures, like the official data, tell us little, if anything, about the number of recidivist criminals in London at this time. For one thing, they are 'implausibly varied'.¹²³ The methodology used to collect them is also unknown. Yet Godfrey, Cox and Farrall have argued that such estimates influenced public opinion. They have said that 'many of the popular conceptions of criminality that date from the mid-to-late Victorian period ... can be traced back either to Mayhew or Binny', Mayhew's collaborator.¹²⁴ It is probable that the work of these commentators, which supported the official judicial statistics in asserting that a sizable body of repeat offenders resided and operated in London, increased the prevalence of this view.

The perceived threat of a so-called criminal class also needs to be understood in the context of the changing penal landscape of the time. The key change was the reduction in the use of the punishment of transportation to Australia, which ultimately ceased in 1868. After British settlement of Australia in 1788, following the refusal of the former American colonies to take further convicts, over 168,000 convicts were sent to New South Wales, Van Diemen's Land and Western Australia during the next eighty years. For the authorities in the UK, a great benefit of this system was that very few convicts returned from half way around the world at the expiration of their sentence. However, this system had been in decline since 1840 when New South Wales took its last convicts. This was largely due to the vigorous opposition of many colonists who desired to rid their adopted homeland of the 'convict stain' and, to a lesser extent, unease in the UK at the costs associated with transportation.¹²⁵ Nonetheless, Van Diemen's Land took convicts for a further thirteen years. Then, until 1868 when transportation to Australia finally stopped completely, comparatively small numbers of convicts were sent to Western Australia. Between 1850 and 1868 only 10,000 British and Irish criminals were sent to the western-most Australian colony. The refusal of New South Wales to accept more convicts meant that from 1840 many who would previously have been transported were instead being punished, usually through incarceration, and released at home. Between 1848 and 1852, of the 16,229 convicts sentenced to transportation, only 10,963 were transported.¹²⁶

---

¹²² H. W. Holland, 'Professional Thieves', *Cornhill Magazine*, vol. 6, no. 35 (1862), p. 640.
¹²³ Godfrey, Cox and Farrall, *Serious Offenders*, p. 87.
¹²⁴ Ibid., p. 17.
¹²⁵ Stephen Nicholas and Peter R. Shergold, 'Unshackling the Past', in Stephen Nicholas (ed.), *Convict Workers: Reinterpreting Australia's Past*, Cambridge: Cambridge University Press, 1988, p. 3; John Gascoigne, *The Enlightenment and the Origins of European Australia*, Cambridge: Cambridge University Press, 2002, pp. 129–38.
¹²⁶ *Report from the Select Committee of the House of Commons on Transportation*, [C 244] HC 1856, xvii, appendix I, p. 179.

This change undoubtedly increased popular anxieties regarding crime.[127] Radzinowicz and Hood have sought to explain the nature of these concerns.

> As long as transportation provided the means for flushing large numbers of England's convicts to the antipodes, there was no necessity to consider how to control or incapacitate them at home. The refusal of Australia's eastern colonies to accept more convicts at the end of the 1840s, combined with the rapid growth of the cities and the expansion and consolidation of the police, made the phenomenon of crime appear more real and more tangible. The perception of a mass of offenders at home, moving about and yet anonymous, fostered an escalating fear of a criminal or dangerous class and a resolve to do something drastic about it.[128]

For its part the government believed what it read about a criminal class. Lord Kimberley specifically referred to the most recent data concerning 'known thieves and depredators' in his second reading speech on the *Habitual Criminal Bill 1869*. He then asked, '[H]ow are we to deal with this vast mass of criminals?' He also claimed that the 'criminal class' was a 'great army'.[129] A new means of defeating this army was needed because of the termination of transportation as a penal option. 'There is at the present time', Kimberley said, 'a special reason for carefully scrutinising and seeing whether we cannot improve our system, and that is the complete cessation of transportation'.[130] A belief in the existence of a large criminal class, no longer subject to transportation, was a key reason for the introduction of the *Habitual Criminals Bill 1869*.

The significant mid-nineteenth-century discourse concerning a criminal class stressed the provenance of this social group. It was a recognizable subgroup, many theorists confidently asserted, of the broader working class.[131] Social investigators Harriet Martineau, Rev. Holland, Henry Mayhew and Mary Carpenter all wrote extensively on the problem of repeat offenders who, they argued, lived by crime. Their writing was informed by first-hand experience, as all boasted that they had lived among criminals in order to better research their subject. They did not have a difficult time locating it. The criminal class was

---

[127] Randall McGowen, 'Civilising Punishment: The End of the Public Execution in England', *Journal of British Studies*, vol. 33, no. 3 (Jul. 1994), p. 275; Emelyne Godfrey, 'Stranglehold on Victorian Society', *History Today*, vol. 59, no. 7 (Jul. 2009), p. 55.
[128] Radzinowicz and Hood, 'Incapacitating the Habitual Criminal', p. 1308.
[129] The Earl of Kimberley (Liberal), 194 *Parl. Deb.*, HL (3rd ser.), col. 338 (26 Feb. 1869).
[130] Ibid., col. 337.
[131] Quennell (ed.), *London's Underworld*, pp. 58, 79, 165; Holland, 'Professional Thieves', p. 645; Harriot Martineau, 'Life in the Criminal Class', *Edinburgh Review*, vol. 122, no. 250 (Oct. 1865), pp. 337, 342, 350.

not a disparate grouping, but, they believed, one concentrated in the poorest quarters of major cities, especially London. Therefore, while the concept of a criminal class was not specifically tied to ethnicity, the Irish were believed to make up a prominent element of this hostile group. This was foremost because so many poor Irish families crowded London's slums in the nineteenth century.[132] Mayhew, with typical English racism, said that Irish cockneys represented 'the most unprincipled part of the population of London'.[133] The class origin of this group, furthermore, was made plain by the appearance of its members. Holland said that what he called professional thieves lived in a 'thieves' quarter' in the most deprived working-class sectors of cities that was 'well known to the police'.[134] And according to Carpenter, the criminals who lived in such areas had both a facial appearance and a more general bearing that was recognizable. They bore, she said, a 'low expression', a point that Mayhew also made repeatedly.[135] As Martineau informed her readers, members of the 'criminal class' were used to an existence 'altogether unlike our own'.[136] The working-class origin of repeat offenders was clearly articulated by numerous mid-nineteenth-century authors.

Up until the late 1880s a further, and insistent, element of this discourse was that members of the criminal class freely chose a life of crime over honest living. Many sources, albeit predominantly drawn from the middle and upper classes, claimed that despite the numerous possible causes of crime, members of the criminal class freely chose to live by crime. For instance, in the 1870s the ordinary of Newgate prison claimed that 'in nine cases out of ten it is choice, and not necessity, that leads to crime'.[137] And in 1894 *The Times*, referring to the rise of Lombrosian criminology that minimized the role of free choice in crime and popularized the idea of the born criminal, lamented the advent of 'modern controversies' about the causes of crime.[138] While there were now 'differences and doubts' concerning the origin of crime, before the 1880s, during which – as will be discussed in later chapters – ideas linking crime to heredity came to be widely recognized, there had been 'an accepted opinion' that crime was a

---

[132] This point is discussed by Jennifer Davis in 'From "Rookeries" to "Communities": Race, Poverty and Policing in London, 1850–1985', *History Workshop*, vol. 27, no. 1 (Spring 1989), pp. 66–89.
[133] Quennell (ed.), *London's Underworld*, p. 79.
[134] Holland, 'Professional Thieves', p. 645.
[135] Mary Carpenter, *Our Convicts*, vol. I, London: Longman, Green, Longman, Roberts and Green, 1864, p. 11; Quennell (ed.), *London's Underworld*, pp. 165, 255.
[136] Martineau, 'Life in the Criminal Class', p. 337.
[137] Edward Cox, *The Principles of Punishment: As Applied in the Administration of the Criminal Law by Judges and Magistrates*, London: Law Times Office, 1877, p. 142.
[138] *Times*, 17 Dec. 1894, p. 9.

matter of 'choice'.[139] Numerous historians have found that this was a prevalent mid-Victorian view. 'It was commonly believed,' one has said, 'that the criminal, exercising his or her free will, chose a life of crime'.[140] Another has argued, 'Individuals were regarded as free to choose whether to build character ... or to fall prey to base character traits.'[141] Despite the distress and poverty of working-class life in London, and elsewhere, freedom of choice was often ascribed to the criminal class.

Commentators addressed the issue of why such a choice might have been made. Repeat offenders apparently calculated that a life of crime, accompanied by the danger of imprisonment, would be both more pleasant and remunerative than one that adopted the respectable norms of self-help and honest hard work. Despite his empathy for many whose experiences he chronicled, Mayhew did much to propagate this notion. Criminals were, according to Mayhew '[t]hose that will not work'.[142] Martineau, after having spent time with the criminal population of London, also said that its members 'show no traces of honorable toil on their hands'.[143] Finally, Holland compiled a report in 1862 based on personal experience of London's underworld. He found that repeat offenders were 'idle' and that honest work would not deliver the requisite compensation to 'satisfy their wants'.[144] These themes were also apparent in crime fiction, which was popular and cheap.[145] The content and importance of this literature will be discussed further in later chapters. One eminent historian of crime and punishment in nineteenth-century Britain is correct in asserting that the idea of a 'criminal class' that simply preferred 'idleness and moments of adventure to a fair day's work ... had become popular in Victorian England'.[146]

Such a criminal class, made up of members of the lowest stratum of the working class and freely choosing an adventurous life of crime, did not in fact

---

[139] Ibid., p. 9. For further discussion of the impact of Lombrosian thought see Daniel Pick, *Faces of Degeneration: A European Disorder, c. 1848–c. 1918*, Cambridge: Cambridge University Press, 1989, p. 17.

[140] David Taylor, 'Beyond the Bounds of Respectable Society: "The Dangerous Classes" in Victorian and Edwardian England', in Judith Rowbotham and Kim Stevenson (eds.), *Criminal Conversations: Victorian Crimes, Social Panic and Moral Outrage*, Columbus: Ohio State University Press, 2005, p. 4.

[141] George Pavlich, 'The Emergence of Habitual Criminals in 19th Century Britain: Implications for Criminology', *Journal of Theoretical and Philosophical Criminology*, vol. 2, no. 1 (2010), p. 23.

[142] Quennell (ed.), *London's Underworld*, pp. 13–27.

[143] Martineau, 'Life in the Criminal Class', p. 342.

[144] Holland, 'Professional Thieves', p. 653.

[145] Rosalind Crone, *Violent Victorians: Popular Entertainment in Nineteenth-Century London*, Manchester: Manchester University Press, 2012, pp. 160–209.

[146] Clive Emsley, *Hard Men: The English and Violence since 1750*, London: Hambleton and London, 2005, p. 16.

exist. It was, rather, a comforting construct that enabled the middle and upper classes to believe crime was overwhelmingly committed by a distinctive group that could be identified and suppressed. This construct also ensured that the middle and upper class could be guilt-free, as the impact of any social causes of crime that they served to exacerbate, such as poverty and a lack of education, was downplayed. The historian J. J. Tobias, however, has argued that the criminal class was a reality, claiming that a large amount of criminality was concentrated within the poorest elements of the working class. He has said that 'the concept of a "criminal class" may be regarded' as an 'acceptable explanation'.[147] Yet court records do not support his position. Instead they show that convicted criminals, although predominantly from the working class, did not emanate from an identifiable subgroup. Emsley has carried out an analysis of court records in London in the 1860s and found that most thefts were 'opportunist' in nature, while crimes of violence predominantly involved 'people who were either related to each other or who were known to each other'.[148] As another historian of crime has claimed, it appears clear that 'all kinds of people' from all social classes committed crimes. Consequently, the concept of a criminal class was a 'myth'.[149] As transportation to the Australian colonies ceased, many members of the middle and upper classes were genuinely fearful of a criminal class, notwithstanding the fact that such a class did not exist.[150]

*

After coming to power in 1868 the Liberal government embraced the notion of a discrete and identifiable section of the working class that was often called the criminal class, which freely rejected honest society. In the House of Lords Kimberley said that members of the 'criminal class' looked upon crime 'as a profession'.[151] And in the Commons the home secretary, H. A. Bruce, said that only 10 per cent of prisoners committed crime 'under some strong temptation'. The rest made a free choice in order to avoid 'vigorous labour'. This view was in keeping with those of commentators and newspapers that I have summarized above. It was used to justify an unprecedented response. Because repeat offenders

---

[147] J. J. Tobias, *Crime and Industrial Society in the Nineteenth Century*, London: B. T. Batsford, 1967, p. 62.
[148] Emsley, *Crime and Society in England*, p. 171.
[149] Pat Carlean, foreword to Godfrey, Cox and Farrall, *Serious Offenders*, p. viii.
[150] Robert B. Shoemaker, *The London Mob: Violence and Disorder in Eighteenth Century England*, London: Hambledon, 2004, pp. xi–xii; John Pratt, *Governing the Dangerous: Dangerousness, Law and Social Change*, Sydney: The Federation Press, 1997, pp. 13–4.
[151] The Earl of Kimberley (Liberal), 194 *Parl. Deb.*, HL (3rd ser.), col. 343 (26 Feb. 1869).

chose to forego honest labour and respectability, 'society was justified in taking vigorous measures of repression'.[152]

The system that the government consequently introduced requires re-analysis. The literature concerning these measures predominantly utilizes models of moral panic and social control in order to explain their genesis and effectiveness. However, these models are not sufficient to fully understand why the government introduced the legislation in the form that it did and the extent to which its aims were achieved. Indeed, adherence to these models has led to conclusions that are partial, contradictory and incorrect. The reality of the motivations for, and effectiveness of, the habitual criminals' legislation of the Gladstone government reveals a significantly more complex state of affairs than the existing literature can account for. Simplistic frameworks are alluring, as they give form to a past that can – in the absence of much detailed research – appear chaotic to the point to utter incomprehension. The facts regarding the genesis of the legislation of 1869, and its alteration and implementation, invite us to step back and appreciate the competing, sometimes muddled and exasperating, interactions that typified mid- and late Victorian efforts to combat the criminal class.

This is the broad theme of this book, which is set out chronologically and draws extensively on Home Office and Metropolitan Police Force files, court reports, parliamentary records, relevant memoirs (of criminals themselves, magistrates, judges and policemen, in particular) and the reporting of London newspapers. The first chapter aims to establish why the Liberal government introduced the *Habitual Criminals Bill 1869*. The role of the SSA in shaping efforts to better control repeat offenders is assessed, given the group's very close relationship to the new government. Chapter 2 analyses the early operation of the new act until 1871, when further changes were made and the key measures of the legislation were re-enacted through the *Prevention of Crime Act 1871*.[153] The final three chapters assess the effectiveness of the major provisions of the 1871 legislation until 1895. Chapter 3 contains an analysis of the habitual criminals' registry and how it was intended to function, as well as of the various other registers created in London. Chapter 4 asks whether members of the Metropolitan Police Force are able to monitor those under supervision in the busy city. Also, how did London's magistrates interpret the provisions of the *Prevention of Crime Act*

---

[152] Henry Bruce (Liberal), 198 *Parl. Deb.*, HC (3rd ser.), col. 1258 (4 Aug. 1869).
[153] For an examination of these amendments, see Melling, 'Cleaning House in a Suddenly Closed Society', pp. 334–42.

1871 concerning police supervision? Finally, the fifth chapter investigates the extent to which the legislation led to longer sentences for repeat offenders, as anticipated by the government. The chapter asks whether magistrates and judges placed the weight upon proven past convictions that the government had hoped they would, and if not, why not.

1

The Origins of the *Habitual Criminals Act 1869*: 'Our Wretched Little Bill'

What shall we do with our convicts?[1]

(The Earl of Carlisle, Liberal peer, 1858)

The *Habitual Criminals Act 1869* was, as Leon Radzinowicz and Roger Hood have argued, a 'heavy baggage of repressive measures'.[2] To understand why such legislation was introduced it will be necessary to examine the role of the press, public opinion in London, and the Social Science Association (SSA), which was an important pressure group with very close ties to the Liberal Party.[3] According to the published criminal statistics, the very significant analytical pitfalls of which have already been discussed, the 1860s were years in which crime decreased in England and Wales, as did the size of the 'criminal class'.[4] Nonetheless, at the end of the decade the government felt it necessary to bring forward legislation that greatly increased the power of the state over repeat offenders and those who had been granted early release from prison on a licence.

Why was this the case? This chapter will begin by describing and analysing legislation from the 1850s and 1860s that sought to deal with repeat offenders and licence-holders. This first section will also seek to explain why successive governments believed these earlier efforts required augmentation and will focus on periods of alarm in London concerning the effects of the ending of

---

[1] The Earl of Carlisle, 'Address on the Punishment and Reformation of Criminals', in *Transactions of the National Association for the Promotion of Social Science 1858*, London: John W. Parker and Son, 1859, pp. 70, 72.
[2] Leon Radzinowicz and Roger Hood, 'Incapacitating the Habitual Criminal: The English Experience', *Michigan Law Review*, vol. 78, no. 8 (Aug. 1980), p. 1340.
[3] Lawrence Goldman, 'The Social Science Association, 1857–1886: A Context of Mid-Victorian Liberalism', *English Historical Review*, vol. 101, no. 398 (Jan. 1986), pp. 95–134.
[4] *Judicial Statistics. 1869. England and Wales. Part 1. Police-Criminal Proceedings-Prisons*, [C 195] HC 1870, lxiii, pp. x, 6.

transportation. It will also address the genesis and ideology of the SSA and analyse the impact of its advocacy. The second section will assess events from 1868 and 1869 and determine how they shaped the *Habitual Criminals Act 1869*. Here the significant role of the SSA, in particular, will again be considered.

The *Habitual Criminals Act 1869* has been interpreted by numerous historians as part of a process of adaptation to changed circumstances, notably the decline and eventual cessation of transportation to Australia, an adaptation that was driven, it is argued, by public alarm in London, stoked by the city's newspapers, about the accumulation of criminals at home.[5] For example, Victor Bailey has argued that following the British government's acceptance in 1840 of the demands of the colonists of New South Wales that they should take no further convicts, the public, especially in London, became increasingly alarmed at newspaper reports of a dangerous criminal class, leading governments to implement legislation in 1853, 1857, 1864 and 1869.[6] According to this account, there was no 'coherent penal policy', rather, as Peter Bartip has said, a kind of 'hand to mouth pragmatism' as governments sought to deal with public unease about crime.[7] Lawrence Goldman has correctly noted the dominance in the relevant historiography of this discourse depicting mid-Victorian penal reform as a 'piecemeal adaptation to essentially pragmatic considerations'.[8] We will see that this view cannot fully explain the reasons for the key penal changes of the 1850s and 1860s regarding the criminal class, including the *Habitual Criminals Act 1869*, and that the sustained advocacy and influence of the SSA were, instead, vital factors.

*

The *Habitual Criminals Act 1869* was not the first legislative measure that sought to deal with the consequences of the cessation of transportation. Acts passed in 1853, 1857 and 1864 were designed to replace transportation with an

---

[5] Drew D. Gray, *London's Shadows: The Dark Side of the Victorian City*, London: Continuum, 2010, p. 112; John Welshman, *Underclass: A History of the Excluded since 1880*, London: Hambledon Continuum, 2006, p. 6; Pete King, 'Moral Panics and Violent Street Crime, 1750–2000: A Comparative Perspective', in Barry Godfrey, Clive Emsley and Graeme Dunstall (eds.), *Comparative Histories of Crime*, Cullompton: Willan, 2003, p. 57; W. G. Runciman, *Very Different, but Much the Same: The Evolution of English Society since 1714*, Oxford: Oxford University Press, 2015, p. 69.

[6] Victor Bailey, 'Introduction', in Victor Bailey (ed.), *Policing and Punishment in Nineteenth Century Britain*, London: Croom Helm, 1981, p. 20.

[7] Ibid., p. 20; Peter Bartrip, 'Public Opinion and Law Enforcement: The Ticket-of-Leave Scares in Mid-Victorian Britain', in Bailey (ed.), *Policing and Punishment in Nineteenth Century Britain*, London: Croom Helm, 1981, p. 174.

[8] Lawrence Goldman, *Science, Reform and Politics in Victorian Britain: The Social Science Association 1857–1886*, Cambridge: Cambridge University Press, 2002, p. 172.

expanded and enhanced penal regime at home. Under the acts, criminals were to be sentenced to longer terms of incarceration, in the hopes of reforming them, while a licence or ticket-of-leave system was also to be introduced. This section will analyse the specific reasons for these legislative changes and what they entailed. The genesis of the *Habitual Criminals Act 1869* can only be properly understood in the context of these earlier pieces of legislation, which, as we shall see, it built upon.

The gradual end of transportation to Australia necessitated a significant reassessment of penal policy. By 1840 transportation had 'almost entirely' replaced capital punishment as the key legal mechanism to deal with those convicted of serious crime.[9] Capital punishment, as Michael Melling has noted, 'proved less and less popular with the public in the nineteenth century'.[10] Consequently, public hangings finally ceased in 1867. Radzinowicz and Hood have estimated that throughout the 1860s fewer than ten people were actually executed in Britain each year.[11] As a result, transportation became 'the ordinary sentence upon conviction' for any felonious offence.[12] However, in the 1850s and 1860s British governments were forced to respond to the imminent ending of transportation to Australia. As those transported were very unlikely to ever return, removing convicts to Australia was 'almost as effective a way of preventing crime in England as was executing them'.[13] However, from 1840 transportation to Australia was progressively ended, largely in response to objections to the practice from the colonists.[14] The refusal of New South Wales to accept more convicts meant that from 1840 many who would previously have been transported were already being incarcerated and then released on home shores.[15] As Randall McGowen has argued, this new reality 'produced an anxiety ... about releasing serious offenders back into society'.[16] Members of the legislature were not immune from

---

[9] Michael Melling, 'Cleaning House in a Suddenly Closed Society: The Genesis, Brief Life and Ultimate Death of the Habitual Criminals Act, 1869', *Osgoode Hall Law Journal*, vol. 21, no. 2 (Sept. 1983), p. 321.
[10] Ibid.
[11] Leon Radzinowicz and Roger Hood, 'Judicial Discretion and Sentencing Standards: Victorian Attempts to Solve a Perennial Problem', *University of Pennsylvania Law Review*, vol. 127, no. 5 (1978-9), p. 1291.
[12] Luke Pike, *A History of Crime in England*, vol. 2, New Jersey: Patterson Smith, 1968 (first published 1876), p. 456.
[13] Melling, 'Cleaning House in a Suddenly Closed Society', p. 322.
[14] This was discussed in the previous chapter. See Stephen Nicholas and Peter R. Shergold, 'Unshackling the Past', in Stephen Nicholas (ed.), *Convict Workers: Reinterpreting Australia's Past*, Cambridge and Sydney: Cambridge University Press, 1988, p. 3.
[15] *First Report from the Select Committee of the House of Commons on Transportation; Together with the Minutes of Evidence, and Appendix*, [C 244] HC 1856, xvii, p. 179.
[16] Randall McGowen, 'Civilising Punishment: The End of the Public Execution in England', *Journal of British Studies*, vol. 33, no. 3 (Jul. 1994), p. 275.

these concerns. Consequently, the cessation of transportation had a significant influence on penal policy. It was, as Barry Godfrey, David Cox and Stephen Farrall have said, 'the catalyst for a new legislative programme'.[17] Martin Wiener has also argued that 'fears induced by the ending of transportation' were the 'most important short-run influence' on the penal legislation of governments in the 1850s and 1860s.[18] Indeed penal measures of 1853, 1857 and 1864, which will be discussed below, were justified primarily on the grounds that transportation was no longer available.

The rise of the penitentiary was the other key change in Britain's penal regime during the early and mid-nineteenth century. Since the late eighteenth century advocates of reform such as Whig politicians Samuel Romilly, Thomas Buxton and William Wilberforce had attacked the state of Britain's prisons with some justification.[19] As A. H. Manchester has claimed, many prisons were 'squalid nurseries of crime' in which old and young offenders mixed freely.[20] In response to such concerns a new type of prison was created. In 1816 the first new model prison, called a penitentiary, was opened at Millbank in London. Pentonville, also in London, followed in 1842. The design of these prisons was partly borrowed from the utilitarian Jeremy Bentham's sketch of 1791, entitled *Panopticon*. His prison design allowed a person standing in a central hexagon to enjoy a clear line of sight into every cell in six pentagons that led from it, enabling an 'omnipresent inspection'.[21] Owing to the perceived benefits of this design at Millbank and Pentonville, a further fifty-six panoptic penitentiaries were constructed throughout the UK by 1848. In these penitentiaries corporal punishment was rarely used and the separation of prisoners was firmly enforced. These elements of the penitentiary regime were accompanied by religious teaching, a strict diet and a total intolerance of the prison subculture of drinking,

---

[17] Barry Godfrey, David Cox and Stephen Farrall, *Serious Offenders: An Historical Study of Habitual Criminals*, London: Oxford University Press, 2010, p. 49.
[18] Martin Wiener, *Reconstructing the Criminal: Culture, Law and Policy in England, 1830–1914*, Cambridge: Cambridge University Press, 1990, p. 141.
[19] McGowen, 'Civilising Punishment', p. 263.
[20] A. H. Manchester, *A Modern Legal History of England and Wales, 1750–1950*, London: Butterworth, 1980, pp. 24, 77. For further information regarding the parlous state of many British prisons before the advent of the penitentiary, and the concern that this elicited, also see Michael Ignatieff, *A Just Measure of Pain: The Penitentiary in the Industrial Revolution, 1750–1850*, London: Macmillan, 1978, p. 77; Philip Priestley, *Victorian Prison Lives*, London: Methuen, 1985, p. 34; Margaret DeLacy, review of Janet Semple, *Bentham's Penitentiary: A Study of the Panoptic Penitentiary*, Oxford: Clarendon Press, 1993, *American Historical Review*, vol. 99, no. 5 (Dec. 1994), p. 1690.
[21] Ignatieff, *A Just Measure of Pain*, p. 78.

gambling and the use of prostitutes that formerly prevailed.[22] Finally, and in contrast to the former, locally run, system, 'no aspect of prison administration was to escape the principle of uniformity'.[23]

Previously the focus of much punishment had been the body of the offender, demonstrating the power of the sovereign in a public display intended primarily to deter, not to reform.[24] The penitentiary was focused instead on the mind and soul of the offender. The various activities described above, which prisoners were forced to undertake, showed the extent of the control that the state could exert over offenders. The intended result, to borrow Michel Foucault's memorable expression, was the creation of 'docile bodies' by wearing prisoners down and convincing them of the futility of rebellion in the face of the power of the state.[25] Indeed, the first of Foucault's seven universal maxims of good penitentiary conditions was that '[p]enal detention must have as its essential function the transformation of the individual's behaviour'.[26] Thus there was a discernible 'shift' in the 'objective of punishment'.[27] The chief concern of penal policy, embodied in the new penitentiaries, was now to 'transform the criminal'.[28]

Legislative recognition of the decline of transportation and the desire to accommodate more offenders in penitentiaries in Britain first came in 1853. In that year Van Diemen's Land stopped receiving convicts, meaning that of the Australian colonies only Western Australia remained a possible destination for transported criminals. This change was met by the introduction of the new punishment of penal servitude as a substitute for sentences of transportation of fewer than fourteen years, which were abolished. Penal servitude was to involve an initial period of nine months' solitary confinement. The remainder of the sentence was then to be served at one of five prisons that had been specially designed or adapted to facilitate employment of prisoners on public works.

---

[22] Sean McConville, 'The Victorian Prison: England, 1865-1965', in Norval Morris and David J. Rothman (eds.), *The Oxford History of the Prison: The Practice of Punishment in Western Society*, New York: Oxford University Press, 1995, p. 144; John Briggs, Christopher Harrison, Angus McInnes and David Vincent, *Crime and Punishment in England: An Introductory History*, London: University College London Press, 1996, pp. 167-9.

[23] Heather Tomlinson, *Victorian Prisons: Administration and Architecture, 1835-1877*, unpublished doctoral thesis, University of London, 1975, p. 66.

[24] Michel Foucault, *Discipline and Punish: The Birth of the Prison*, Alan Sheridan (trans.), London: Allen Lane, 1977 (first published 1975), pp. 8-10, 32-54; V. A. C. Gatrell, *The Hanging Tree: Execution and the English People 1770-1868*, Oxford and New York: Oxford University Press, 1994, pp. 396-408.

[25] Foucault, *Discipline and Punish*, p. 138.

[26] Ibid., p. 269.

[27] David Garland, 'Foucault's "Discipline and Punish" – An Exposition and Critique', *American Bar Foundation Journal*, vol. 11, no. 4 (Autumn 1986), p. 850.

[28] Ibid.

These facilities were at Borstal, Chatham, Dartmoor, Portland and Portsmouth.[29] As Peter Bartrip has noted, this was a 'classic case' of 'reform through pressure of events'.[30] When introducing the bill's second reading in the House of Lords on 11 July 1853, Lord Cranworth, Lord Chancellor in Lord Aberdeen's Whig/Peelite coalition government, made it clear that the end of transportation was the reason for the legislation.[31] A minimum of three years' penal servitude in a large penitentiary augmented magistrates' and judges' existing sentencing option of two years or less in one of the country's numerous small, local gaols.[32] The Lord Chancellor explained that penal servitude had been introduced to keep criminals off the streets for longer, as a deterrent, and to provide the best chance of reformation.[33]

The 1853 act, which covered the entire UK, also borrowed an Australian innovation. Any criminal sentenced to penal servitude would be eligible for 'a licence to be at large in the United Kingdom and the Channel Islands'.[34] The main effect of these licences, commonly called tickets-of-leave, was to reduce the length of the initial sentence. Using this mechanism judges could approve a remission of between one-sixth and one-third of the total sentence, based upon reports from prison staff. The measure was a significant departure from past practice, as this was the first time the notion of remission for good behaviour had been introduced into law in the UK. The government hoped that licences would aid reformation, as prisoners would be aware that good behaviour would be rewarded. Licences could be revoked at Her Majesty's pleasure.[35] There was also a pragmatic reason for the introduction of the ticket-of-leave system. Indeed, it was primarily put in place 'to keep faith' with several thousand convicted criminals, sentenced to transportation but serving prison sentences in the UK with the expectation of ultimate release on licence in the colonies.[36] Due to the fact that very few criminals were now being transported, these convicts were serving their sentences at home. The directors of convict prisons feared a breakdown of discipline would be the result of keeping these

---

[29] Helen Johnston, 'Victorian Prison', in Yvonne Jewkes and Jamie Bennett (eds.), *Dictionary of Prisons and Punishment*, Cullompton: Willan, 2008, p. 306.
[30] Bartrip, 'Public Opinion and Law Enforcement', p. 153.
[31] 129 *Parliamentary Debates*, HL (3rd ser.), col. 7 (11 Jul. 1853).
[32] Briggs, Harrison, McInnes and Vincent, *Crime and Punishment in England*, pp. 169, 173.
[33] 129 *Parliamentary Debates*, HL (3rd ser.), col. 7 (11 Jul. 1853).
[34] *Penal Servitude Act*, 16 & 17 Vict., c. 99, 1853, s. 9.
[35] Ibid., s. 11.
[36] *General Report on the Convict Prisons, with Observations on Several Questions Connected with Management and Disposal of Convicts, Tickets-of-Leave, Supervision of the Police, Irish System, Etc., 1860–61*, [C 3055] HC and HL 1862, xxv, p. 6.

inmates confined for the full period of their sentence and urged the government to introduce a system of remission.[37] Finally, licencing was also a cheaper option than continued incarceration, which was another – albeit lesser – reason for its introduction.[38] The legislation received bipartisan support and came into effect on 1 September 1853.

The changes to the *Penal Servitude Acts* were heavily criticized by a commentator who would become very influential over the course of the rest of the 1850s and the 1860s. Matthew Davenport Hill, the recorder of Birmingham, or principal magistrate in the city, was 'a leading penal reformer of the period'.[39] As Bartrip has noted, this position gave Hill a 'public platform from which, through his addresses or charges to grand juries, he could air his views, particularly on matters of penal and criminal law reform'. Consequently, by 1850 Hill was widely known 'as a "criminologist" and penal reformer'.[40] He championed a set of ideas that he had first set out in 1846, albeit to much opprobrium.[41] Hill argued that, for recidivists, short periods of imprisonment achieved little. While he believed incorrigible offenders should be detained until 'released by death', if freed, 'known criminals' should remain the object of 'just and unavoidable suspicion' through supervision.[42] This, in Hill's view, should be facilitated by a register of known criminals. He borrowed this idea from his brother Frederic, himself a prison inspector, who had proposed it in 1845 as a means to ensure that repeat offenders were recognized as such when they appeared before the courts.[43]

---

[37] This body had been established in 1850 in order to oversee the running of convict prisons, where prisoners were sent while awaiting transportation. It replaced various smaller bodies. See Clive Emsley, 'Jebb, Sir Joshua (1793–1863)', in H. C. G. Matthew and Brian Harrison (eds.), *Oxford Dictionary of National Biography*, Oxford: Oxford University Press, 2004; online ed., Lawrence Goldman (ed.), May 2012, http://www.oxforddnb.com/view/article/14683 (accessed 25 Nov. 2015); Joshua Jebb to Horatio Waddington, undersecretary at the Home Office, 10 Feb. 1853, TNA, HO 12/4/362.

[38] For the significant cost of incarceration in the nineteenth century see G. Larry Mays and L. Thomas Winfrey Jnr., *Essential of Corrections*, 4th ed., Belmont: Wadsworth, 2009, p. 39.

[39] Radzinowicz and Hood, 'Incapacitating the Habitual Criminal', p. 1317.

[40] P. W. J. Bartrip, 'Hill, Matthew Davenport (1792–1872)', in H. C. G. Matthew and Brian Harrison (eds.), *Oxford Dictionary of National Biography*, Oxford: Oxford University Press, 2004; online ed., Lawrence Goldman (ed.), 2004, http://www.oxforddnb.com/view/article/13286 (accessed 24 Nov. 2015).

[41] Matthew Davenport Hill, *Draft Report on the Principles of Punishment: Presented to the Committee on Criminal Law Appointed by the Law Amendment Society, in December, 1846*, London: William Clowes and Sons, 1847, pp. 1–19.

[42] Matthew Davenport Hill, *Suggestions for the Repression of Crime*, London: Patterson Smith, 1857, p. 182.

[43] *Tenth Report of the Inspectors Appointed under the Provisions of the Acts 5 & 6 Will. IV c. 38, to Visit Different Prisons of Great Britain, IV. Scotland, Northumberland, and Durham*, [C 688] HC and HL 1845, xxiv, p. viii.

Hill criticized the act of 1853, in particular, on the grounds that something should be done to control those released on tickets-of-leave before the expiry of their sentences.[44] No mechanism was in place to do this. For example, police forces were not notified when a licence-holder was released into their district.[45] The Home Office believed that surveillance of licence-holders was incompatible with the liberty of the subject.[46] It appears this view was widely held, as Hill's proposals were denounced in various quarters on the same grounds.[47] Unlike many of the countries of continental Europe, Britain did not have a history of organized police forces with covert functions. However, some private forces had carried out detective work. London's so-called Bow Street runners, which were formed by the magistrate Henry Fielding in 1749 and ultimately disbanded in 1839, often engaged in surveillance.[48] Nonetheless, 'spy systems' were heavily criticized by many British writers due to a perceived threat to individual liberty.[49] Bernard Porter provides numerous examples from Britain in the nineteenth century of revulsion at police surveillance in other European countries.[50] For example, in 1850 the novelist Charles Dickens criticized the use of spies in Italian states. He said, 'They assume no distinctive dress – make no sign; they walk in darkness, and move like the pestilence.' Englishmen, Dickens approvingly continued, spoke 'not under the terror of an organized spy system'.[51] From the regular articulation of such views, it is likely that they were widely held.[52] Therefore, as Radzinowicz and Hood have argued, when first put forward in the 1840s and 1850s, many people found Hill's surveillance proposals 'quite unacceptable'.[53] They 'ran counter to deeply held notions of justice'.[54]

Despite the opposition to Hill's views, by 1855 London's newspapers were expressing concerns that the ticket-of-leave system was fundamentally flawed. As

---

[44] Hill, *Suggestions for the Repression of Crime*, p. 182.
[45] *Report from the Select Committee of the House of Commons on Transportation*, p. 25.
[46] Ibid.
[47] *Times*, 24 Oct. 1850, p. 4; Joshua Jebb, 'Reports of the Directors of the Convict Prisons on the Discipline and Management of Pentonville, Millbank, and Parkhurst Prisons, and of Portland, Portsmouth, Dartmoor, Chatham, and Brixton Prisons, with Fulham Refuge and the Invalid Prison at Woking, for the year 1860. With memorandum by Sir Joshua Jebb, K.C.B., Chairman, &c', *Justice of the Peace, and County, Borough, Poor Law Union, and Parish Law Recorder*, vol. 26, no. 11 (15 Mar. 1862), p. 170.
[48] J. M. Beattie, *The First English Detectives: The Bow Street Runners and the Policing of London, 1750–1840*, Oxford: Oxford University Press, 2012, pp. 60–76.
[49] Charles Dickens, 'Spy Police', *Household Words*, vol. 1 (21 Sept. 1850), p. 611.
[50] Bernard Porter, *The Origins of the Vigilant State: The London Metropolitan Police Special Branch before the First World War*, London: Weidenfeld and Nicolson, 1987, p. 2.
[51] Dickens, 'Spy Police', p. 611.
[52] Porter, *The Origins of the Vigilant State*, pp. 2–3.
[53] Radzinowicz and Hood, 'Incapacitating the Habitual Criminal', p. 1322.
[54] Radzinowicz and Hood, 'Judicial Discretion and Sentencing Standards', p. 1327.

several historians have noted, numerous London newspapers argued that violent crime was increasing in the capital, particularly that of 'garotting'.[55] Holders of tickets-of-leave were held to be responsible. The *Standard*, a conservative daily newspaper, argued that violent attacks were being perpetrated in London by 'convicts who have been liberated under the ticket-of-leave system'.[56] The *Era*, a liberal weekly newspaper, in discussing possible remedies for this situation, condemned the idea of early release as 'morbidly tender' and argued instead that 'every judicial sentence should be fully executed'.[57] While various newspapers expressed concern about the new system, *The Times*, which – of course – was highly influential, was most vocal.[58] Rob Sindall has carried out an analysis of newspaper reports of violent crime and the ticket-of-leave system and found that during the winter months of 1856 *The Times* published seven editorials and thirty-one letters on the subject.[59] It is unclear exactly why newspaper reports of the ticket-of-leave system became so numerous and negative in 1855 and 1856. Bartrip has undertaken an assessment of the judicial statistics and has found that, while the number of indictments rose in the first half of the 1850s, in London and elsewhere, 'it is hard to maintain that there was a significant trend towards more "serious" crime, particularly given the population increase'.[60] Furthermore, there was no data to corroborate the supposed link between violent crime and holders of tickets-of-leave. Nevertheless, as we will see, this connection was readily accepted, by politicians at least. The key factor that precipitated the spate of reports of garottings was probably the desire to sell newspapers. Several reports of attacks in 1855, allegedly carried out by licence-holders, were exploited in order to do this.[61] Notwithstanding the lack of any firm statistical basis, violent crime in London was used by various newspapers of differing political leanings to criticize the 1853 legislation.

As a result of this perceived link between violent crime in London and the licence system, in April 1856 an inquiry was instigated by Francis Scott MP, the

---

[55] A thorough discussion of the reporting of violent crime in London in 1855–6, by various newspapers, is contained in R. Sindall, 'The London Garotting Panics of 1856 and 1862', *Social History*, vol. 12, no. 3 (Oct. 1987), pp. 351–9. Also see Bartrip, 'Public Opinion and Law Enforcement', p. 156.
[56] *Standard*, 7 Jul. 1854, p. 4.
[57] *Era*, 14 Oct. 1855, p. 9.
[58] For the great influence of *The Times*, especially among the middle class and politicians, see Richard Shannon, *The Age of Disraeli, 1868–1881: The Rise of Tory Democracy*, London and New York: Longman, 1992, p. 128.
[59] Sindall, 'The London Garotting Panics of 1856 and 1862', p. 352.
[60] Bartrip, 'Public Opinion and Law Enforcement', p. 156.
[61] See two letters to the editor of *The Times* by correspondents who claimed they had been the victims of garotte attacks. Jacob Bueler, 'Garotte Robberies', *Times*, 19 Feb. 1855, p. 7; J. L. C. H., 'A Garotte Attack in Fleet Street', *Times*, 22 Sept. 1855, p. 6.

Conservative member for the Scottish constituency of Berwickshire. This was necessary, he said, because of the effects of the gradual end of transportation as a penal option. Since transportation to Australia was drawing to a close, a 'criminal population' had built up in London that 'formed a distinct educated, well-trained class'.[62] The activity of this class, according to Scott, had led to a significant increase in violent crime. In calling for a select committee he argued that part of the remedy for this supposed problem was greater surveillance of licence-holders and repeat offenders, as Hill had been advocating.[63] Scott's motion received bipartisan support and the committee that was established as a result noted that as 'transportation must cease, the whole mind of England' was 'awakened' to the question of how to get 'quit of the criminals'.[64] The committee heard from magistrates and judges, prison staff, police and civil servants, who all agreed that more could be done to answer this question. The most common suggestions brought before the committee in order to strengthen the 1853 system were the use of longer terms of imprisonment and police supervision of repeat offenders upon release. The committee heard evidence from five witnesses that the punishment of repeat offenders was too lenient.[65] For example, Sir William Erle, a judge of the court of the Queen's Bench, criticized his colleagues' current practice, asserting that 'a heavy sentence ought to be passed on confirmed depravity'. He claimed that 'the periods of imprisonment' imposed by many magistrates and judges 'have been too short'.[66] Supervision was also discussed as a possible remedy for the perceived defects of the 1853 legislation. Sir Richard Mayne, commissioner of the Metropolitan Police Force, was asked whether licence-holders and repeat offenders should be subject to police surveillance in order to encourage rehabilitation and prevent further crime. The commissioner thought not, as surveillance was 'inconsistent with our habits here and offensive'.[67] Yet Hill's ideas were now being seriously discussed.

The select committee's conclusion was measured. It did not accept that the 1853 legislation required wholesale change, finding that licensing 'has been too short a time in operation in this country to enable the committee to form a clear and decided opinion either as to the effects which it has already produced, or as

[62] 141 *Parliamentary Debates*, HC (3rd ser.), col. 395 (3 Apr. 1856).
[63] Ibid., col. 395.
[64] *Second Report from the Select Committee of the House of Commons on Transportation; Together with the Minutes of Evidence, and Appendix*, [C 296] HC 1856, xvii, pp. 36, 55.
[65] These were Sir Richard Mayne, Matthew Davenport Hill, William Hart, the procurator fiscal at the sheriff court in Lanarkshire, and Sir William Erle, a judge of the court of the Queen's Bench. See the *Second Report from the Select Committee of the House of Commons on Transportation*, pp. 17, 68, 128.
[66] Ibid., p. 128.
[67] Ibid., p. 142.

to its probable ultimate working'.[68] It endorsed the principle behind the ticket-of-leave system, namely 'that of enabling a convict to obtain ... the remission of a portion' of the initial sentence.[69] But the committee was critical of the way this new system had been administered, noting the lack of any mechanism to enforce licence conditions.[70] While the committee did not recommend Hill's controversial schemes of indeterminate sentences and supervision, it did criticize the 1853 legislation. Its findings were made law by the *Penal Servitude Act 1857*, which received royal assent on 1 July.

The act, reflecting the committee's report, steered a middle course between the earlier legislation and the ideas of Hill. Principally, it sought to increase the length of sentences by equating terms of penal servitude to the previous terms of transportation. The committee had recommended that 'sentences of penal servitude should be changed and lengthened so as to be identical with the terms of transportation for which they are respectively substituted'.[71] Whereas four years' penal servitude had been deemed equivalent to seven years' transportation under the 1853 act, the new equation was therefore seven to seven. A Home Office circular of 27 July 1857 complemented this provision by laying down longer minimum periods of confinement before release on licence.[72] Moreover, holders of tickets-of-leave were required to notify the police when moving to a different area of the country. As Sindall has said, some of the 'slack administration of the 1853 act was tightened up'.[73] The legislation did not seek to fundamentally alter penal policy. Nonetheless, it was a step towards the establishment of greater police control over released criminals. Bartrip and Sindall, the two historians to most fully investigate the genesis of the 1857 legislation, have argued correctly that it was largely a response to a perceived panic about crime.[74] However, this legislation also represented an increasing acceptance within parliament of the views that Hill had been consistently advocating for over a decade.

The 1857 changes to the *Penal Servitude Act of 1853* did not satisfy Hill and his supporters, who were now able to utilize a powerful vehicle to push for the

---

[68] *Third Report from the Select Committee of the House of Commons on Transportation; Together with the Minutes of Evidence, and Appendix*, [C 355] HC 1856, xvii, p. iii.
[69] Ibid., p. iv.
[70] Ibid.
[71] Ibid., p. iii.
[72] *Report of the Commissioners Appointed to Inquire into the Operation of the Acts Relating to Transportation and Penal Servitude. Vol 1. Report*, [C 3190] HC 1863, xxi, p. 12.
[73] R. Sindall, *Street Violence in the Nineteenth Century: Media Panic or Real Danger?* Leicester: Leicester University Press, 1990, p. 135.
[74] Sindall, 'The London Garotting Panics of 1856 and 1862', p. 353; Bartrip, 'Public Opinion and Law Enforcement', pp. 155–62.

further changes they desired. This vehicle was the SSA, which was formed in 1857. From mid-century onwards there was a growth in the number of middle-class pressure groups, such as the SSA, the Vigilance Association for the Defence of Personal Rights, the Law Amendment Society and the National Reformatory Union. As Stefan Petrow has noted, these groups sought to exploit 'the widening of the franchise' in 1832 and then again in 1867 by presenting themselves as the representatives of the newly enfranchised middle class in an effort to alter government policy.[75] The changes desired by these groups, many of whose members were influenced by evangelicalism or utilitarianism, were often those that would aid individuals to choose conduct consistent with the middle-class norm of respectability.[76] This was certainly the case with the SSA, which was conceived in the autumn of 1856. George Hastings, the lawyer and general secretary of the SSA, told the group's first annual congress that

> it was suggested to Lord Brougham that he should take the lead in founding an association for affording to those engaged in all the various efforts now happily begun for the improvement of the people, an opportunity for considering social economics as a great whole.[77]

Many of the association's early members were, as Hastings said, already actively pursuing various reforms designed to raise the moral standards of the people. The SSA drew members from two particular pressure groups: the Law Amendment Society and the National Reformatory Union. The former campaigned, primarily, for the creation of a ministry of justice and married women's property rights, while the latter sought the establishment of reformatory schools for young offenders as a way to break up the criminal class as transportation came to an end.[78] The concerns of these pre-existing pressure groups became central to the programme of the new association. As John Stuart Mill, himself a member of the governing body of the SSA, said, it was a forum for the expression of 'all opinions consistent with the profession of a desire for social change'.[79]

---

[75] Stefan Petrow, *Policing Morals: The Metropolitan Police and the Home Office 1870–1914*, Oxford: Clarendon Press, 1995, p. 17; Goldman, 'The Social Science Association', pp. 95–134.

[76] Petrow, *Policing Morals*, p. 17; Wiener, *Reconstructing the Criminal*, pp. 52–83; Wiener, review of A. P. Donajgrodzki (ed.), *Social Control in Nineteenth Century Britain*, London: Croom Helm, 1977, *Journal of Social History*, vol. 12, no. 2 (Winter 1978), pp. 314–21.

[77] G. W. Hastings, 'Introduction', *Transactions 1857*, p. xxi.

[78] Goldman, 'The Social Science Association', p. 98.

[79] J. S. Mill to Thomas Bayley Potter, 17 Mar. 1864, in Francis E. Mineka and Dwight N. Lindley (eds.), *The Later Letters of John Stuart Mill 1849–1873*, vol. 15, Toronto: University of Toronto Press, 1972, pp. 632–3.

Those who joined the SSA and expressed such opinions were often highly influential. Many were drawn from the 'class of professional men with expert knowledge', a significant number being lawyers or doctors.[80] The inaugural council of the SSA included numerous people of great influence, including Edwin Chadwick, the social reformer, and John Simon, the surgeon and public health reformer.[81] The SSA was intended as a meeting place for people such as these, men and some women, and key political leaders, thereby increasing the likelihood of legislative action that was in line with the aims of the association.[82] Indeed, many more members were politicians themselves. For example, the original patrons of the association were Lord John Russell, twice a Liberal prime minister, Lord Stanley, an influential Tory who would later serve as foreign secretary in both Conservative and Liberal cabinets, and Lord Brougham, the campaigner for parliamentary reform and the abolition of slavery. Eighteen peers were members of the association's inaugural council, as were twenty-eight MPs.[83] Most politicians who became members of the SSA were Liberals. In 1867 eighty-five members of the association's governing council, whose total membership was 266, were politicians. Of these, sixty-four were Liberals.[84] Consequently, the SSA was well placed to influence policy, and especially when the Liberal Party was in power.

The association held its first congress in Birmingham in July 1857. The president, Lord Brougham, explained that the purpose of the association was 'to aid legislation by preparing measures, by explaining them, by recommending them to the community, or, it may be, by stimulating the legislature to adopt them'.[85] Such efforts were focused on five areas of policy, each of which had its own department within the association. These were penal policy, legal reform, education, public health and social economy. Penal policy, which is of most interest here, was therefore a key area in which the association sought to influence the government and the legislature, and from its inception its efforts to do so were vigorous. For instance, the chair of the department of penal policy gave an address at every annual SSA congress. As Goldman has noted, penal reform was a 'central theme' of the SSA.[86]

---

[80] Goldman, *Science, Reform and Politics in Victorian Britain*, p. 2.
[81] Hastings, 'Introduction', *Transactions 1857*, pp. xv–i.
[82] Petrow, *Policing Morals*, p. 50.
[83] Hastings, 'Introduction', *Transactions 1857*, pp. xv–i.
[84] Petrow, *Policing Morals*, p. 50.
[85] Lord Brougham, 'Inaugural Address', in *Transactions of the National Association for the Advancement of Social Science, 1857*, London: John W. Parker and Son, 1858, p. 23.
[86] Goldman, 'The Social Science Association', p. 143.

From its establishment the SSA aligned itself with the then unpopular ideas of Hill, which were now being put into practice in Ireland by Sir Walter Crofton, the director of Irish prisons since 1854.[87] In response to the cessation of transportation and the introduction of the ticket-of-leave system through the *Penal Servitude Act 1853*, Crofton implemented Hill's ideas of a register of known criminals and supervision of holders of tickets-of-leave.[88] There were different systems for Dublin and the rest of the country. In Dublin James Organ, whose chief employment was as a lecturer in the city's prisons, was responsible for supervision. Commencing these latter duties in January 1856, Organ visited every licence-holder in Dublin once a fortnight and furnished regular reports to Crofton. Crofton was very happy with the results of this system, arguing that 'nothing can be more strict' than the supervision carried out by Organ and that when licence conditions are breached the ticket-of-leave is 'revoked immediately'.[89] The female staff of Dublin's women's prisons carried out this same task for female licence-holders, with, according to Crofton and the other directors, similarly satisfactory results.[90] A different system, which came into effect on 1 January 1857, operated outside Dublin. Licence-holders had to report themselves to a designated local constabulary barracks on the first day of every month. If the local police had information suggesting that the licence-holder was 'leading an idle, irregular life' then this would be reported to the directors, who, upon investigation, could revoke the licence.[91] Despite this supervision, rates of revocation were very low. By August 1857 the licences of only 1 per cent of women under supervision had been revoked, while for men the figure was 3 per cent.[92] Crofton could therefore argue that his system was leading to the reformation of criminals.[93]

Crofton's assertions of the success of registration and supervision in Ireland found a sympathetic audience in the SSA. The example of the so-called Irish system was taken as proof that the gaze of the police, or other functionaries, discouraged crime.[94] Members of the SSA then used the apparent success of the Irish system to push for similar reforms throughout the rest of the UK.

---

[87] Patrick Carroll-Burke, *Colonial Discipline: The Making of the Irish Convict System*, Dublin: Four Courts Press, 2000, pp. 102–3, 125.
[88] Ibid.
[89] *Report of the Commissioners Appointed to Inquire into the Operation of the Acts Relating to Transportation and Penal Servitude. Vol. 2. Minutes of Evidence*, [C 3190] HC 1863, xxi, p. 274.
[90] *Fourth Report of the Directors of Convict Prisons in Ireland*, [C 2376] HC 1857, xxx, p. 30.
[91] Ibid., p. 14.
[92] Ibid., p. 30.
[93] *Report of the Commissioners Appointed to Inquire into the Operation of the Acts Relating to Transportation and Penal Servitude. Vol. 2*, p. 274.
[94] *General Report on the Convict Prisons*, pp. 1, 22.

For example, the Earl of Carlisle, a Liberal member of the House of Lords, delivered a lengthy address to the 1858 congress in which he praised the Irish system, offered Crofton 'my admiration' and also recognized Hill as 'a foremost authority' on reform. He described the registration and supervision of members of the 'criminal class' as 'sound', arguing that such measures were, at least in part, the answer to the question of 'what shall we do with our convicts?' now that transportation to Australia was coming to an end.[95] Such sentiments were expressed every year from 1857 until 1862.[96] As Sir Joshua Jebb – chairman of the board of directors of convict prisons – said, the 'Irish system' was being 'pressed' upon the public and the parliament by the SSA.[97]

It is worth briefly noting that policy 'improvisations' involving increased state intervention were not unusual in nineteenth-century Ireland.[98] Therefore, it is not surprising that it was there that Hill's ideas were first taken up. Numerous examples of a centralizing tendency in the government of Ireland, which was far more marked than in Britain, can be found. These include the establishment of dispensaries to provide free medical care to the poor in 1805, a national school system in 1831 and prison reform in 1856, all of which were 'stages ahead' of Britain.[99] Oliver MacDonagh, who has most fully analysed this phenomenon, provides various reasons for what he calls the 'centralised authoritarianism' of Irish government, including a governing class that was few in number and separated from the bulk of the Irish population by religion.[100] The result of these factors was a greater readiness of the state to intervene than in Britain, where supervision was widely condemned in the 1850s and 1860s. In the case of the registration and supervision of licence-holders, Crofton's claims for the success of the system in Ireland allowed the SSA to advocate from a position of strength for the same measures to be applied throughout the UK.

*

[95] The Earl of Carlisle, 'Address on the Punishment and Reformation of Criminals', *Transactions 1858*, pp. 70, 72.
[96] For example, see the address of Arthur Kinnaird, Liberal MP, to the 1860 congress, in which he praised the 'beneficial results' of the Irish system, which can be found in *Transactions 1860*, p. 114. Also see a paper that Baron Holtzendorff, the Prussian academic, contributed to the 1861 *Transactions*, 'On Police Supervision'. He argued that supervision, along the lines of that which was operational in Ireland, was necessary as criminals lacked self-control. See *Transactions 1861*, p. 415.
[97] *General Report on the Convict Prisons*, pp. 1, 22.
[98] Oliver MacDonagh, *Early Victorian Government: 1830-1870*, London: Weidenfeld and Nicholson, 1977, p. 181.
[99] Oliver MacDonagh, 'The Economy and Society, 1830–45', in W. E. Vaughan (ed.), *A New History of Ireland, vol. 5, Ireland under the Union, I: 1801–1870*, Oxford: Clarendon Press, 1989, pp. 209, 212, 233.
[100] MacDonagh, *Early Victorian Government*, pp. 180–1.

In 1862, once again, London's press increased its reporting of violent crime in the capital. Reports of garottings allegedly carried out by licence-holders led to greater parliamentary support for the ideas that the SSA had been pursuing since its inception, and Hill longer still. A garotte attack on Liberal parliamentarian James Pilkington was the first of many similar reported offences in London in 1862 and early 1863 which, it was argued in the press, were the work of licence-holders.[101] Numerous historians have argued that reports of violent crime in newspapers informed and often altered the views of their readers.[102] To determine the opinions of the public concerning crime is, of course, a difficult task. As Bartrip has noted, it is hard to ascertain what 'public opinion' actually was in the nineteenth century, beyond 'the sentiments expressed in parliament or the pages of the newspapers', which represented, far more often than not, the interests of the middle and upper classes.[103] Nonetheless, he argues that the alarm expressed in the newspapers had a role in forming the views of many Londoners.[104] There is good reason to believe that newspapers moulded the views of a largely middle-class readership.[105] Newspapers themselves certainly argued that they had shaped the views of the public in their reporting of an increase in violence on London's streets. For example, the liberal journal *All The Year Round* said that news of 'garotte' attacks had 'created quite a panic in the town' and the *Illustrated London News*, which was a conservative weekly newspaper, argued that '[g]arotting is the talk of the town'.[106]

As several historians have said, the increased level of reporting of violent crime in London in 1862 was part of a 'moral panic' in the capital, during which alarm was increased in the minds of many Londoners.[107] A moral panic can be defined as a period of exaggerated public alarm, which is often caused by media reports and usually focuses upon a social group that is perceived as dangerous and a

---

[101] This was discussed in the previous chapter. For examples of this reporting see *The Times*, 14 Aug. 1862, p. 8; *Daily News*, 2 Dec.1862, p. 4.
[102] Godfrey, Cox and Farrall, *Serious Offenders*, p. 12; Bartrip, 'Public Opinion and Law Enforcement', pp. 150–81; Jennifer Davis, 'The London Garotting Panic of 1862: A Moral Panic and the Creation of a Criminal Class in Mid-Victorian England', in V. A. C. Gatrell, Bruce Lenman and G. Parker (eds.), *Crime and the Law: The Social History of Crime in Western Europe since 1500*, London: Europa Publications, 1980, pp. 190–213.
[103] Bartrip, 'Public Opinion and Law Enforcement', p. 173.
[104] Ibid., pp. 150–81.
[105] This was discussed in the previous chapter. Also see Sindall, *Street Violence in the Nineteenth Century*, p. 36.
[106] 'Small Beer Chronicles', *All the Year Round*, vol. 8, no. 189 (6 Dec. 1862), p. 296; *The Illustrated London News*, 29 Nov. 1862, p. 571.
[107] Godfrey, Cox and Farrall, *Serious Offenders*, p. 12; Bartrip, 'Public Opinion and Law Enforcement', pp. 150–81; Davis, 'The London Garotting Panic of 1862', pp. 190–213; Briggs, Harrison, McInnes and Vincent, *Crime and Punishment in England*, p. 170.

threat to the rest of society. Many contemporaries, of course, already perceived licence-holders as deviant – members of a hostile criminal class.[108] Such alarm, moral panic theory argues, may lead to and be reinforced by reactive legislation, as indeed was the case following alarm in London in 1855 and 1856, which has been discussed above.[109] The renewed panic in 1862 was probably most marked among members of the middle class in London. As Sindall has explained:

> For the middle classes, knowledge of events in London's streets was restricted to their own limited personal experience and the vicarious experience of reported events in the press. The importance of an event in the public mind is largely dictated by the proportion of coverage it receives in the daily press. Consequently, the increase in reports of garotte attacks led the middle classes to feel insecure in the face of this perceived threat.[110]

At least partly as a consequence of this public alarm, the government was soon under pressure to act.

In December 1862 the Liberal home secretary, Sir George Grey, instituted an inquiry into the efficacy of the *Penal Servitude Acts*. He did so at the urging of London's magistrates. On 15 December Grey received a deputation of London magistrates, led by the lord mayor, eager to discuss the state of the law as it applied to 'the class of hardened criminals'.[111] Prior to the meeting, London's magistrates had resolved that 'the present system of dealing with the criminal population of this country is defective'.[112] They believed that many repeat offenders and those released on licence, who would previously have been deposited in one of the Australian penal colonies, now found their way back to their old haunts in London. In coming chapters it will be shown that London's magistrates often interpreted legislation in a manner that minimized its negative impact upon members of the working class, largely due to the role of London's so-called police courts in dispensing justice, and a range of other services, to

---

[108] S. J. Stevenson, 'The "Habitual Criminal" in Nineteenth-Century England: Some Observations on the Figures', *Urban History*, vol. 13 (May 1986), pp. 37–60; Donald Thomas, *The Victorian Underworld*, London: Hodder and Stoughton, 1998, p. 3; Lynda Nead, *Victorian Babylon: People, Streets and Images in Nineteenth-Century London*, New Haven and London: Yale University Press, 2000, pp. 3–10, 71–2.
[109] Charles Krinsky, 'Introduction', in Charles Krinsky (ed.), *The Ashgate Research Companion to Moral Panics*, Farnham and Burlington: Ashgate Publishing, 2003, p. 1.
[110] Sindall, 'The London Garotting Panics of 1856 and 1862', p. 359.
[111] *Times*, 16 Dec. 1862, p. 6.
[112] Ibid.

the poor.[113] Their unusual intervention in 1862 in favour of harsher measures is, therefore, further evidence of a panic regarding crime in London. When the group of magistrates expressed the same views to the home secretary that newspapers had been expounding since the attack on Pilkington, Grey readily accepted that the post-1853 penal system required investigation and appointed a commission to inquire into the *Penal Servitude Acts*.[114]

The committee of five Conservatives, five Liberals and two legal experts acknowledged the existence of public unease in London and recommended legislative change. It noted that recent acts of 'violence in the Metropolis' had 'caused great alarm to the public'.[115] The committee heard that the best way to quell this alarm was to better enforce licence conditions and sentence repeat offenders to longer periods in gaol in the first place. There were some grounds to inquire into the administration of the licence system. Horatio Waddington, undersecretary at the Home Office, admitted that in practice licence-holders experienced no disabilities. He conceded that licences were only revoked when fresh offences were committed, not for contravention of the various conditions that were stipulated on the licence. Consequently, these conditions were 'a dead letter'.[116] Mayne, the commissioner of the Metropolitan Police Force, also made it clear that there were no mechanisms to enforce licence conditions in London. He said that 'the reverse of inspection' took place and admitted that 'the police are actually directed not to interfere with "ticket-of-leave men"' in order, in particular, to ensure that they were able to gain employment.[117] In addition, Crofton criticized this present system. Now the vice-president of the department of penal policy within the SSA, Crofton was called by the committee and questioned at length. His evidence, provided over two days, fills fifty-eight pages of the committee's report. He was questioned for longer than any other witness. Crofton described the system of surveillance that had been in operation in Ireland since January 1856 and argued that supervision of repeat offenders was imperative in order to 'surround, by every possible means, the commission

---

[113] Jennifer Davis, 'A Poor Man's System of Justice: The London Police Courts in the Second Half of the Nineteenth Century', *Historical Journal*, vol. 27, no. 2 (Jun. 1984), p. 313; Hugh Gamon, *The London Police Court Today and Tomorrow*, London: J. M. Dent, 1907, pp. 226–7; H. T. Waddy, *The Police Court and Its Work*, London: Butterworth and Co., 1925, p. 1; Lydia Murdoch, *Imagined Orphans: Poor Families, Child Welfare, and Contested Citizenship in London*, New Jersey and London: Rutgers University Press, 2006, pp. 105–6.

[114] *Report of the Commissioners Appointed to Inquire into the Operation of the Acts Relating to Transportation and Penal Servitude. Vol. 1*, pp. 5–8.

[115] Ibid., p. 20.

[116] *Report of the Commissioners Appointed to Inquire into the Operation of the Acts Relating to Transportation and Penal Servitude. Vol. 2*, p. 31.

[117] Ibid., p. 433.

of crime by obstructions'.[118] Furthermore, as in 1856, longer sentences for repeat offenders were suggested as another way to deal with the public alarm. In all, five witnesses took up this position.[119] The SSA itself also called for police supervision and longer sentences for recidivists at this time.[120]

A second select committee, also in 1863, made similar findings after, once again, being heavily influenced by the SSA. On 19 February 1863, while the penal servitude acts commissioners were still hearing evidence, the Earl of Carnarvon called for the establishment of a further inquiry, this time to investigate discipline in local prisons. Carnarvon, who sat in the House of Lords as a Tory, took a keen interest in penal policy.[121] He was also a senior member of the SSA, rising to become its president in 1868.[122] This additional inquiry, the establishment of which, again, received bipartisan support, was also put in place due to a belief that violent crime in London had increased of late due to the accumulation of a criminal class. Carnarvon said there had been a 'startling increase in crime' and that 'during a very recent period there was such insecurity in the streets of London that it was dangerous to walk about after nightfall'.[123] The Lords accepted Carnarvon's arguments and appointed a select committee to inquire into 'the Present State of Discipline in Gaols and Houses of Correction' on 20 February.[124] The twelve-man select committee had equal representation from Conservatives, including Carnarvon who chaired the committee himself, and Liberals. Despite narrow terms of reference, Carnarvon ensured that the committee served as a forum for the programme of the SSA as Crofton, once again, discussed the benefits of police supervision at length. He was supported by the prison inspector John Perry, who said that the only way to restrain repeat offenders was to 'obtain a repressive power' over such men when 'discharged from prison'.[125] There was also much debate about the difficulty of identifying repeat offenders as such. Three witnesses said that many recidivists used aliases

---

[118] Ibid., p. 254.
[119] These were Mayne, Waddington, Jebb, Sydney Gurney, the clerk of assize on the Western circuit, and John Avery, the clerk of arraigns at the central criminal court. See *Report of the Commissioners Appointed to Inquire into the Operation of the Acts Relating to Transportation and Penal Servitude*. Vol. 2, pp. 77, 134, 150, 154–6.
[120] *The Transportation of Criminals: Being a Report of a Discussion at a Special Meeting of the Association Held at Burlington House, on the 17th February, 1863*, London: Emily Faithfull, 1863, pp. 1–30.
[121] Sean McConville, *English Local Prisons 1860-1900: Next Only to Death*, London: Routledge, 1995, p. 97.
[122] Ibid., pp. 87–9.
[123] 169 Parliamentary Debates, HC (3rd ser.), col. 477 (19 Feb. 1863).
[124] *The Daily News*, 9 Jan. 1863, p. 4.
[125] *Report from the Select Committee of the House of Lords, on the Present State of Discipline in Gaols and Houses of Correction; Together with the Proceedings of the Committee, Minutes of Evidence, Appendix and Index*, [C 499] HC 1863, ix, p. 71.

in order to convince magistrates and judges that they were first offenders, thereby escaping with shorter sentences.[126]

The first select committee, two of whose members were actively involved in the SSA, made recommendations concerning both the treatment of licence-holders and the punishment of penal servitude.[127] These mirrored the evidence cited above. It did so having accepted that crime was increasing and that this was

> at least partly attributable to defects in the system of punishment now in force, and to the fact that there has been an accumulation of discharged convicts at home, owing to the comparatively small number sent to a penal colony since 1853.[128]

As discussed above, there was no evidence to substantiate this position, which had been promulgated by numerous newspapers during the recent period of alarm. For instance, in November 1862 a leading article in *The Times* blamed the supposed increase in the crime of 'garotting' on the ticket-of-leave system, which, it argued, 'seems to be established solely to catch thieves and let them go again'.[129] Notwithstanding the lack of evidence that those released from prison on a licence were responsible for the alleged increase in violent crime in London, the commission concluded that penal servitude was not 'sufficiently dreaded', predominantly because convicted criminals were, in their view and the view of numerous witnesses, subject to sentences that were too short.[130] The final report stated that 'the want of sufficient efficacy in the present system of punishment … [is] mainly attributable to the shortness of punishment generally inflicted upon convicts'.[131] In particular, the 'principle' of awarding a heavier punishment to a criminal on a second conviction 'should be more fully acted upon'.[132] The commission sought to deal with this perceived issue by increasing the minimum term of penal servitude from three to seven years. A mandatory minimum sentence for 'habitual criminals' of seven years' penal servitude was also

---

[126] These were Crofton, William Musson, the governor of Leicester gaol, and William Linton, the governor of West Sussex county gaol.
[127] The Conservative Sir John Pakington had been the first head of the association's department of public health and was still an active member at this time. Spencer Walpole, again a Conservative, was also a member. See Goldman, *Science, Reform and Politics in Victorian Britain*, pp. 65, 195.
[128] *Report of the Commissioners Appointed to Inquire into the Operation of the Acts Relating to Transportation and Penal Servitude.* Vol. 1, p. 23.
[129] *Times*, 5 Nov. 1862, p. 8.
[130] *Report of the Commissioners Appointed to Inquire into the Operation of the Acts Relating to Transportation and Penal Servitude.* Vol. 1, p. 23.
[131] Ibid.
[132] Ibid., p. 72.

recommended, although what 'habitual' precisely meant was left undefined.[133] Police supervision was recommended as well. The commissioners called for 'strict' and 'effective' supervision of licence-holders.[134] They said that the 'best prospect of giving to society a real protection against criminals' would be to place the holders of tickets-of-leave 'under effective control and supervision'.[135] The Carnarvon committee also supported the registering and supervision of repeat offenders, reporting that

> [i]t is of the greatest importance that those offenders who are commencing a course of crime should be made aware that each repetition of it, duly recorded and proved, will involve a material increase of punishment, pain, and inconvenience to them.[136]

Two parliamentary committees, which had been convened due to concern expressed in newspapers regarding violent crime in London, therefore gave their sanction to key elements of a controversial policy that Hill had been pursuing since 1846 and the SSA since its establishment in 1857.

The work of these committees, influenced (and occasionally populated) as they were by the SSA, precipitated significant legislative change. Contrary to the arguments of numerous historians, these changes were part of a coherent programme.[137] The *Penal Servitude Act 1864*, which received bipartisan support after being introduced by the Liberal government of Lord Palmerston and covered the whole UK, put in place many of their recommendations. As a result, it 'provided for substantial mechanisms of control over recidivistic offenders'.[138] First, it enacted a system of monthly, in-person reporting by licence-holders to the police and mandatory notification of change of address to the chief of police. Non-compliance with either of these provisions would result in a return to penal servitude.[139] These provisions put 'teeth', as Bartrip has said, into the ticket-of-leave system.[140] Secondly, the act conferred upon a policeman the very significant new power to arrest without warrant any licence-holder 'whom he may reasonably suspect of having committed

---

[133] Ibid.
[134] Ibid.
[135] Ibid.
[136] *Report from the Select Committee of the House of Lords, on the Present State of Discipline in Gaols and Houses of Correction*, p. xvi.
[137] Gray, *London's Shadows*, p. 112; Welshman, *Underclass*, p. 6; King, 'Moral Panics and Violent Street Crime', p. 57; Runciman, *Very Different, but Much the Same*, p. 69; Bailey, 'Introduction', p. 20.
[138] Melling, 'Cleaning House in a Suddenly Closed Society', p. 323.
[139] *Penal Servitude Act*, 27 & 28 Vict., c. 47, 1864, s. 4.
[140] Bartrip, 'Public Opinion and Law Enforcement', p. 169.

any offence, or having broken any of the conditions of his licence'.[141] This provision – enabling arrest on suspicion alone – represented a major expansion of the power of the state.[142] Thus, it demonstrated the great desire within parliament to suppress the perceived threat from criminals who would previously have been transported. Thirdly, the act responded to the committee's recommendation to alter the sentencing regime. The minimum period of penal servitude was raised to five years. Those convicted of a felony who had previously been found guilty of committing a felonious offence were also to be subject to a mandatory minimum period of seven years' penal servitude.[143] Felony was a broad category of crime including all offences that had previously been punishable by death. Various forms of theft were the most commonly committed felonious offences.[144] So, for example, someone convicted twice of stealing an item from a shop, such as a piece of fruit or a loaf of bread, would face seven years' penal servitude. These legislative changes, which predominantly resulted from the recommendations of the penal servitude acts commissioners, significantly augmented the power of the state over certain offenders. Indeed, Wiener has justifiably argued that no more influential parliamentary inquiry regarding the penal system was conducted until 1895.[145]

These reforms were a triumph, albeit a partial one, for the SSA. As Goldman has said, the 1864 legislation enacted several 'longstanding elements of its [the SSA's] programme'.[146] The association claimed victory. At the 1864 congress in York, Hill himself noted that 'we have zealously assisted in bringing over the largest part of the Irish system into our own island'.[147] Hastings also argued that the association's views concerning penal policy had now been 'substantially accepted by Parliament, and adopted by the Home Office'.[148] This was correct. Measures that had been dismissed since Hill first articulated them in the 1840s had now been accepted, after much advocacy by the SSA. Of course, other

---

[141] *Penal Servitude Act*, s. 6.
[142] Bartrip, 'Public Opinion and Law Enforcement', p. 169.
[143] *Penal Servitude Act*, s. 2.
[144] *Judicial Statistics. 1862. England and Wales. Part 1. Police-Criminal Proceedings-Prisons*, [C 3025] HC 1863, lvi, p. 16; *Judicial Statistics. 1863. England and Wales. Part 1. Police-Criminal Proceedings-Prisons*, [C 3370] HC 1864, lvii, p. 16.
[145] Wiener, *Reconstructing the Criminal*, p. 344. Wiener is referring to the *Prisons Committee: Report from the Departmental Committee on Prisons*, [C 7702] HC 1895, lvi. The significance of this inquiry will be discussed in the later chapter concerning police supervision.
[146] Goldman, *Science, Reform and Politics in Victorian Britain*, p. 160.
[147] Matthew Davenport Hill, 'On the Penal Servitude Acts', *Transactions 1864*, London: Longman, Green, Longman, Roberts and Green, 1865, p. 242.
[148] Hastings, 'Introduction', *Transactions 1864*, p. xxxvi.

factors were at play. There had been much debate in the press and in parliament, which members of the SSA had participated in, about the adequacy of Britain's penal system since New South Wales refused to accept further convicts in 1840. This debate was informed by the notion that many criminals formed a distinct and hostile class. Then in 1862 a panic caused by exaggerated reports of violent crime in London led to the establishment of parliamentary committees, which recommended harsher measures against certain types of criminals, including repeat offenders. As numerous historians have argued, the legislative actions that followed can only be understood in this context of changed circumstances and public alarm.[149] Nonetheless, these historians have failed to fully recognize that the specific actions that were taken were adopted from the programme of the SSA, demonstrating its significant influence. As we will shortly see, the legislation of 1864, which built on that of 1857 and 1853 before it, was altered once more by the Gladstone government's *Habitual Criminals Act 1869*, and as we will also see below, the SSA was to play an even greater role in the passage of that act.

*

This section investigates the factors that led directly to the introduction of the *Habitual Criminals Bill 1869* into parliament in February of that year. Did renewed public alarm in London play a major role in pressuring the government to implement further legislative changes, as several historians have argued?[150] It also asks whether the SSA had sufficient influence over the new government, which took office in November 1868 to successfully push for the adoption of further elements of its agenda. Finally, the contents of the bill will also be considered.

The 1864 legislation put in place several provisions that the SSA had advocated since its inception. Nonetheless, its members continued to agitate for further reform. In a speech to the SSA in September 1864 that was published as a pamphlet, Hill cautioned that it was not the case 'that our penal code has arrived at perfection'.[151] Numerous parts of his and the association's programme

---

[149] Runciman, *Very Different, but Much the Same*, p. 69; Gray, *London's Shadows*, p. 112; Welshman, *Underclass*, p. 6; King, 'Moral Panics and Violent Street Crime', p. 57.

[150] Runciman, *Very Different, but Much the Same*, p. 69; King, 'Moral Panics and Violent Street Crime', p. 57; Gray, *London's Shadows*, p. 57; Goldman, *Science, Reform and Politics in Victorian Britain*, p. 154.

[151] Matthew Davenport Hill, *Papers on the Penal Servitude Acts: And on the Regulations of the Home Department for Carrying Them into Execution*, London: Longman, Green, Longman, Roberts and Green, 1864, p. 3.

had not been adopted. These included supervision of repeat offenders not in possession of a licence and a register of criminals. Hill believed these further measures were necessary in order to ensure all members of the criminal class, not just holders of a licence, were watched over by the police as a means to prevent crime and aid reformation.[152] So, Hill could truthfully say that the association had not 'accomplished all it has attempted'.[153] In addition, one element of the 1864 legislation was questioned by Hill. He believed that the five-year minimum term of penal servitude might be ineffective, as judges still had the option of sentencing criminals to a term of imprisonment of two years or less in a local gaol. Judges might 'shrink' from inflicting a lengthy term of penal servitude if they felt it was unjust.[154] Nonetheless, it was possible that additional legislative changes would be able to be made more quickly and easily than those of 1864. This was because, as Hill said, there would be no need to 'establish new principles'.[155] The government, the parliament and many members of the public had accepted that there was a growing body of repeat offenders in London who lived by crime.[156] What is more, the principles of police surveillance and mandatory sentences for those deemed to be habitual criminals had already been enshrined in legislation. This argument of Hill's would be validated before the end of the decade.

Key figures within the SSA believed that 1868 presented the opportunity to ensure the completion of their penal project. At its congress that year, held in Birmingham in early October, Crofton gave an address arguing that the time had come for further reform. Two reasons were given. In the first place, enough time had elapsed since the enactment of the 1864 legislation in order to judge whether police supervision infringed upon the liberty of those under surveillance and, in particular, damaged their chances of gaining and maintaining employment. Crofton said that 'practical experience has scattered to the winds those bugbears of "interfering with the liberty of the subject"'.[157] The police certainly maintained that this was the case. Colonel Henderson, the commissioner of the Metropolitan

---

[152] Matthew Davenport Hill, *Two Charges: Delivered by the Recorder, to the Grand Juries of Birmingham, at the Michaelmas Quarter Sessions for the years 1850 & 1851*, Bristol: n.p., 1851, p. 3.
[153] Hill, *Papers on the Penal Servitude Acts*, p. 12.
[154] Ibid., p. 9.
[155] Ibid., p. 3.
[156] Peter Quennell (ed.), *London's Underworld: Being Selections from 'Those That Will Not Work', the Fourth Volume of 'London Labour and the London Poor' by Henry Mayhew*, vol. 7, London: Hamlyn, 1969, pp. 58, 79, 165; H. W. Holland, 'Professional Thieves', *Cornhill Magazine*, vol. 6, no. 35 (Nov. 1862), p. 645; Harriot Martineau, 'Life in the Criminal Class', *Edinburgh Review*, vol. 122, no. 250 (Oct. 1865), pp. 337, 342, 350.
[157] Walter Crofton, 'Address on the Criminal Class and Their Control', *Transactions 1868*, London: Longmans, Green, Reader, and Dyer, 1869, p. 300.

Police Force, said that after each monthly attendance at a designated police station, 'no further steps are taken by the police' to monitor holders of tickets-of-leave. Only if there was a suspicion that a licence-holder was leading 'an irregular life' would closer attention be paid. Furthermore, he said that 'employers are never informed by the police that they are employing a licence-holder'.[158] An absence of substantiated complaints to the contrary would appear to bolster Crofton and Henderson's position that the liberty of licence-holders had not been infringed by the 1864 legislation. Secondly, Crofton said that after the complete cessation of transportation, which occurred earlier in 1868, police supervision was now the key defence against the 'criminal classes'. He argued that its 'completeness' and 'thoroughness', by way of its extension to those other than 'actual licence-holders', was imperative.[159] He also called for the establishment of a register of those who were criminals by 'repute and habit'.[160] In a discussion of Crofton's address nine of ten participants backed his call for further reform, including Carnarvon, the congress's president, and Frederic Hill.[161] In short, the SSA threw its weight behind the final accomplishment of its long-held penal agenda: police surveillance of all those deemed part of the criminal class.

The association's success was made more likely by the election of a Liberal government in November 1868, with William Gladstone at its helm. As discussed, many members of the Liberal Party were also active within the SSA, and the association had very strong links to the new home secretary, the Welsh MP Henry Bruce. Bruce's involvement with the SSA commenced in 1866, when the former education minister delivered a speech on educational reform to the SSA congress in Manchester, for which he was roundly congratulated.[162] Having met with various members, including the Tory reformer Lord Shaftesbury, Bruce reported to his wife that 'I am very glad that I have come here'.[163] With this sympathizer now home secretary the SSA sought to capitalize. Crofton led a deputation of senior members of the SSA to meet Bruce on 14 December 1868, only five days after he took up office. The conservative *Pall Mall Gazette* reported that the deputation urged

---

[158] Memorandum by Commissioner Henderson, 1869, quoted in James Greenwood, *The Seven Curses of London*, London: Stanley Rivers and Co., 1869, p. 294.
[159] Crofton, 'Address on the Criminal Class and Their Control', pp. 301, 303.
[160] Ibid., p. 303.
[161] The only participant to oppose Crofton was the Liberal peer Lord Houghton, who argued that as the police had significant knowledge of the 'criminal classes' further supervisory powers were unnecessary. See 'The Criminal Classes. Discussion', *Transactions 1868*, London: Longmans, Green, Reader, and Dyer, 1869, p. 350.
[162] Henry Bruce to Nora Bruce, his wife, 4 Oct. 1866, in *Letters of the Rt. Hon. Henry Austin Bruce, G.C.B., Lord Aberdare of Duffryn*, vol. 1, Oxford: Horace Hart, 1902, p. 242.
[163] Bruce to Bruce, 6 Oct. 1866, in *Letters of the Rt. Hon. Henry Austin Bruce*, p. 243.

the importance of taking more active measures for dealing with our criminal classes. Sir W. Crofton was the spokesman ... Mr. Bruce expressed great interest in the important subject brought before him, and after putting various questions, promised that the matter should have the attention of the Government.[164]

Key members of the SSA were therefore quick to push the new home secretary to build upon the *Penal Servitude Act 1864*.

Crofton and the other delegates were sufficiently encouraged by their meeting to commence drafting legislation. He invited a small group, including Frederic Hill and Barwick Baker, a Gloucestershire magistrate, to London to draft a bill. Baker, whose autobiography contains an account of the meeting, recalled that

> in a couple of hours, we had got the principles of an utterly unworkable Bill; but I said 'that it did not signify, for that it would only be in the Home Office Closet for 10 years & before it was called out, we could have got a better Bill into shape', and I came home well satisfied with having made a very small beginning, which might come to something after many years. What was my astonishment & I may say disgust, though certainly mingled with great pleasure! when I found our wretched little Bill actually printed to be brought before parliament.[165]

It is not surprising that Baker described the bill that he worked on in such disparaging terms. He was writing long after its failure, which will be discussed at length in the next chapter. These comments therefore appear to be an attempt to deny responsibility for that failure. It was in Baker's interests to argue that the bill presented to the home secretary by members of the SSA was nothing but a 'small beginning'.[166] There are further reasons to believe that the thrust of this account is probably correct: that is, prominent members of the association quickly drafted a bill that was then introduced into parliament with very few alterations. After all, the *Habitual Criminals Bill 1869* was introduced into the House of Lords, given the heavy schedule of the Commons, very early in the life of the new government, on 26 February 1869. Moreover, during the debate that followed one Liberal peer, Lord Houghton, himself a member of the SSA, argued that Crofton was principally responsible for the legislation. 'The real author of this Bill', he said, 'is Sir Walter Crofton'.[167] Bruce also acknowledged Crofton's role. In 1875, the year after the defeat of the Gladstone government, Bruce told

---

[164] *Pall Mall Gazette*, 15 Dec. 1868, p. 8. This account was reproduced in *The Times* the next day. See *Times*, 16 Dec. 1868, p. 7.
[165] Thomas Barwick Lloyd Baker, 'My Life: 1856–79', vol. II, pp. 174–5. Gloucestershire Archives, D3549/25/7/1.
[166] Ibid., p. 175.
[167] 194 *Parl. Deb.*, HL (3rd ser.), col. 333 (26 Feb. 1869).

the SSA congress that although he had been the minister responsible for the preparation of the *Habitual Criminals Act 1869* and the *Prevention of Crime Act 1871*, Sir Walter Crofton was 'entitled to a great share in the authorship of those measures'.[168] Two historians agree that the bill was, in all probability, the work of Crofton's delegation. Goldman, in reference to Baker's account, has argued that the SSA 'dictated the terms of the Habitual Criminals Act in 1869'.[169] And Melling, while he does not actually mention the association, has argued that given the striking similarity between the recommendations made by Crofton's delegation and the ultimate bill, it appears that 'a small group of interested individuals succeeded in influencing the newly-elected Government to act on an issue of concern to them, largely in a manner suggested by them'.[170] Bruce was a new cabinet minister with a demanding portfolio. He, as we know, also had strong connections to the SSA. Consequently, it is not surprising that he allowed a small group of SSA members, led by Crofton, to draft the *Habitual Criminals Bill 1869*.

The *Habitual Criminals Bill 1869* was introduced into the House of Lords on 26 February 1869 by the Earl of Kimberley, lord privy seal and, consequently, a member of Gladstone's cabinet. The measures it contained, as Melling said, were very similar to those discussed on 14 December. The clauses of the bill were grouped into five parts. The first concerned licence-holders. It empowered any policeman to take licence-holders into custody and then bring them before a magistrate on suspicion of living by 'dishonest means'. Failure to prove otherwise would lead to the forfeiture of the convict's licence. The first part also stipulated that a register of licence-holders should be created, for their 'better supervision'. The second created new powers over 'habitual criminals'. Those convicted of a second felony and not sentenced to penal servitude would be subject to a mandatory period of seven years' police supervision. If the individual being monitored was 'suspected' of living by dishonest means and could not prove otherwise to a magistrate, imprisonment with hard labour, for any period less than one year, would follow. Habitual criminals would be similarly punished if found 'about to commit or aid in the commission of any crime' or in any building whatsoever without a satisfactory explanation. Thrice-convicted felons who had ceased their last term of imprisonment within the last five years would receive a mandatory minimum term of seven years' penal servitude. Part three

---

[168] Henry Bruce, 'The President's Address', *Transactions 1875*, London: Longmans, Green and Co., 1876, p. 323.
[169] Goldman, *Science, Reform and Politics in Victorian Britain*, p. 3.
[170] Melling, 'Cleaning House in a Suddenly Closed Society', p. 318.

reversed the onus of proof on anyone in possession of stolen goods who had previously been found guilty of an offence punishable by penal servitude. Part four increased the penalty for assaulting a police officer from 5 to 20 pounds or six months' imprisonment on default of payment. Finally, part five contained some 'general provisions'. They stated that a previous conviction need not be proved by a written record but could be done so by any 'credible witness'.[171]

As the undersecretary of state for the Home Office, E. H. Knatchbull-Hugessen, explained in a letter to the lord mayor of London:

> [T]he Act has been formed with a view to the protection of the public from the depradations [sic] of detected offenders by restraining them from lapsing into the old habits of crime. For this purpose greatly enhanced powers have been entrusted to the police.[172]

In short, the bill sought to significantly increase the power of the state over licence-holders and repeat offenders in a range of ways that were consistent with the programme of the SSA.

However, the direct role of the SSA in the genesis of this bill is little recognized in the literature concerning the changing penal system of the mid-nineteenth century.[173] As Goldman has argued, 'the organisation has been largely forgotten'.[174] Numerous scholars, such as W. G. Runciman, Pete King and Drew D. Gray, have recently argued that the legislation was introduced, primarily, in response to a 'moral panic' in London about crime in the capital and garotting in particular. These scholars claim that this panic was linked to the increased reporting of crime in London's press.[175] Petrow also refers to the significance of public unease as a causal factor of the 1869 legislation, although he does note that the SSA played a major part in advocating for and preparing the measure.[176] There is some limited evidence that concern about violent crime may have increased in the period directly before the bill was introduced. Goldman, who also recognizes the important role played by the SSA, refers to an increase in references in *The Times* to the crime of garotting between October 1868 and April 1869. He has noted that in the first nine months of 1868, *The Times* carried only two reports of trials of those suspected of garotting,

---

[171] *Habitual Criminals Bill*, 32 & 33 Vict., c. 99, 1869.
[172] E. H. Knatchbull-Hugessen, undersecretary at the Home Office, to Robert Besley, Lord Mayor of London, 8 Nov. 1869, reproduced in *Law Times: The Journal and Record of the Law and Lawyers*, vol. 48 (Nov. 1869–Apr. 1870), p. 52.
[173] This was discussed in the previous chapter.
[174] Goldman, 'The Social Science Association', p. 96.
[175] Runciman, *Very Different, but Much the Same*, p. 69; King, 'Moral Panics and Violent Street Crime', p. 57; Gray, *London's Shadows*, p. 57.
[176] Petrow, *Policing Morals*, p. 17.

whereas in the next seven months fourteen such reports appeared.[177] Eight letters concerning the need for further measures to control criminals appeared in the newspaper between October and April, as did six leading articles.[178] The paper called for greater police powers, including supervision of all repeat offenders and arrest based only on suspicion, as a way of 'dealing with the criminal classes'.[179] Thus, Goldman has argued that 'if the coverage of garottings in *The Times* is any guide, there was a sudden crisis of crime and panic from October 1868 to April 1869'.[180]

Yet the notion that a crisis existed in the months of late 1868 and early 1869 does not bear scrutiny. When Goldman's device of counting the cases of garotting referred to before and after October is used with other London newspapers no significant increase can be discerned. From October 1868 to April 1869 five other major London newspapers, the *Daily News*, the *Standard*, *Lloyd's Weekly Newspaper*, the *Morning Post* and *Reynolds's Newspaper*, only covered four cases of suspected garotting.[181] In the preceding seven months three cases had been referred to.[182] There was also no increase in the number of relevant letters and leading articles. All these newspapers continued to occasionally express concern about the effects of the cessation of transportation and the ability of the authorities to deal with licence-holders and repeat offenders.[183] However, this was not a new state of affairs. Other than in *The Times*, no evidence is available to suggest an increase in the reporting of violent crime in London or the presence of an especial panic in late 1868 and early 1869. In fact, the opposite may have been the case. In a leading article regarding the *Habitual Criminals Bill 1869*, the *Daily News* argued that 'the public mind is pretty much at ease as to the classes with which it deals'.[184] It does not seem defensible to assert that there was a general state of alarm in London solely on the basis of reporting in

---

[177] Goldman, *Science, Reform and Politics in Victorian Britain*, p. 154.
[178] *Times*, 4 Nov. 1868, p. 5; 7 Dec. 1868, p. 5; 17 Dec. 1868, p. 6; 7 Jan. 1869, p. 5; 12 Jan. 1869, p. 5; 13 Jan. 1869, p. 5; 2 Feb. 1869, p. 5; 29 Oct. 1869, p. 9; 4 Nov. 1868, p. 5; 2 Dec. 1868, p. 6; 22 Dec. 1868, p. 7; 30 Dec. 1868, p. 6.
[179] *Times*, 2 Dec. 1868, p. 5.
[180] Goldman, *Science, Reform and Politics in Victorian Britain*, p. 154.
[181] *Daily News* and *Reynolds's Newspaper* each referred to two cases. See *Daily News*, 12 Nov. 1868, p. 6 and 8 Dec. 1868 p. 6, and *Reynolds's Newspaper*, 17 Jan. 1869, p. 1 and 25 Apr. 1869, p. 6. The other three newspapers did not report on any cases.
[182] *Daily News*, *Standard* and the *Morning Post* each referred to one case. See *Daily News*, 3 Apr. 1868, p. 7; *Standard*, 8 Aug. 1868, p. 7; *Morning Post*, 3 Apr. 1868, p. 7. *Lloyd's Weekly Newspaper* and *Reynolds's Newspaper* did not report on any cases.
[183] For example see *Daily News*, 30 Mar. 1869, p. 4; *Morning Post*, 9 Dec. 1868, p. 4; *Reynolds's Newspaper*, 22 Nov. 1868, p. 2; *Lloyd's Weekly Newspaper*, 29 Nov. 1868, p. 2; *Standard*, 5 Jan. 1969, p. 4.
[184] *Daily News*, 6 Aug. 1869, p. 4.

The Times. Public alarm, caused by newspaper reporting, was an important factor in precipitating legislative changes in 1857 and 1864, but not in 1869.

It appears more likely that the SSA was leading the push for further penal changes and using *The Times* to do so. It is no coincidence that *The Times* commenced its calls for further regulation of repeat offenders in October 1868. The SSA congress, at which Crofton called for the completion of the SSA's long-held penal programme, concluded on 7 October. Only then did *The Times* commence its campaign against garroting. A closer analysis of the letters published in *The Times* from October 1868 is also instructive. Of the eight letters five were by Baker and one was by Edwin Hill, Matthew's brother who had been part of Crofton's deputation to Bruce.[185] These letters called for police supervision of all repeat offenders, a central office to enable the monitoring and identification of recidivists and more deterrent sentences – exactly what Crofton had advocated at the recent congress. It appears that *The Times* was being used as an organ of opinion by members of the SSA. It is therefore not correct to argue that the press created a state of anxiety among Londoners that the SSA could then exploit. Rather one newspaper in particular took its lead from the SSA in repeating and publicizing the association's calls for the completion of its long-standing agenda.

*

The *Habitual Criminals Act 1869* was largely the result of much advocacy by the SSA as transportation to the Australian colonies was ceasing to be a penal option. Firstly, the act must be seen in the context of a changing penal system. The gradual end of transportation fostered concern in London, and throughout the UK, that a large body of offenders, who previously would have been deposited in Australia, were now to be released at home. This anxiety was stoked by arguments, common in the press, that many of the convicted criminals now to be released after completing their sentences were repeat offenders who formed a distinct and hostile class.[186] Such a class, in reality, did not exist. Yet the idea of a criminal class was a very powerful and widely accepted one. The government was explicit that the *Habitual Criminals Act 1869* was a response to the cessation of transportation and resulting accumulation of what it believed was a criminal class.

---

[185] *Times*, 4 Nov. 1868, p. 5; 7 Dec. 1868, p. 5; 17 Dec. 1868, p. 6; 7 Jan. 1869, p. 5; 13 Jan. 1869, p. 5; 2 Feb. 1869, p. 5. Of the other two letters, one was from 'A Chairman of Quarter Sessions', arguing that men 'addicted to robbery' are allowed to 'freely' contravene the law. See *The Times*, 4 Nov. 1868, p. 5. The other was by G. L. Fenwick, the chief constable of Cheshire, who believed that further, unspecified, impediments must be placed in the way of 'robbers'. See *The Times*, 12 Jan. 1869, p. 5.
[186] *Times*, 14 Aug. 1862, p. 8; *Daily News*, 2 Dec. 1862, p. 4.

The key measures contained in the 1869 legislation built upon earlier legislative efforts that were designed to mitigate the impact of the end of transportation. Legislation of 1853, 1857 and 1864 introduced the new punishment of penal servitude, put in place and refined the licence system, and sought to institute a tailored sentencing regime for recidivists. In doing so, these acts adapted measures that were already in operation in Australia and Ireland. The *Habitual Criminals Bill 1869* expanded the powers of the state over licence-holders and repeat offenders. It augmented the ticket-of-leave system that had been first introduced in 1853 by increasing the supervisory power of the police, and it also extended mandatory sentences for recidivists, first introduced by the act of 1864. The *Habitual Criminals Bill 1869* contained, as Radzinowicz and Hood have noted, a 'heavy baggage of repressive measures'.[187] But perhaps it would be more correct to say that it added further weight to the baggage of measures that had been introduced from 1853.

One of the reasons that the governments of 1857 and 1864 deemed these legislative changes to be necessary was because of public alarm in London concerning violent crime. In one respect, then, the development of this post-transportation penal system was ad hoc, as Bartrip has claimed.[188] However, more and more of the consistent policy of Hill, Crofton and the SSA was enacted, including longer sentences for recidivists, police supervision after release and a register of criminals. This has been largely overlooked by historians of mid-Victorian crime and penal policy. Governments were clearly influenced by the reporting of crime in the 1850s and 1860s, and the increased public concern that such reporting precipitated. This is a point that numerous historians have made.[189] Yet the actions that were then taken were often borrowed from the agenda of the SSA. Thus the main argument in the relevant literature – that penal legislation in the period was a piecemeal and uncoordinated attempt to respond to altered circumstances – is not accurate.[190]

This is especially true of the *Habitual Criminals Act 1869*. The SSA called for further legislation in October 1868, based on its long-standing view that the ultimate end of transportation to Australia made an expansion of the

---

[187] Radzinowicz and Hood, 'Incapacitating the Habitual Criminal', p. 1340.
[188] Bartrip, 'Public Opinion and Law Enforcement', p. 174.
[189] Runciman, *Very Different, but Much the Same*, p. 69; King, 'Moral Panics and Violent Street Crime', p. 57; Gray, *London's Shadows*, p. 57; Godfrey, Cox and Farrall, *Serious Offenders*, p. 12; Bartrip, 'Public Opinion and Law Enforcement', pp. 150–81; Davis, 'The London Garotting Panic of 1862', pp. 190–213.
[190] Goldman, *Science, Reform and Politics in Victorian Britain*, p. 172.

power of the state over criminals at home vital. *The Times* subsequently took up this cause. Then the election of the Gladstone government in November further strengthened the position of the SSA due to its ties to the new home secretary, whom it quickly and successfully sought to influence. As a result, the *Habitual Criminals Bill* was introduced into the House of Lords in February 1869. It really was, as Baker said, the association's 'wretched little bill'.[191] The prevailing interpretation of the genesis of the *Habitual Criminals Act 1869* is therefore wrong. While public panic caused by London's press had been an important factor in precipitating earlier legislation, this was not the case in 1868 and 1869. Instead the SSA was principally responsible for the 1869 legislation. The passage of the bill and its early operation will be the subject of the next chapter.

---

[191] Thomas Barwick Lloyd Baker, 'My Life: 1856–79', vol. II, p. 174. Gloucestershire Archives, D3549/25/7/1.

2

Repeal and Reintroduction: Parliamentary Debate and the Question of Liberty

> [M]easures are not unfrequently passed through the Legislature with so much haste and so little consideration, that they are found to contain ambiguties [sic] and complications which render action upon them extremely difficult. This is the case with the Act of 1869, for some of its clauses are full of contradictions and defects.[1]
>
> (The Earl of Carnarvon, Conservative peer, 25 Apr. 1871)

The government had high hopes that the *Habitual Criminals Act 1869* would help to answer the key question arising from the cessation of transportation: 'What shall we do with our convicts?'[2] However, within two years the same government considered it necessary to repeal the legislation and, after significant changes, reintroduce its principal measures through the *Prevention of Crime Act 1871*. There appeared to be much agreement that the *Habitual Criminals Act 1869* would do a great deal to curtail the activities of the criminal class. Positive early appraisals of the legislation were provided by, among others, cabinet ministers, the overwhelming majority of the press and senior police officers.[3] For instance, the *Pall Mall Gazette*, a conservative newspaper, said the act would 'materially facilitate the operations' of the police, and the superintendent of the Southwark division of the Metropolitan Police Force said it would prevent 'the various classes of persons whom it is designed to reach' from 'carrying out

---

[1] The Earl of Carnarvon (Conservative), 205 *Parliamentary Debates*, HL (3rd ser.), col. 1678 (25 Apr. 1871).
[2] The Earl of Carlisle, 'Address on the Punishment and Reformation of Criminals', in *Transactions of the National Association for the Promotion of Social Science 1858*, London: John W. Parker and Son, 1859, pp. 70, 72.
[3] For example see the *Daily News*, 6 Aug. 1869, p. 4; *Morning Post*, 30 Aug. 1869, p. 9; *Times*, 27 Feb. 1869, p. 9.

their evil designs'.[4] Nonetheless, within months of the legislation's enactment the government commenced drafting a new measure.[5] Why was the repeal of the *Habitual Criminals Act 1869* deemed necessary? In seeking to answer this question, this chapter will, initially, provide an assessment of the parliamentary debate on the *Habitual Criminals Bill 1869* and the numerous amendments that were made. The second section will analyse the working of the legislation until its repeal. Finally, the third section will provide an explanation of the new legislation of 1871.

Many historians have claimed that the *Habitual Criminals Act 1869* was a repressive measure that led to unreasonable interference with a designated section of the working class by firstly police and, subsequently, magistrates and judges. While numerous historians have noted several flaws in the 1869 legislation, such as the failure to mandate monthly reporting for those under supervision and an overly broad definition of habitual criminal that meant the registers were needlessly large, they nonetheless argue that the act represented a significant increase in the power of the state over certain offenders.[6] For example, Stefan Petrow has claimed that as a result of the Gladstone government's habitual criminals' legislation 'police power over habitual criminals was immeasurably enhanced: the police thereafter had the potential to beset their every move'.[7] Magistrates and judges, Petrow suggests, supported the police in this endeavour. He has said that 'police testimony largely determined whether a convict deserved rescue from, or was consigned to, a life of crime', as magistrates and judges would convict recidivists even on the basis of questionable evidence.[8] Several historians argue that through the application of these powers the police, supported by magistrates and judges in sentencing, actually created a criminal class.[9] The 'stigmatising' effect of the legislation, it is said, acted to 'reproduce'

---

[4] *Pall Mall Gazette*, 21 Dec. 1869, p. 4; *Report of the Commissioner of Police of the Metropolis*, [C 358] HC 1871, xxxvii, p. 50.
[5] The Earl of Kimberley (Liberal), 200 *Parliamentary Debates*, HL (3rd ser.), cols. 568–70 (24 Mar. 1870).
[6] Stefan Petrow, *Policing Morals: The Metropolitan Police and the Home Office 1870–1914*, Oxford: Clarendon Press, 1995, p. 82; Martin Wiener, *Reconstructing the Criminal: Culture, Law and Policy in England, 1830–1914*, Cambridge: Cambridge University Press, 1990, pp. 303–7; Barry Godfrey, David Cox and Stephen Farrall, *Serious Offenders: An Historical Study of Habitual Criminals*, London: Oxford University Press, 2010, p. 67.
[7] Petrow, *Policing Morals*, p. 51.
[8] Ibid.
[9] This was discussed in Chapter 1. Also see Godfrey, Cox and Farrall, *Serious Offenders*, p. xii; Clive Emsley, *Crime and Society in England: 1750–1900*, 2nd ed., London: Longman, 1996, pp. 172–4; Helen Johnston, *Crime in England 1815–1880: Experiencing the Criminal Justice System*, Abingdon: Routledge, 2015, p. 36.

criminality.[10] To what extent is this argument valid for the initial period after the introduction of the *Habitual Criminals Act 1869* in London? Does it exaggerate the power of the police? And were the government, the Metropolitan Police Force and magistrates united in a desire to monitor and control the criminal class? This chapter illuminates a state divided. It thereby provides answers to these questions that do not fit the neat framework of social control and that are significantly at odds with the prevailing consensus.

*

The *Habitual Criminals Bill 1869* was intended to bolster the post-transportation penal regime in order to ensure, primarily, that the supposedly growing group of licence-holders and repeat offenders was subject to police monitoring following their release from prison.[11] Despite the vocal support of numerous London newspapers, several of the bill's provisions, such as police supervision and mandatory minimum sentences, were nonetheless controversial. This section will analyse the legislation's highly contested passage through parliament, with a particular focus on how the bill was amended in response to objections regarding the novelty and severity of the measure.[12] The impact of the legislation can only be fully understood in light of these changes, which, as we shall see, were significant.

The Liberal Earl of Kimberley gave notice of the *Habitual Criminals Bill* in the House of Lords on 22 February 1869. The bill was, as rarely occurred, introduced into the Lords due to a lack of business in that chamber compared to the Commons. Kimberley presented it on 26 February. He explained that the bill was not a response to any sense of public alarm, but rather an attempt to deal with a problem that had been increasing for some time: the expansion of the criminal class at home due to the cessation of transportation. He said that an effective system of supervision of repeat offenders, based on the Irish model, was the principal object of the bill.[13] In the nineteenth century policy 'improvisations' involving increased state intervention were often implemented in Ireland before they were tried in Britain.[14] Kimberley conceded that the

---

[10] Johnston, *Crime in England*, p. 36.
[11] This was discussed in the previous chapter.
[12] This was not unusual. Legislation in the nineteenth century was often amended significantly during its passage through parliament. Oliver MacDonagh has argued that 'almost invariably, there was compromise ... in the committee stage in parliament'. MacDonagh says this was primarily due to the advocacy of those impacted by the legislation. In this case – as we shall see – one such group was pawnbrokers. See Oliver MacDonagh, 'The Nineteenth Century Revolution in Government: A Reappraisal', *Historical Journal*, vol. 1, no. 1 (Mar. 1958), p. 58.
[13] 194 *Parl. Deb.*, HL (3rd ser.), col. 335 (26 Feb. 1869).
[14] Oliver MacDonagh, *Early Victorian Government: 1830–1870*, London: Weidenfeld and Nicholson, 1977, p. 181.

bill contained harsh measures but assured the Lords that it would effectively target 'habitual criminals', who were, he asserted, determined to wage 'war on society'.[15] The Conservative Earl of Shaftesbury spoke in reply, foreshadowing the bipartisan support that the bill was to enjoy. He said that Kimberley had exaggerated the threat from the 'criminal class' and criticized the failure of the bill to clearly define habitual criminality. Yet he enthusiastically welcomed the focus on receivers of stolen goods as a means to reduce crime.[16] He presumably believed, like numerous commentators whose views have been discussed in earlier chapters, the axiom that without the receiver there could be no thief.[17]

The bill came up for second reading on 5 March and strong arguments were put for and against several measures contained in it. The Tory Earl of Carnarvon supported the bill on the grounds that it corrected perceived flaws in the present system: the inability to adequately track repeat offenders and to police the terms of tickets-of-leave. He believed a mandatory period of penal servitude to be followed by supervision would remedy this defect.[18] Lord Romilly and the Duke of Cleveland, both Liberals, also supported the introduction of a mandatory minimum sentence of seven years' penal servitude for a second felony conviction. Both believed that repeat offenders were too often sentenced to very short periods of imprisonment.[19] However, Lords Houghton and Hylton, a Liberal and Conservative respectively, opposed the bill on the grounds that it placed too much power in the hands of policemen and that repeat offenders would become marked men, unable to obtain employment.[20] This was a common criticism of police surveillance.

On March 15 the bill went to a committee of the whole House of Lords. At this stage several important amendments were made, including an alteration to the reporting arrangements attached to tickets-of-leave. The change made by the Lords, as we shall see, came to be much criticized. The original bill contained no provision regarding reporting conditions for licence-holders and others deemed habitual criminals. Had the bill passed into law unchanged in this respect the monthly reporting clause of the *Penal Servitude Act 1864* would have remained in force. By this earlier legislation licence-holders were

---

[15] 194 *Parl. Deb.*, HL (3rd ser.), col. 338 (26 Feb. 1869).
[16] Ibid., cols. 345–6.
[17] Patrick Colquhoun, *A Treatise on the Police of the Metropolis*, London: Patterson Smith, 1795, p. 4; Arthur Morrison, *Child of the Jago*, 3rd ed., Woodbridge: The Boydell Press, 1982 (first published 1896), p. 124; *Standard*, 12 Oct. 1870, p. 4.
[18] 194 *Parl. Deb.*, HL (3rd ser.), cols. 703–8 (5 Mar. 1869).
[19] Ibid., cols. 695, 712.
[20] Ibid., cols. 695–6, 709–11.

required to report monthly and in person to a designated police station. Shaftesbury stated that according to a 'minute inquiry' into the operation of monthly reporting he believed it was 'nearly an absolute failure'.[21] He had a particular concern that it sometimes led to the discovery of licence-holders' criminal pasts by their employers, thereby jeopardizing their jobs. Due to such concerns about employment, Shaftesbury believed it would be wise to abolish reporting altogether. Kimberley noted Shaftesbury's concern and agreed that it would be a 'great hindrance' for those under supervision to have to report themselves each month.[22] Hence Kimberley introduced an amendment to the *Penal Servitude Act 1864* in committee to remove the reporting requirement for licence-holders.[23] The amendment was agreed to.

A further amendment again reduced the power bestowed upon the police and, on this occasion, the magistrates also. The bill gave any policeman the power to arrest, without a warrant, a licence-holder whom he suspected of earning his or her livelihood by dishonest means. If such a person, when brought before a magistrate, failed to establish that he or she was not earning a living in this way the licence would be revoked and the individual would be committed to return to prison for a period of up to a year. It was in reference to this provision that Kimberley had approvingly noted that the legislation created a 'different code' for those who set the 'laws of society at defiance'.[24] However, both Liberals and Conservatives voiced objections to reversing the onus of proof in this way.[25] To alleviate this concern, Kimberley offered a compromise in committee. He proposed an amendment requiring the written authority of the chief officer of police of the relevant police district to arrest on suspicion. This amendment was accepted.[26]

Changes were also made to the bill's provisions regarding receivers of stolen goods – once more lessening the severity of the bill. Under the bill any person previously convicted of an offence punishable by imprisonment and subsequently discovered to have stolen goods in their possession was deemed to have known them to be stolen until they proved the contrary. This measure was aimed at curbing the activities of professional fences who many, including the principal architects of the legislation, believed sat atop the criminal

---

[21] Ibid., col. 697.
[22] Ibid., col. 713.
[23] 195 *Parl. Deb.*, HL (3rd ser.), col. 222 (6 Apr. 1869).
[24] 194 *Parl. Deb.*, HL (3rd ser.), col. 340 (26 Feb. 1869).
[25] Lord Romilly (Liberal), Lord Shaftesbury (Conservative) and Lord Hylton (Conservative), 194 *Parl. Deb.*, HL (3rd ser.), cols. 693–9 (5 Mar. 1869).
[26] 194 *Parl. Deb.*, HL (3rd ser.), col. 1310 (15 Mar. 1869).

hierarchy.[27] Nonetheless, the measure did not find much favour in the House of Lords. Carnarvon proposed an amendment deleting the words 'punishable by imprisonment' and replacing them with 'involving fraud or dishonesty' in order to reduce the number of people brought within the scope of the provision. Kimberley concurred that this new language would better target receivers of stolen goods. The amendment was agreed to, as was a further change proposed by Romilly requiring seven days' notice to be given to the accused of the intent to prove the previous conviction.[28] Any less time, it was argued, would not be sufficient to enable the accused to prepare a defence.

The Lords also substantially altered the bill's provisions regulating pawnbrokers. In the nineteenth century pawnbroking services were primarily used as a means for poor families to gain access to cash through pawning, with the intention of later redeeming, their own property.[29] An 1872 select committee heard from a London missionary that half of the working class pawned their property.[30] Pawnbrokers were therefore a vital source of funds for the poor. Yet, as Alannah Tomkins has noted, the press and other commentators often argued that many pawnbrokers aided thieves who used their shops as 'a way to dispose of stolen goods'.[31] Under the initial bill pawnbrokers were to be bound, at any time during business hours, to produce for the police books describing all articles currently pawned with them and all goods that the officer reasonably suspected to be stolen or fraudulently obtained. If required by the officer, the pawnbroker was compelled to deposit all such articles with the chief of police. In addition, if any officer provided information to a pawnbroker describing a certain stolen article and it subsequently came into the pawnbroker's possession, he was bound to inform the police.[32] These measures were designed to mitigate the risk of pawnbrokers acting as receivers of stolen goods.[33] London's pawnbrokers reacted angrily, quickly pledging around 800 pounds to fund a campaign opposing the bill. While they objected to the additional police powers,

---

[27] Matthew Davenport Hill, *Suggestions for the Repression of Crime: Contained in Charges Delivered to Grand Juries of Birmingham; Supported by Additional Facts and Arguments*, London: John W. Parker and Son, 1857, pp. 66–7.

[28] 194 *Parl. Deb.*, HL (3rd ser.), cols. 1341–2 (15 Mar. 1869).

[29] Melanie Tebbut, *Making Ends Meet: Pawnbroking and Working-Class Credit*, New York: St. Martin's Press, 1983, pp. 37–67.

[30] *Report from the Select Committee on the Pawnbrokers Bill; Together with the Proceedings of the Committee and Minutes of Evidence*, [C 288] HC 1872, xii, p. 47.

[31] Alannah Tomkins, 'Pawnbroking and the Survival Strategies of the Urban Poor in 1770s York', in Steven King and Alannah Tomkins (eds.), *The Poor in England 1700–1850: An Economy of Makeshifts*, Manchester: Manchester University Press, 2003, p. 172.

[32] *Habitual Criminals Act*, 32 & 33 Vict., c. 99, 1869, sec. 4.

[33] The Duke of Cleveland (Liberal), 194 *Parl. Deb.*, HL (3rd ser.), col. 1346 (15 Mar. 1869).

the chief objection of pawnbrokers was to having their trade referred to in a bill targeting habitual criminals. This, they believed, would damage their reputation as honest businessmen.[34] Because of this opposition the Liberal Lord Lyveden successfully proposed an amendment to strike out the relevant clauses.[35] The impact of all major amendments in the House of Lords was to lessen the severity or scope of the bill – or both. Despite widespread anxiety about the cessation of transportation, classical notions of justice continued to be strongly held by many, Conservatives and Liberals alike.[36] Punishment, argued numerous peers across party lines, should be proportionate to the crime, and reformation should be its ultimate aim. The bill was accepted as amended by the committee, which reported its amendments to the House of Commons on 16 April.

The Home Secretary, H. A. Bruce, presented the amended bill to the House of Commons on 12 April; at which point it was read for the first time without debate. No debate accompanied the second reading on 26 July. The bill was first debated in the Commons, albeit briefly, on 4 August in committee. Bruce outlined the bill's key measures to the house: police supervision, a system of registration and mandatory minimum sentences for those convicted of a third felonious offence. The present law concerning the 'criminal class' was, he complained, 'too lenient'. The accumulation of this class in large cities due to the ending of transportation meant that society now needed to 'arm itself with more effectual weapons'. However, Bruce noted concerns already expressed in the Lords regarding threats to the liberty of the subject. He was therefore 'anxious' not to carry 'this repressive legislation' any further than was necessary.[37]

The Conservative Sir Charles Adderley spoke next and opposed the bill. He disapproved of police supervision, mandatory minimum sentences and the reversal of the onus of proof. These measures, he said, took the principle of deterrence 'to an outrageous extent', at the expense of reformation.[38] Adderley found support from every other speaker in the Commons bar one. Five further members, two Conservatives, two Liberals and a Radical, argued that the

---

[34] *Times*, 17 Mar. 1869, p. 12; A. Hardaker, *A Brief History of Pawnbroking: With Full Narrative of How the Act of 1872 Was Fought for and Obtained and the Stolen Goods Bill Opposed and Defeated*, London: Jackson, Ruston and Keeson, 1892, pp. 162–3.
[35] 194 *Parl. Deb.*, HL (3rd ser.), cols. 1344–6 (15 Mar. 1869).
[36] This has been discussed in the previous chapters.
[37] 198 *Parl. Deb.*, HC (3rd ser.), cols. 1251–60 (4 Aug. 1869).
[38] Ibid., cols. 1260–5.

legislation was unduly severe and based on new and obnoxious principles.[39] Only the Conservative Sir George Jenkinson approved of the bill as amended by the Lords.[40] The middle-class men and women of the Social Science Association (SSA) were drawn overwhelmingly from the liberal professions and were near unanimous in their support of the measures contained in the *Habitual Criminals Bill 1869*.[41] The parliament, with its more diverse membership, was home to a greater variety of views. As a result of the strength of the criticism that the bill received in the House of Commons the government was forced to agree to a number of further amendments. These, as was the case in the Lords, were generally intended to mitigate the legislation's severity. A major objection to the bill in the House of Commons was regarding police supervision. Several members were strongly opposed to this measure. Bruce suggested an amendment to give the courts the discretion to order a lesser period than seven years. He did this to 'meet the objections'. This amendment was accepted.[42]

The imposition of a mandatory sentence of seven years' penal servitude following a third conviction for a felony also attracted strong opposition, which was expressed not only in the House of Commons but also in the press. Notably, this measure was deemed to be too severe by two people who had been instrumental in the bill's genesis. In *The Times* the Gloucestershire magistrate and SSA member Barwick Baker voiced concern that a sentence of seven years might be considered to be too harsh by judges and juries, leading to evasion through a refusal to convict. He recommended that the clause be amended.[43] Matthew Davenport Hill, the penal reformer whose ideas had – to a very great extent – influenced the position of the government on the question of habitual criminals, wrote to England's principal legal magazine, the *Law Times*, regarding the legislation. In the pages of the conservative magazine he pointed out that 'taking an apple which had fallen from a tree' was a felony and that to pass a mandatory sentence of seven years for three such crimes was unjustifiable. He cited several recent cases in which he believed a sentence of seven years' penal servitude would be too harsh and echoed the concern that unjust acquittals

---

[39] Ibid., cols 1266–73.
[40] Ibid., col. 1273.
[41] Lawrence Goldman, 'The Social Science Association, 1857–1886: A Context for Mid-Victorian Liberalism', *English Historical Review*, vol. 101, no. 398 (Jan. 1986), pp. 95–134; Francis E. Mineka and Dwight N. Lindley (eds.), *The Later Letters of John Stuart Mill 1849–1873*, vol. 15, Toronto: University of Toronto Press, 1972, pp. 632–3.
[42] 198 *Parl. Deb.*, HC (3rd ser.), col. 1278 (4 Aug. 1869).
[43] *Times*, 8 Mar. 1869, p. 4.

could be the only result of such a provision.⁴⁴ While Baker and Hill were both important figures in the drafting of the *Habitual Criminal Bill 1869*, Crofton had been its key author. This explains how the two men could oppose one its provisions. The government, as the previous chapter demonstrated, was most susceptible to the views of Baker and, in particular, Hill.⁴⁵ In committee Bruce noted that 'great objection had been taken to this clause'. After a brief discussion it was agreed that the clause should be omitted entirely.⁴⁶ The key mechanism to achieve one of the bill's major objectives – longer sentences for repeat offenders – was therefore removed.

A substantial change was also made respecting registration. The original bill stipulated that a central register of 'convicts' – meaning licence-holders – was to be kept in London. Bruce moved an amendment substituting the word 'criminals' for 'convicts', in order to provide for the registration of more offenders. The legislation's definition of crime included all felonies and numerous misdemeanours. The misdemeanours were obtaining money by false pretences, conspiracy to defraud and being at large at night with the intent of committing a crime, with either housebreaking instruments or a disguised face.⁴⁷ Bruce said that at present many repeat offenders escaped being sentenced as such due to imperfect knowledge of their history of offending. Broadening the scope of registration would, Bruce argued, solve this problem. However, we will see that it created others. No further discussion is recorded regarding this amendment, which was agreed to.⁴⁸

Finally, further amendments were made regarding receivers of stolen goods. In the bill as amended by the Lords the burden of proof fell upon anyone found in possession of stolen goods who had a previous conviction for a crime involving fraud or dishonesty. George Young, the solicitor general for Scotland, proposed amending the clause so that a previous conviction would be 'admissible as evidence', but no longer prima facie evidence of guilt. He provided no reason for his amendment, which lessened the severity of the clause. With no discussion the amendment was accepted. John Stapleton, Liberal MP for Berwick, also introduced an amendment seeking to make it easier for policemen to gain

---

⁴⁴ Matthew Davenport Hill, 'Habitual Criminals Bill', *Law Times: The Journal and Record of the Law and Lawyers*, vol. 47 (May–Oct. 1869), p. 115.
⁴⁵ Edward Cox, a Middlesex judge, and the *Law Times* itself made similar points to Hill. See Edward Cox, 'The Habitual Criminals Bill', *Law Times*, vol. 46 (Jan.–Apr. 1869), p. 404; 'The Habitual Criminals Act', vol. 47, p. 323.
⁴⁶ 198 *Parl. Deb.*, HC (3rd ser.), col. 1279 (4 Aug. 1869).
⁴⁷ See *Habitual Criminals Act*, s. 20.
⁴⁸ 198 *Parl. Deb.*, HC (3rd ser.), cols. 1276–8 (4 Aug. 1869).

access to premises thought to house stolen property. Stapleton believed gaining written authorization from the chief officer of police would be a quicker and simpler process than applying to a magistrate for a warrant. His amendment, which, as we will see, proved problematic in practice, was also agreed to without discussion.[49]

The committee reported on 5 August and, after a short debate, the report was accepted by the house. The bill was considered on August 6, without debate, and was read for the third time. As Baker recalled being told by an opposition MP, Conservative members 'said nothing but "Aye", and it passed very pleasantly'.[50] The amendments made in the House of Commons were reported to the Lords on August 9 and accepted after a brief discussion. The measure was therefore supported by both major parties, despite the vigorous objections of numerous Conservatives and Liberals to the original bill. The bill received royal assent on 11 August 1869, the last day of the session. Given the strength of the British discourse regarding the liberty of the subject it is not surprising that so many members of parliament objected to the original bill and forced the government to accept alterations. However, this necessarily rushed process at the very end of a session that had been full of significant legislative measures meant the final act contained numerous defects, the significance of which will be discussed in the next section.[51]

*

The *Habitual Criminals Act 1869* was quickly hailed a success by London's press, the Metropolitan Police Force, the government and the Home Office. Yet during the course of the act's first year, strong criticisms of its operation began to appear publicly in the press and privately in letters to the Home Office. This section will examine the way the new act functioned during 1879–80.

Several London newspapers welcomed the habitual criminals' legislation. It was widely argued in London's press that the measures contained in the legislation, principally the registry and police supervision, were appropriately stringent.[52] It was claimed that the post-transportation penal regime put in place by the *Penal Servitude Acts* of 1853, 1857 and 1864 was not harsh enough.

---

[49] Ibid., cols. 1281–2.
[50] Thomas Barwick Lloyd Baker, 'My Life: 1856–79', vol. 2, pp. 177–8. Gloucestershire Archives, D3549/25/7/1.
[51] For further information regarding the significant legislation of this session see Richard Shannon, *Gladstone: 1865–1898*, vol. 2, Chapel Hill: North Carolina University Press, 1999, pp. 62–105.
[52] *Pall Mall Gazette*, 21 Dec. 1869, p. 4; *Daily News*, 6 Aug. 1869, p. 4; *Times*, 27 Feb. 1869, p. 9; *Times*, 16 Mar. 1869, p. 11.

Through inadequate prison terms and early release, the rights of members of the criminal class, it was said, were being upheld at the expense of those of respectable citizens.[53] Tougher legislation that restricted the freedom of this group of offenders by significantly increasing the power of the police was now necessary, primarily due to the end of transportation.[54] For example, in a leading article from December 1869 the *Pall Mall Gazette* said, 'This is a pretty good bill of fare,' as registration and supervision would 'materially facilitate the operations' of the police.[55] The liberal *Morning Post* also approved of the legislation, arguing that through registration and supervision it would be a 'terror' to 'those who prey on society'.[56] The *Daily News*, another liberal paper, referred to the accumulation of a criminal class in London, claiming that this had occurred due to the cessation of transportation. The newspaper bemoaned the fact that 'our forefathers hung them [repeat offenders] and got rid of them; we imprison them, and then bid them go forth'.[57] Consequently, the stern measures contained in the *Habitual Criminals Act 1869* were now needed.

The government claimed, very early in the life of the legislation, that the *Habitual Criminals Act 1869* had been a success. In the House of Commons Bruce robustly defended his legislation twice in the first half of 1870. On 29 April Bruce was questioned by Richard Assheton Cross, the Conservative MP for South West Lancashire, about the failure of the *Habitual Criminals Act 1869* to define what police supervision actually meant. Bruce admitted that the omission left the legislation 'open to criticism', but nonetheless confidently predicted that the registration of criminals, 'which was now being carefully pursued', and police supervision would 'have excellent effects'.[58] On 5 May Bruce received a pre-arranged question, this time from Stapleton – a friendly Liberal MP – seeking information on the working of the legislation. Bruce approvingly informed the House of Commons that between 9 August 1869 and 28 March 1870 a total of 12,277 criminals had been registered, 2,501 of these in London. What was more, within the Metropolitan Police District thirty people had been convicted under the act for receiving stolen goods, eight of harbouring thieves, six of purchasing small amounts of metal, sixty-four of assaulting a policeman (where the sentence was greater than two months in duration), and 287 for

---

[53] *Morning Post*, 25 Aug. 1869, p. 4; *Standard*, 4 Sept. 1869, p. 4.
[54] *Daily News*, 6 Aug. 1869, p. 4; *Pall Mall Gazette*, 21 Dec. 1869, p. 4; *Morning Post*, 25 Aug. 1869, p. 4; *Times*, 27 Feb. 1869, p. 9; *Times*, 16 Mar. 1869, p. 11; *Morning Post*, 25 Aug. 1869, p. 4.
[55] *Pall Mall Gazette*, 21 Dec. 1869, p. 4.
[56] *Morning Post*, 10 Aug. 1869, p. 4.
[57] *Daily News*, 6 Aug. 1869, p. 4.
[58] 200 *Parliamentary Debates*, HC (3rd ser.), col. 2134 (29 Apr. 1870).

loitering and vagrancy. This data demonstrated, according to Bruce, that 'the enforcement of the Act has had a beneficial influence'.[59] Kimberley also said, albeit without recourse to any evidence, that, 'in the metropolis' in particular, the legislation 'had been made [sic] instrumental in breaking up many haunts of thieves, and in otherwise putting a check upon the criminal classes'.[60] These claims were repeated in a Home Office report of 1872 regarding the effectiveness of the Gladstone government's habitual criminals' legislation.[61] However, Bruce's statistics are of questionable worth when assessing the impact of the legislation. Other than the purchase of small amounts of metal, each of the other crimes he listed were offences prior to the enactment of the habitual criminals' legislation, and he provided no evidence of the success of the legislation's two principal provisions: registration and police supervision. Many criminals had been registered, he said, but no evidence was provided that more crimes were being prevented or repeat offenders recognized as a result. Nonetheless, according to the government, its efforts against repeat offenders were succeeding.

The leadership of the Metropolitan Police Force also believed that the *Habitual Criminals Act 1869* provided the police with useful tools in order to combat recidivism. The commissioner claimed that the act had led to less loitering, fewer assaults on the police and a reduction in theft. These apparently good results, it was argued, were enabled by the new system of registration, which facilitated the identification of repeat offenders.[62] Between 1 May and 31 December 1870, 262 applications had been received by staff at the registry of habitual criminals from all the police forces of England and Wales, to search through their records in order to ascertain if an individual was a repeat offender. Thirty-nine of these applications led to a positive identification.[63] While the commissioner conceded that these results 'hardly appear satisfactory', he nonetheless argued that a 'consideration of the facts' would 'change such an impression'.[64] Chief among these, Henderson believed, was that police forces were not accurately recording the number of positive identifications.[65] In any case, the number of applications and successful identifications was far higher in London than elsewhere, presumably because the registry was housed in the capital and,

---

[59] 201 *Parliamentary Debates*, HC (3rd ser.), cols. 272–3 (5 May 1870).
[60] *Standard*, 25 Mar. 1870, p. 2.
[61] *Memorandum Respecting the Decrease in Crime in England and Wales, Especially in the Crimes Affected by the Habitual Criminals Act, 1869, and the Prevention of Crime Act, 1871*, [C 665] HC and HL 1872, i, pp. 1, 3–4.
[62] *Report of the Commissioner of Police of the Metropolis*, 1871, pp. 38, 44, 56.
[63] Ibid., p. 27.
[64] Ibid., p. 8.
[65] Ibid.

therefore, was easier for members of the Metropolitan Police Force to access. Of all 262 applications, 145 had been made by members of the Metropolitan Police Force, leading to twenty-five identifications. This seemingly low number of identifications across an eight-month period was nevertheless sufficient for Henderson to pronounce in 'favour of the working of the "Habitual Criminals Act"'.[66] The Home Office, most of London's newspapers and the Metropolitan Police Force had all strongly supported the Gladstone government in its efforts to overcome the perceived threat from repeat offenders. It is not surprising, therefore, that any early indications of success were hailed from these quarters, and by the government itself, as evidence of the legislation's effectiveness. Despite these positive appraisals of the functioning of the *Habitual Criminals Act 1869*, the legislation – as we will see – was in fact deeply flawed.

Concerns about the act were raised in correspondence between senior officers of the Metropolitan Police Force and the Home Office, in the parliament and the press. These concerns were primarily regarding two issues: errors and impracticalities resulting from the process of amendment, and the actions of London's magistrates to lessen the severity of the legislation.

Various pieces of correspondence between senior members of the Metropolitan Police Force and the Home Office pointed out serious problems regarding the regime of police supervision that the *Habitual Criminals Act 1869* had ushered in and also the conduct of magistrates. Many licence-holders and repeat offenders were escaping longer sentences and police supervision, Commissioner Henderson argued, as a result of a failure on behalf of magistrates and judges to properly examine their past. With their criminal histories unknown, many recidivists were thus escaping the provisions of the legislation. This view was put to Henderson in May 1870 by C. Kendall, the man charged with compiling the register of habitual criminals. He said that 'as a rule' magistrates refused to remand defendants so that their background could be checked. Additional time was needed, said Kendall, so that the registry of habitual criminals could be thoroughly searched. He provided two examples of cases in which repeat offenders had been sentenced as if first offenders by London magistrates when information concerning their past offences was contained in the register.[67] The Home Office had already been informed by prison officials that there were 'many cases' in which London magistrates did not allow for fulsome checks to

---

[66] Ibid.
[67] C. Kendall, registrar of criminals, to Edmund Henderson, 6 May 1870, TNA, HO 12/184/85459A/40.

be made.⁶⁸ Consequently, Henderson recommended the act should be amended mandating a week's remand for any 'suspected persons'.⁶⁹ The Home Office thought the issue was pressing enough to immediately draft a circular to all magistrates calling for 'a more frequent resort on the part of magistrates to the practice of remanding for further enquiry' all those suspected of 'living a life of habitual crime'.⁷⁰ Therefore, due to the actions of London magistrates and for reasons that will be discussed below, the *Habitual Criminals Act 1869* did not prove initially effective in ensuring repeat offenders in the capital were identified and sentenced as such, which was one of its key objectives.

According to Henderson, magistrates and judges were also undermining police supervision. On 19 May 1870 the commissioner received further correspondence from Kendall, in which he complained that he was often 'unable to obtain relevant information' about those under supervision because magistrates and judges did not make it sufficiently clear in sentencing if they were imposing police supervision.⁷¹ This meant that prison wardens did not send information about these offenders to the registry before their release from prison, which was the practice for those about to be released under police supervision. Henderson forwarded Kendall's letter to the Home Office and himself argued that there were many cases in which licence-holders and repeat offenders had escaped surveillance even though the magistrate or judge who sentenced them intended police supervision to be applied. Because of this problem he asked that the amending legislation should stipulate that supervision be pronounced as part of the sentence.⁷²

Henderson made various other complaints to the Home Office about a lack of cooperation from London's magistrates which, in the commissioner's view, significantly undermined the effectiveness of the 1869 legislation. Indeed, the evidence he put to the Home Office shows that in numerous instances in London the *Habitual Criminals Act 1869* was not being enforced in the manner that the government and the parliament had intended. Henderson first complained to the Home Office about the conduct of London's magistrates on 30 December 1869. He referred to a recent case that had come before the magistrate John Paget in which the police were alleging that two defendants, Thomas Riley and

---

[68] Lord Monson, deputy lieutenant of Lincolnshire, to Adolphus Liddell, permanent under-secretary at the Home Office, 27 Apr. 1870, TNA, HO 12/184/85459A/38.
[69] Edmund Henderson to Adolphus Liddell, 6 May 1870, TNA, HO 12/184/85459A/40.
[70] Draft circular, 6 May 1870, TNA, HO 12/184/85459A/40.
[71] C. Kendall to Edmund Henderson, 19 May 1870, TNA, HO 12/184/85459A/45.
[72] Edmund Henderson to Adolphus Liddell, 20 May 1870, TNA, HO 12/184/85459A/45.

Jeremiah Calden, had been found loitering with intent to commit a felony, which was a crime under section 9 of the legislation. The two men, Henderson claimed, were known thieves, had run away from the police and were observed concealing themselves while watching people's pockets. Despite this Paget had found both men not guilty. Henderson, as if to confirm the criminality of the men, noted that they went on to commit and be convicted of theft within a month of their acquittal. He argued that 'the view taken by the magistrate appears to nullify the power of the police to carry into effect the law according to the intention of parliament'.[73] While the Home Office was concerned enough to seek legal advice regarding Paget's verdict, Adolphus Liddell, the permanent under-secretary, told Henderson that the home secretary 'cannot interfere with their [the magistrates'] discretion'.[74] As will be discussed in the later chapter on sentencing, judicial discretion was a long-standing principle of the British justice system.[75] No actions were taken, therefore, in regard to some London magistrates who were failing to fully implement the *Habitual Criminals Act 1869*.

Henderson and other senior officers within the Metropolitan Police Force were also frustrated by the way London's magistrates interpreted the sections of the legislation regarding receivers of stolen goods. Numerous London magistrates read the statute in a way that, as far as possible, limited the powers of the police. For example, on 11 November 1869 the *Daily News* reported on the recent proceedings at London's magistrates' courts, including an application by Inspector Rutt of N division to W. Cooke, the magistrate at the Clerkenwell police court, for a search warrant. Rutt told the magistrate that he had information that stolen door knockers were being hidden at a certain address. However, Cooke refused the application on the grounds that under part four of the *Habitual Criminals Act 1869* 'the police had ample powers' to authorize searches.[76] On hearing of the matter Henderson immediately sought legal advice from the chosen solicitors of the Metropolitan Police Force, Ellis and Ellis. He was told that he did not have the power to authorize a search in this case.[77] Therefore the magistrate, either out of ignorance or, more probably given the clarity of section 11 of the act, quite deliberately, used the legislation to limit the power

---

[73] Edmund Henderson to Adolphus Liddell, 30 Dec. 1869, TNA, MEPO 3/88.
[74] Adolphus Liddell to Edmund Henderson, 14 Jan. 1870, TNA, MEPO 3/88.
[75] Leon Radzinowicz and Roger Hood, 'Judicial Discretion and Sentencing Standards: Victorian Attempts to Solve a Perennial Problem', *University of Pennsylvania Law Review*, vol. 127, no. 5 (1978-9), pp. 1288-349.
[76] *Daily News*, 11 Nov. 1869, p. 6.
[77] *Habitual Criminals Act*, s. 11; Ellis and Ellis, solicitors, to Edmund Henderson, 11 Nov. 1869, TNA, MEPO 3/88.

of the police rather than increase it as the parliament intended. Moreover, on 13 January 1870 Russell Gurney, the recorder of London, disallowed an attempt by members of the Metropolitan Police Force to prove former convictions against several men charged with burglary. The police did this in order to 'avail themselves of a provision of the Habitual Criminals Act' that made it clear that anyone in possession of stolen goods who had previous convictions could be treated by the court as a 'habitual criminal' and, as a result, be made subject to police supervision. However, the accused had to be given seven days' notice of police attempts to prove prior convictions.[78] Gurney argued that such notice had to be in writing, despite the act not stating as much, and refused the request of the police. Again, a magistrate had acted to mitigate the severity of the new act. Gurney may have done so out of a desire to keep faith with members of the working class, who appeared in police courts far more than members of other classes, often used these courts as a source of legal advice and were the target of the *Habitual Criminals Act 1869*.[79] If magistrates had vigorously enforced the legislation they would have risked alienating members of the working class, for whom the courts had been established. This, and other reasons for the manner in which the legislation was interpreted by London magistrates, will be discussed in detail below.

Metropolitan Police files contain one further example of magistrates frustrating their efforts to enforce the new legislation. On 18 May 1870 the superintendent of F division wrote to the commissioner regarding a matter that had been brought before a police magistrate the day before. Francis Peppiatt was charged with, and admitted to, purchasing 42 pounds of lead in contravention of the *Habitual Criminals Act 1869*, which specified that no lesser quantity than 112 pounds of the metal could be bought. Peppiatt claimed that he was ignorant of the law and, nonetheless, knew the seller to be honest. The magistrate, Thomas Arnold, had strong views regarding the need for London's working class to have ready access to the services of second-hand dealers in order to gain access to money when their wages were insufficient to meet their everyday needs.[80] He said that he 'did not think' the act was intended to 'prevent metal dealers' from purchasing goods from 'respectable persons' and dismissed the

---

[78] *Times*, 13 Jan. 1870, p. 11; *Habitual Criminals Act*, sec. 11.
[79] Jennifer S. Davis, 'Law Breaking and Law Enforcement: The Creation of a Criminal Class in Mid-Victorian London', unpublished Ph.D. thesis, Boston College, 1984, pp. 262–3; Alfred Plowden, *Grain or Chaff?: The Autobiography of a Police Magistrate*, London: T.F. Unwin, 1903, p. 266.
[80] See his comments concerning pawnbroking, which will be quoted below, in the *Report from the Select Committee on the Pawnbrokers Bill*, pp. 20–2.

charge.⁸¹ Thus a clear breach of the legislation was ignored. The police believed that these examples were indicative of the attitude of police magistrates across the board towards the enforcement of the legislation and it seems likely that they were correct. In 1869 Sir Thomas Henry, London's chief magistrate, informed Liddell that he and his fellow magistrates would place no weight upon evidence of recidivism garnered from the registers. He said that London's magistrates looked 'upon "Photographs" and "descriptive returns" as a very dangerous class of evidence'. They did not, he argued, prove identity and could even lead to cases of mistaken identity.⁸² Consequently, prisoners in London were not remanded so past offending could be investigated.⁸³ As the superintendent of H division, whose remarks Henderson forwarded to the Home Office, said, there was a failure of 'all magistrates' to fully implement the legislation.⁸⁴

Complaints about the operation of the act were also made in parliament. A debate on the working of the *Habitual Criminals Act 1869* took place in the House of Lords on 24 March 1870 as a result of a question from Carnarvon, who had a deep interest in effective remedies to the perceived problems of an accumulation of repeat offenders in Britain.⁸⁵ In this debate a number of serious problems with the drafting of the act were identified. Section 14 wrongly stated that several forms to be used in the act's administration were in the second schedule, while they were, in fact, in the third. Therefore this clause 'was inoperative'.⁸⁶ There were also problems with section 11, regarding receivers of stolen goods. Before amendment in the House of Commons the clause had said that anyone in receipt of stolen goods would, before being tried, have seven days in which to prove that they had no knowledge of the goods' provenance. While these words were omitted in the final legislation after alterations made in the Commons, they were left in the form of notice which was to be given to the prisoner. Judicial opinion, Carnarvon reported, was that the clause was inoperative because of this discrepancy.⁸⁷ The Earl of Albemarle, a Liberal peer, also said that confusion had been created as the legislation did not say whether 'legal proof' of former convictions was required at trial. As a magistrate himself he could attest to the fact that in some cases repeat offenders were not being recognized and sentenced as such due to uncertainty about what constituted

---

⁸¹ Superintendent of F division to Edmund Henderson, 18 May 1870, TNA, MEPO 3/88.
⁸² Thomas Henry, chief magistrate of London, to Adolphus Liddell, 13 Mar. 1869, TNA, HO 12/184.
⁸³ C. Kendall to Edmund Henderson, 6 May 1870, TNA, HO 12/184/85459A/40.
⁸⁴ Edmund Henderson to Adolphus Liddell, 30 December 1869, TNA, MEPO 3/88.
⁸⁵ This was discussed in the previous chapter.
⁸⁶ 200 *Parliamentary Debates*, HL (3rd ser.), col. 563 (24 Mar. 1870).
⁸⁷ Ibid., col. 564.

proof of a criminal history.[88] Kimberley responded to these issues on behalf of the government and said that the provisions of the legislation were not as clear as was 'desirable'.[89] Indeed, the government accepted that the 'defects pointed out by' Carnarvon were significant enough to necessitate 'a Bill to amend the Habitual Criminals Act'.[90]

Evidence was also presented in London's press that suggested the legislation's flaws were extensive. In particular, it was argued that police supervision – in London especially – was not being carried out effectively. Following news that the government was to introduce an amending bill an article appeared in the *Law Times* articulating what the magazine thought the focus of the new act should be. The magazine argued that as it stood the legislation was 'singularly defective'. The key reason for this was the administration of police supervision. It was correctly noted that there was very little hope of maintaining surveillance over anyone who did not wish to be monitored. Those under supervision neither had to inform police of a change of address nor ever report themselves, personally or in writing, to the police. The *Law Times* urged the government to include a clause in the new act mandating that supervision should entail monthly reporting.[91] Crofton, a key architect of the original legislation, backed this call for a more rigorous approach to police supervision. He penned a letter to *The Times* in February 1871 arguing that unnamed 'improvements' were required to the act that he had played such a significant role in developing. He was careful not to appear critical of the government and noted that it would be 'unreasonable' to think that 'a statute containing such novel and stringent principles should at once be made perfect'.[92] In an address to the annual congress of the SSA later that year Crofton detailed what he believed were the legislation's defects. While 'impracticabilities' had certainly arisen because of drafting errors, he said police supervision had also been largely ineffective. He supported the reintroduction of monthly reporting in order to enable a closer surveillance by the police.[93] The SSA, which had so persistently and successfully advocated for this legislation, was still seeking to influence government through monitoring its impact.

A further issue that was raised in the press, as it had been by the police, concerned the alleged failure of London's magistrates to properly enforce the

---

[88] Ibid.
[89] Ibid.
[90] Ibid.
[91] 'The Habitual Criminals Act', vol. 49, p. 63.
[92] Walter Crofton, 'Habitual Criminals', letter to the editor of *The Times*, 7 Feb. 1871, p. 9.
[93] Walter Crofton, 'International Prison Congress', *Transactions 1871*, p. 320.

legislation by neither acting upon nor seeking information about the criminal history of defendants. The *Law Times* argued strenuously that this was the case. In June 1870 the magazine said that magistrates 'notoriously' failed to properly inquire into the background of those brought before them. The consequence of this, purportedly, was that many repeat offenders were presumed to be first offenders and, as a result, received shorter sentences. Serious offenders were generally referred by magistrates to the Middlesex sessions or London's central criminal court at which a jury trial would occur and long sentences of penal servitude could be handed down. However, according to the *Law Times*, the 'indiscriminate' application of magistrates' summary jurisdiction meant that for many repeat offenders no such referral was being made. They were therefore escaping with sentences of imprisonment, which were of a maximum duration of two years.[94] Shortly after making this claim the magazine produced some evidence. In September 1870 it reported on a case that had been heard by the London magistrate Edmund Woolrych. Two boys, one sixteen and the other fifteen, were brought before Woolrych charged with picking pockets at the Crystal Palace. At the trial a warder from Coldbath Fields Prison confirmed that both boys had previous convictions for theft. They were sentenced to periods of three months' imprisonment. Despite the youth of the two defendants the *Law Times* responded angrily to the brevity of the sentences, which it argued undermined the 'purpose of the Habitual Criminals Act': to subject repeat offenders to periods of penal servitude followed by police supervision.[95]

The reluctance of London's police magistrates to enforce the *Habitual Criminals Act 1869* as the parliament had intended requires explanation. When the purpose and various roles of London's magistrates' courts are considered, it is not surprising that magistrates often sought to lessen the severity of the legislation. Stipendiary magistrates' courts, commonly called police courts, were first established in London in 1792 as a consequence of the passage of the *Middlesex Justices Act 1792*. They were courts of summary jurisdiction and wielded immense power. Without the aid of a jury, police magistrates had a large say in deciding the fate of all those charged with a crime in the Metropolitan Police District. Persons convicted of crime came overwhelmingly from the working class.[96] While initially police magistrates could only convict for a misdemeanour, their jurisdiction was greatly expanded by the *Juvenile Offenders Act* and the

---

[94] 'The Habitual Criminals Act', vol. 49, p. 140.
[95] Ibid., p. 359.
[96] Emsley, *Crime and Society in England*, p. 171; Pat Carlean, foreword to Godfrey, Cox and Farrall, *Serious Offenders*, p. viii.

Criminal Justice Act, both of 1855, which enabled them to punish numerous felonies including larceny. When defendants were brought before them, London's twenty-three police magistrates had three options: acquit, sentence offenders to a period of imprisonment of two years or less in a local gaol, or refer defendants to a higher court, at which a jury trial would occur and a heavier sentence could be administered.[97] A contemporary observer noted, 'Within that margin your discretion is unfettered.'[98] In short, the power of London's police magistrates over the predominantly working-class cohort brought before them was enormous.

However, London's thirteen police courts were not solely oppressive institutions. They conducted a vast amount of business, both criminal and non-judicial, at the behest of members of the working class, including its poorest members who were often believed to form part of a criminal class.[99] This point is not sufficiently recognized by historians who have analysed the working of London's police courts. As Jennifer Davis has said, there is a significant level of agreement among such historians that these courts reflected the 'values and concerns' of the middle class.[100] Numerous historians, such as David Philips and R. D. Storch, have utilized social control interpretations and argued that London's police courts were part of a broader system designed to control the working class.[101] However, this analysis is undermined by the fact that the police courts were, in many respects, a working-class resource. As the late nineteenth-century police magistrate Henry Waddy explained:

> The Act of Parliament by which they were authorised described them as offices which were to be 'available for the poor,' the word 'poor' being used to denote, not the pauper or the outcast, but the working-man of the period, uneducated, ignorant of his legal rights, and unable to enforce them even when he understood them, unless a court should be provided for him, where he might find both guidance and redress. To be 'available for the poor' was the original purpose

---

[97] Jennifer Davis, 'A Poor Man's System of Justice: The London Police Courts in the Second Half of the Nineteenth Century', *Historical Journal*, vol. 27, no. 2 (Jun. 1984), p. 313.
[98] Hugh Gamon, *The London Police Court Today and Tomorrow*, London: J. M. Dent, 1907, pp. 226–7.
[99] Davis, 'A Poor Man's System of Justice', p. 326.
[100] Davis, 'Law Breaking and Law Enforcement', p. 265.
[101] D. Philips, 'A New Engine of Power and Authority: The Institutionalisation of Law Enforcement in England 1780–1830', in Gatrell, Lenman and Parker (eds.), *Crime and the Law*, London: Europa Publications, 1980, p. 178; Allan Silver, 'The Demand for Order in a Civil Society: A Review of Some Themes in the History of Urban Crime, Police and Riot', in David Bordua (ed.), *The Police: Six Sociological Essays*, New York: John Wiley and Sons, 1967, pp. 1–24; J. Brewster, 'The Wilkites and the Law, 1763–1774: A Study of Radical Notions of Governance', in J. Brewster and J. Styles (eds.), *An Ungovernable People: The English and Their Law in the Seventeenth and Eighteenth Century*, London: Hutchinson, 1980, p. 170; Robert D. Storch, 'The Policeman as Domestic Missionary: Urban Discipline and Popular Culture in Northern England, 1850–1880', *Journal of Social History*, vol. 9, no. 4 (1976), pp. 481–90.

of the police courts. It has never been lost sight of since, and abides as the one essential justification for their continuance.[102]

Police courts were indeed available for the poor in a wide range of ways. A huge amount of the courts' time involved hearing complaints from members of the working class, especially against allegedly violent husbands, bad neighbours and unscrupulous employers.[103] These complainants were overwhelmingly drawn from the working class.[104] To cite just one example, in 1868 Mrs Wilson, who was a resident in a well-known rookery called Jennings' Buildings, applied to the Hammersmith police court for a summons against her abusive husband.[105] People also came in large number to use the police courts as a free source of legal advice.[106] As Lydia Murdoch has shown, the views of magistrates were often sought regarding how to deal with troublesome children.[107] Finally, magistrates regularly provided funds to those in need from the poor boxes that were housed in London's thirteen police courts.[108] Davis's work clearly demonstrates that many members of London's working class viewed the courts as a resource, bringing criminal and non-criminal matters to them far more often than members of the middle or upper classes. She has correctly noted that this has been 'largely overlooked by historians' who instead see the police courts as part of penal system specifically designed to control the working class.[109]

The purpose and roles of London's police magistrates led them to be anxious to make sure members of the working class did not view the courts as manifestations of an oppressive class. Firstly, police magistrates took their role supporting London's poor very seriously: a function that was explicitly articulated in the legislation that established the courts. This meant that, as Davis has shown, the police courts were not 'merely expected to function in tandem with the metropolitan police as an efficient engine for the suppression' of the working class. Indeed, London's police magistrates often sided with the

---

[102] H. T. Waddy, *The Police Court and Its Work*, London: Butterworth and Co., 1925, p. 1.
[103] Gamon, *The London Police Court Today and Tomorrow*, pp. 55, 83–4. Across England and Wales nineteenth-century complainants at magistrates' courts were largely members of the working class. See Stephen Banks, *Informal Justice in England and Wales, 1760–1914: The Courts and Popular Opinion*, Woodbridge: The Boydell Press, 2014, p. 21.
[104] Davis, 'Law Breaking and Law Enforcement', pp. 262–3; Plowden, *Grain or Chaff?* p. 266.
[105] Regarding the notoriety of Jennings' Buildings see Davis, 'A Poor Man's System of Justice', p. 320. *West London Observer*, 6 Jun. 1868, p. 2.
[106] Waddy, *The Police Court and Its Work*, pp. 1, 4; Lydia Murdoch, *Imagined Orphans: Poor Families, Child Welfare, and Contested Citizenship in London*, New Jersey and London: Rutgers University Press, 2006, pp. 105–6.
[107] Murdoch, *Imagined Orphans*, p. 105.
[108] Ibid.
[109] Davis, 'A Poor Man's System of Justice', p. 315. Also see Philips, 'A New Engine of Power and Authority', p. 178.

working class in opposition to policies and practices that were widely supported by the middle and upper classes.[110] For instance, they refused to condemn the use of pawnbrokers, instead noting their role in providing finance to the working class. The magistrate Arnold told a select committee in 1872 that 'the poor are so often short of money and wanting money for ordinary purposes'.[111] Davis has noted that such views were 'in contrast to a fairly general middle-class attitude'.[112] Police magistrates also refused to enforce the provisions of the *Metropolitan Street Act 1839* by convicting petty street traders – commonly called costermongers – as doing so would deprive very poor members of the working class of any means of subsistence.[113] London's police magistrates, as S. J. Stevenson has said, often demonstrated a 'liberal paternalism' when dealing with the working class.[114] Additionally, they had a vested interest in ensuring working-class cooperation. It has been demonstrated above that members of the working class generated the vast majority of the police courts' work. The widespread use of these courts by the working class shows that they were generally regarded as legitimate sources of authority and power. One contemporary observer went so far as to say that police magistrates were 'loved' by the poor.[115] Yet the affection of the working class could not be taken for granted. The strict application of statutes that explicitly targeted members of the working class risked disaffecting the courts' key constituency, as actions by various police forces in the mid-nineteenth century had often angered working-class communities.[116] As police magistrate Alfred Plowden noted, he had 'to walk very warily to avoid accusation of over severity'.[117] For these reasons London's police magistrates often failed to fully implement the *Habitual Criminals Act 1869*, which, of course, specifically targeted a portion of the working class.

In an effort to pressure the government to remedy some of the defects of the *Habitual Criminals Act 1869* the Conservative Party, in this instance led by Carnarvon, initiated another debate on the legislation on 25 April 1871.

---

[110] Davis, 'A Poor Man's System of Justice', pp. 315, 325.
[111] *Report from the Select Committee on the Pawnbrokers Bill*, p. 21.
[112] Davis, 'A Poor Man's System of Justice', p. 325.
[113] Ibid.
[114] S. J. Stevenson, 'The "Habitual Criminal" in Nineteenth-Century England: Some Observations on the Figures', *Urban History*, vol. 13 (May 1986), pp. 47–8.
[115] Gamon, *The London Police Court Today and Tomorrow*, p. 103.
[116] Robert D. Storch, 'The Plague of Blue Locusts', *International Review of Social History*, vol. 20, no. 1 (Apr. 1975), pp. 67, 77; A. P. Donajgrodzki, '"Social Police" and the Bureaucratic Elite: A Vision of Order in the Age of Reform', in A. P. Donajgrodzki (ed.), *Social Control in Nineteenth Century Britain*, London: Croom Helm, 1977, pp. 54–5; Storch, 'The Policeman as Domestic Missionary', pp. 481–2.
[117] Plowden, *Grain or Chaff?* p. 232.

In asking when the promised amending legislation would be forthcoming, he condemned the working of police supervision under the act. Because the section of the *Penal Servitude Act 1864* that mandated monthly reporting had been repealed in the House of Commons supervision was, according to Carnarvon, 'a complete nullity'. He correctly noted that those leaving prison to be supervised in the community were under no compulsion to inform the police where they were going. Their name and brief description were included in the *Police Gazette*, a biweekly publication of the Metropolitan Police Force that carried details of stolen property and individuals wanted for crime. However, this was all the information police forces had at their disposal in order to facilitate the supervision of licence-holders and repeat offenders who were at liberty to move around the country without informing the police. 'All pretence of supervision', therefore, had been 'abandoned'. Brandishing 'a large number of letters from the police authorities of the principal towns' in his support, Carnarvon called for monthly reporting to form part of the amending legislation. Others agreed that the provisions regarding police supervision needed to be strengthened. The Duke of Richmond, another Conservative, argued that at present 'there was no supervision at all' as criminals leaving prison were not required to give authorities an address. Finally, the Liberal Morley agreed that the provisions of the 1869 act regarding supervision were unsatisfactory. Despite their non-cooperation with the act, there was no criticism of London's magistrates during these debates. This was probably the case due to the respect with which judicial discretion was regarded by members of parliament across party lines.[118] Kimberley responded on behalf of the government and conceded that Bruce was 'not quite satisfied with the stringency of the regulations with respect to criminals reporting themselves'.[119] The government was therefore forced to acknowledge that the principal measure of the *Habitual Criminals Act 1869* had not led to the close monitoring of licence-holders and designated repeat offenders. As a result of this and other acknowledged flaws in the *Habitual Criminals Act 1869* the government introduced the *Prevention of Crime Bill 1871*. This new bill, and its passage through parliament, will be analysed in the next section.

*

[118] Sir Charles Adderley (Conservative) and Henry Bruce (Liberal), 198 *Parl. Deb.*, HC (3rd ser.), cols. 1260–5, 1279 (4 Aug. 1869).
[119] 205 *Parliamentary Debates*, HL (3rd ser.), cols. 1678–83 (25 Apr. 1871).

The *Prevention of Crime Bill 1871* sought to improve the *Habitual Criminals Act 1869* in two keys ways: by making the registration of criminals more likely to lead to their identification and by strengthening the system of police supervision. Regarding registration, section 6 of the bill stipulated that the register of habitual criminals should include photographs of all those listed: a development that will be discussed further in the next chapter. The government hoped this would make it easier to carry out searches at the registry. The other significant change was to police supervision. Monthly reporting by licence-holders and repeat offenders under police supervision was introduced – or reintroduced in the case of the former – in sections 5 and 8. By agreement between the individual under supervision and their local police force this could be done in writing. The same two sections said that licence-holders and repeat offenders under police supervision must inform the police of their address on leaving prison and of subsequent changes of address. In addition, section 7 made the imposition of police supervision optional for twice-convicted felons who had not been sentenced to penal servitude. While judges could previously sentence this cohort of criminals to seven years' supervision or less, they could not sentence them to no supervision at all. Although the government did not explain the reason for this change, it was presumably an attempt to limit the huge number of offenders who had been made subject to supervision.[120] In numerous other ways the bill attempted to address the ambiguities of the earlier legislation. Section 19, for instance, altered the language regarding receivers of stolen goods in order to clarify that the police needed to give an accused receiver seven days' notice in writing if they intended to introduce evidence of prior convictions for crimes of fraud or dishonesty.[121]

In parliament the government explained that the legislation would hopefully remedy the faults of the early act. Unlike the legislation of 1869, the *Prevention of Crime Bill 1871* had an uncomplicated passage through parliament. After being read for the first time on 23 June 1871, the bill was second-read and debated in the House of Lords on 4 July, during which no opposition to the measure was expressed.[122] Subsequently, Bruce introduced the bill into the House of Commons on 26 July and the second reading took place on 14 August, albeit without debate. In the Commons, as the Lords, the views of members

---

[120] This is also the conclusion of Leon Radzinowicz and Roger Hood in 'Incapacitating the Habitual Criminal: The English Experience', *Michigan Law Review*, vol. 78, no. 8 (Aug. 1980), p. 1344.
[121] *Prevention of Crime Act*, 34 & 35 Vict., c. 112, 1871, s. 19.
[122] 207 *Parl. Deb.*, HL (3rd ser.), cols. 1082–8 (4 Jul. 1871).

concerning the measure were overwhelmingly positive.[123] The committee reported on 18 August, when the bill was read a third time without debate. The legislation came into force on 2 November after having received royal assent on 21 August. While the *Prevention of Crime Act 1871* improved the earlier legislation in a number of ways, it was also, as we shall see in the coming chapters, an imperfect instrument. Numerous errors of drafting in the 1869 act were corrected. The mandated photographing of all those registered as habitual criminals and the re-introduction of monthly reporting also had the potential to enable a closer monitoring of repeat offenders by policemen. However, once again, criticisms were soon made regarding the functioning of both registration and police supervision under the new act. These will be discussed at length in the coming chapters.

*

In London the *Habitual Criminals Act 1869* was a highly ineffective instrument of social control. To some extent this was because of numerous major amendments that were hurriedly made as the legislation passed through parliament. Some Liberals, Conservatives and Radicals argued that the principles embodied in the bill went against important norms of justice. Consequently, multiple alterations were made, with the effect that the final act was significantly less severe. These amendments – rushed through at the end of the session – also introduced errors. While early assessments of the legislation's operation were predominantly positive, several significant problems soon became apparent. The regime of police surveillance, in particular, was heavily criticized on the basis that those being supervised were under no obligation to inform the police of their address or to report themselves, the latter being due to an amendment in the House of Commons. Registration was also far less effective in enabling the identification of licence-holders and repeat offenders than the government had hoped. This was at least partly due, as the government argued when introducing the new legislation of 1871, to the vast number of those registered. Once again, this resulted from an amendment to the original bill. The Metropolitan Police Force also collected much evidence to suggest that London's police magistrates, on many occasions, were failing to fully enforce the legislation.

As numerous historians have claimed, despite its many amendments the legislation did give the Metropolitan Police Force significant additional

---

[123] 208 *Parl. Deb.*, HC (3rd ser.), cols. 1756–9 (16 Aug. 1871).

powers.[124] Yet both flaws in the legislation and the actions of police magistrates meant that the impact of these additional powers upon habitual criminals in London was much more limited than its sponsors had hoped. The dominant position in the relevant literature is that, despite some defects, the *Habitual Criminals Act 1869* was an oppressive instrument of control that enabled the monitoring and even creation of a criminal class. The historians who make this case claim that the state, represented, in this case, by members of parliament, magistrates, judges and the police, sought to control the working class and met with significant success in this endeavour. They utilize social control interpretations to claim that this legislation was part of a much larger apparatus of control.[125] In this chapter it has been shown that, at least in London, this thesis is incorrect. A lack of time to fully consider the many amendments to the original legislation meant numerous errors were introduced, making parts of the act inoperative. Furthermore, police magistrates took their role as purveyors of justice to London's poor very seriously and consequently were loath to alienate them by enforcing harsh measures. However, in 1871 the Gladstone government sought to strengthen the measures contained in the earlier legislation. Whether it did so successfully will be the subject of the coming chapters. We shall start with an analysis of the registration of licence-holders and repeat offenders.

---

[124] Petrow, *Policing Morals*, p. 51; Wiener, *Reconstructing the Criminal*, p. 149; Godfrey, Cox and Farrall, *Serious Offenders*, p. 205.

[125] Godfrey, Cox and Farrall, *Serious Offenders*, p. xii; Emsley, *Crime and Society in England*, pp. 172–4; Johnston, *Crime in England*, p. 36; Petrow, *Policing Morals*, p. 51.

3

Registering Habitual Criminals: A 'Salutary Control'?

Sir Walter Crofton ... proceeded to advocate for the establishment of a central office for the registration of licence-holders, which should be in communication with the various police authorities throughout England, and thus make supervision more uniform and effective. But, further, Sir Walter Crofton pointed out that this salutary control should not be confined to convicts, but be extended to all those who are criminals by habit and repute; in other words, that society should undertake its legitimate defence against the class whose livelihood it is to prey on honest industry. [1]

(George Hastings, barrister and member of the Social Science Association, 1869)

One of the key means by which the Gladstone government envisioned the *Prevention of Crime Act 1871* would curtail the activities of the criminal class was through a system of registration. As was the case with the legislation of 1869, the new act mandated the keeping of registers of 'habitual criminals' throughout the UK.[2] The government hoped these registers, which were now to include photographs, would aid the police in identifying and then supervising licence-holders and repeat offenders. The registers were also intended to ensure that magistrates and judges had full information before them regarding a defendant's criminal past, hopefully resulting in the application of longer sentences as fewer repeat offenders would be able to escape recognition.[3] The extent to which the various registers accessible to the Metropolitan Police Force were, as the

---

[1] George Hastings, 'Address on Jurisprudence and Amendment of the Law', in *Transactions of the National Association for the Promotion of Social Science 1869*, London: Longman, Green, Reader and Dyer, 1870, pp. 36–7.
[2] *Prevention of Crime Act*, 34 & 35 Vict., c. 112, 1871, s. 6.
[3] Henry Bruce (Liberal), 198 *Parliamentary Debates*, HC (3rd ser.), cols. 1251–60, 1276–8 (4 Aug. 1869); 200 *Parl. Deb.*, HC (3rd ser.), col. 2134 (29 Apr. 1870); *Prevention of Crime Act*, s. 6.

legislation's chief architect Sir Walter Crofton hoped, a 'salutary control' and defence against the criminal class will be assessed in this chapter.[4]

Most historians have claimed that the registration of 'habitual criminals' as a result of the legislation of 1869 and 1871 had a stigmatizing effect, leading to harsh treatment at the hands of police, magistrates and judges.[5] Stefan Petrow, for one, has said that registration served to 'brand certain criminals as habitual'.[6] There is agreement among the historians who have investigated registration that, prior to the decision to introduce fingerprinting in 1895, the means of identifying licence-holders and repeat offenders were imperfect, as the registers were cumbersome and inexact.[7] Nonetheless, most historians who have analysed the working of registration claim that many people unfortunate enough to have their names listed in one or more of the many registers and, therefore, to be branded a habitual criminal were, as a consequence, hounded by the police and subjected to severe treatment by magistrates and judges.[8] This chapter will show that they are incorrect, at least when it comes to London, and will present and analyse new evidence regarding the conciliatory disposition of many policemen, magistrates and judges towards the criminal class. The chapter will commence by describing the system of registration that was put in place as a result of the habitual criminals' legislation. How effective was the registry in London up until 1880? In 1880, a new Convict Supervision Office (CSO) was created at Scotland Yard that augmented the system of registration in London.[9] The second section, therefore, will assess the effectiveness of registration in London up to 1895.

*

[4] Hastings, 'Address on Jurisprudence and Amendment of the Law', pp. 36–7.
[5] D. J. V. Jones, 'The New Police: Crime and People in England and Wales, 1829–1888', in *Transactions of the Royal Historical Society*, 5th series, vol. 33 (1983), p. 162; David Garland, *Punishment and Welfare*, London: Gower, 1985, p. 62; Donald Thomas, *The Victorian Underworld*, London: Hodder & Stoughton, 1998, p. 285; Helen Johnston, *Crime in England 1815–1880: Experiencing the Criminal Justice System*, Abingdon: Routledge, 2015, pp. 37–8; Stefan Petrow, *Policing Morals: The Metropolitan Police and the Home Office 1870–1914*, Oxford: Clarendon Press, 1995, p. 51.
[6] Petrow, *Policing Morals*, p. 85.
[7] Ibid., p. 84; Leon Radzinowicz and Roger Hood, 'Incapacitating the Habitual Criminal: The English Experience', *Michigan Law Review*, vol. 78, no. 8 (Aug. 1980), p. 1348; Johnston, *Crime in England*, p. 37; Christopher Harding, '"The Inevitable End of a Discredited System"? The Origins of the Gladstone Committee Report on Prisons, 1895', *Historical Journal*, vol. 31, no. 3 (Sept. 1988), p. 599; Cicely Craven, 'The Progress of English Criminology', *Journal of Criminal Law and Criminology*, vol. 24, no. 1 (May–Jun., 1933), p. 231.
[8] Barry Godfrey, David Cox and Stephen Farrall, *Serious Offenders: An Historical Study of Habitual Criminals*, London: Oxford University Press, 2010, p. xii; Clive Emsley, *Crime and Society in England: 1750–1900*, 2nd ed., London: Longman, 1996, pp. 172–4; Johnston, *Crime in England*, p. 36.
[9] *Report of a Committee Appointed by the Secretary of State to Inquire into the Best Means Available for Identifying Habitual Criminals; with Minutes of Evidence and Appendices*, [C 7263] HC and HL 1894, lxxii, pp. 1–16.

The Liberal government and the Conservative opposition hoped that the registration of 'habitual criminals' would enable police monitoring of a group of offenders – licence-holders and repeat offenders – who were often called a criminal class.[10] This was largely not achieved in London between 1869 and 1871 due, primarily, to the huge numbers who were registered.[11] New legislation was introduced in 1871 that mandated the photographing of all 'habitual criminals' in an effort to make searches at the registry less time-consuming and more likely to result in a successful identification.[12] This section will analyse the extent to which the changes made through the *Prevention of Crime Act 1871* were effective up to 1880, at which point the CSO was established in London.

The registry was intended to complement an existing system of identification, the basis of which was personal recognition of offenders by police officers and prison warders. Since the inception of the Metropolitan Police Force, members had been encouraged to hone their knowledge of criminals by conducting visits to prisons to view prisoners before release and to courts in order to ascertain if those about to be tried were known to them.[13] In the 1860s any person committed for trial in London or remanded in custody by a police magistrate was sent to Holloway prison, and these prisoners were viewed three times a week during an hour set aside for exercise. Warders from all London prisons along with detectives from every division of the Metropolitan Police Force attended at these times.[14] Metropolitan police orders, which were issued daily from the commissioner's office, also show that the police and warders were deployed to courts for the purpose of recognizing repeat offenders.[15] The memoirs of senior detective Frederick Wensley show that these duties were taken very seriously.[16] Some policemen, according to Wensley, spent much time increasing their 'knowledge of crooks by going to the courts and noting hundreds of professional thieves'.[17] Information gleaned from these visitations was used as part of a register kept at the main station of

---

[10] Douglas Straight (Conservative), 208 *Parl. Deb.*, HC (3rd ser.), cols. 1756–9 (16 Aug. 1871).
[11] The Earl of Morley (Liberal), 207 *Parl. Deb.*, HL (3rd ser.), cols. 1082–6 (4 Jul. 1871).
[12] *Prevention of Crime Act*, s. 6.
[13] Metropolitan Police Orders, 2 Dec. 1832, TNA, MEPO 7/131.
[14] *Report of the Commissioners Appointed to Inquire into the Operation of the Acts Relating to Transportation and Penal Servitude. Vol. 2. Minutes of Evidence*, [C 3190] HC 1863, xxi, p. 129; *Report of a Committee Appointed by the Secretary of State to Inquire into the Best Means Available for Identifying Habitual Criminals*, pp. 10–1.
[15] Metropolitan Police Orders, 14 Sept. 1857, TNA, MEPO 7/19; Metropolitan Police Orders, 29 Apr. 1865, TNA, MEPO 7/26; Metropolitan Police Orders, 29 Jul. 1865, TNA, MEPO 7/26.
[16] Frederick Wensley, *Forty Years of Scotland Yard*, New York: Greenwood Press, 1968 (first published 1932), p. 13.
[17] Ibid.

each Metropolitan Police Force division.[18] The registers that were introduced as a result of the Gladstone government's habitual criminals' legislation were built upon this system.

This legislation led to the creation of a registry in London, which housed two registers and albums of photographs of habitual criminals from across England. The *Prevention of Crime Act 1871* stipulated that registers of 'all persons convicted of crime' should be kept under the management of the commissioner of the Metropolitan Police Force.[19] The legislation's definition of crime included all felonies and numerous misdemeanours. The misdemeanours were obtaining money by false pretences, conspiracy to defraud and being at large at night with the intent of committing a crime, with either housebreaking instruments or a disguised face.[20] The legislation also mandated that inmates of all British prisons convicted of crime should be photographed, as the government believed this would prove 'very useful' in proving whether a certain individual was a repeat offender.[21] Initially two registers were created in London and housed at a new habitual criminals' registry at Scotland Yard. From 1871 to 1895 the processes for the maintenance of the registers were the same. Shortly before the release of any habitual criminal (as defined by the 1871 act) or other prisoner completing a period of penal servitude, a form was prepared by the prison in which they were incarcerated and forwarded to the registry. This return, called a Form R, contained a physical description of the prisoner, a list of his or her previous convictions and a description of any distinctive marks on the prisoner's body, such as scars and tattoos.[22] One London prisoner who wrote anonymously in 1877 confirmed that this work was carried out conscientiously by prison staff, as 'marks upon' the bodies of prisoners were 'noted in their descriptions'.[23]

This information was then used to compile two registers, which were updated annually and contained the details of all those liberated during the previous calendar year. The habitual criminals' register contained a list of all names in alphabetical order and, in columns alongside each name, the person's distinctive marks, details of previous convictions, their address on release, if known, and the

---

[18] Metropolitan Police Orders, 2 Dec. 1832, TNA, MEPO 8/3.
[19] *Prevention of Crime Act*, s. 6.
[20] Ibid., s. 20.
[21] The Earl of Morley (Liberal), 207 *Parl. Deb.*, HL (3rd ser.), cols. 1082–6 (4 Jul. 1871).
[22] *Report of a Committee Appointed by the Secretary of State to Inquire into the Best Means Available for Identifying Habitual Criminals*, pp. 6–7.
[23] Anonymous, *Five Years' Penal Servitude by One Who Has Endured It*, London: Richard Bentley and Son, 1877, p. 157.

prison from which they were liberated.²⁴ A second register, of distinctive marks, was intended to enable the identification of an individual whose name was unknown, based on bodily marks. The register used nine divisions: the head and face, the throat and neck, the chest, the belly and groin, the back and loins, the arms, the hands and fingers, the thighs and legs, and the feet and ankles. Various categories were then listed under each of these divisions so that a policeman could easily search for tattoos, amputations, burns, fractures and numerous other types of marks.²⁵ For example, it was noted that Thomas Brown, who was sentenced to seven years' penal servitude in London on 16 September 1878 for larceny, had a fractured nose, a blue mark behind his left ear and scars on the end of his thumb.²⁶ Albums of photographs were also compiled. By 3 July 1872 the Home Office had issued instructions to all British prisons on the photographing of 'habitual criminals'.²⁷ Policemen from any force could request a search based on a name, distinctive mark or other details of appearance, or they could attend the registry personally to carry out a search themselves.²⁸ The government and opposition believed that – with the addition of albums of photographs – the registry would better facilitate the identification of 'habitual criminals', but not all relevant parties were of this view.²⁹ Sir Thomas Henry, London's chief magistrate until his death in 1876, believed that the type of information contained in the registers did not conclusively prove identity and could lead to cases of mistaken identity.³⁰ As we will see, the hostility of London's most senior police magistrate to the new system of registration did not augur well for its success. Indeed, as a Home Office inquiry of 1895 found, while evidence from the registers was admissible in court, magistrates and judges generally believed that identity could only be proved by additional evidence from a policeman or prison warder who personally recognized the defendant.³¹

[24] Ibid., p. 7; 'Alphabetical Register of Habitual Criminals Who Have Been Liberated, Subject to the Penalties of the 8th Clause of "The Habitual Criminals Act, 1869;" or of the 7th or 8th Clauses of "The Prevention of Crimes Act, 1871," to the 31st March 1876', 1877, TNA, PCOM 2/404.
[25] For an extract from the register, copies of which are no longer in existence, see *Report of a Committee Appointed by the Secretary of State to Inquire into the Best Means Available for Identifying Habitual Criminals*, p. 7.
[26] *Police Gazette*, 2 Jan. 1885, p. 5.
[27] Photographs were to be taken in a standard size and attached to forms entitled, 'Particulars of a Person Convicted of a Crime Specified in the 20th Section of the Prevention of Crimes Act, 1871'. See 'Prevention of Crime Act, 1871. Instructions', 28 Oct. 1871, TNA, HO 158/3; Adolphus Liddell, permanent undersecretary at the Home Office, to local prison governors, 3 Jul. 1872, TNA, HO 158/3.
[28] *Report of a Committee Appointed by the Secretary of State to Inquire into the Best Means Available for Identifying Habitual Criminals*, pp. 6–8.
[29] The Earl of Morley (Liberal), 207 *Parl. Deb.*, HL (3rd ser.), cols. 1082–6 (4 Jul. 1871).
[30] Thomas Henry, chief magistrate of London, to Adolphus Liddell, 13 Mar. 1869, TNA, HO 12/184.
[31] *Report of a Committee Appointed by the Secretary of State to Inquire into the Best Means Available for Identifying Habitual Criminals*, p. 14.

The system of registration put in place as a result of the *Prevention of Crime Act 1871* was noted with satisfaction by a small number of sources. In their contributions to the annual reports of the commissioner of the Metropolitan Police Force, several superintendents argued that the registry was enabling the identification of repeat offenders. In 1871 the superintendent of the Southwark division claimed that the registers were effective and that 'this system appears to work well'. The superintendent of the Clapham division agreed, writing that the new system 'aid[s] Police in tracing offenders', as did the superintendent of the Whitechapel division in 1872.[32] One London newspaper, the liberal *Morning Post*, also argued that the registry was working well. A leading article of August 1872 on the publication of the commissioner's annual report said, albeit without evidence, that the registry was 'a decided improvement on the previous state of things'.[33] In 1873 these views were reiterated in another leading article on the decrease of recorded crime.[34] These three senior police officers, whose remarks presumably influenced the *Morning Post*, clearly believed that the registry aided their work, as it indeed had done in ten cases that had been identified in the Southwark division.[35]

Despite a small number of positive assessments of the registry, there is far more evidence to suggest that it was highly ineffective in the early years of its operation. The compilation of the two registers was still being carried out in strict keeping with the wording of the act. This meant that all those convicted 'of crime', including numerous petty misdemeanours, were listed.[36] By 1876, 169,521 criminals were registered, and this figure was growing by 28,000 names each year.[37] As a result, searches were very time-consuming and rarely led to positive identifications, as noted by numerous officials, including senior members of the Metropolitan Police Force, and several London newspapers. For example, the chairman of the board of directors of convict prisons, Sir Edmund Du Cane, criticized the working of the registry in an address to the Social Science Association (SSA) in August 1875. He said, 'It has not been made much use' of due to the fact that it was 'too cumbersome'.[38] In his memoirs Du Cane

---

[32] *Report of the Commissioner of Police of the Metropolis*, [C 652] HC 1872, xxx, pp. 63, 69; *Report of the Commissioner of Police of the Metropolis: For the Year 1873*, [C 1059] HC 1874, xxviii, p. 98.
[33] *Morning Post*, 19 Aug. 1872, p. 4.
[34] *Morning Post*, 29 Jan. 1873, p. 6.
[35] *Report of the Commissioner of Police of the Metropolis*, 1872, p. 63.
[36] *Prevention of Crime Act*, s. 20.
[37] Sir Henry Selwin-Ibbetson (Conservative), 229 *Parliamentary Debates*, HC (3rd ser.), col. 1596 (8 Jun. 1876).
[38] *Morning Post*, 8 Oct. 1875, p. 2.

also claimed that the registry was overly bulky.³⁹ This was also the view of both senior members of the Metropolitan Police Force and the Home Office. Possible changes to the way the registry functioned were broached by the commissioner of the Metropolitan Police Force with the Home Office in 1874. Commissioner Edmund Henderson wrote to the Home Office on 22 June 1874 detailing his concerns. He thought too many names appeared in the register and advised that only those 'who can reasonably be called Habitual Criminals' should be listed.⁴⁰ The Home Office agreed. Godfrey Lushington, a senior clerk in the criminal department of the Home Office, wrote a paper for the home secretary in January 1875, in which he argued that the registry had been a 'comparative failure'. This was, in Lushington's view, because of the 'enormous number' of registered criminals. He said that 'the present statutory requirement to register and photograph all persons convicted of "crime" ... is a reductio ad absurdum of the system of registration' and that a choice needed to be made between the 'total abolition of the system of registration and a complete reconstitution of it'.⁴¹ He favoured the latter, via a change to the definition of crime in the legislation to reduce the size of the registers. Given the vast number of criminals whose details were kept at the registry, there is every reason to accept the negative assessment of these officials.

The available data further demonstrates that the registry was of very limited use in identifying licence-holders and repeat offenders in London. For a four-year period from 1870 to 1873 detailed data was compiled regarding the number of applications made by members of the Metropolitan Police Force to the registry concerning people already in custody who were suspected of being repeat offenders.

When weighed against the fact that official reports numbered the known thieves at large in London at 3,467 in 1873, and that 140,000 people were registered, the number of successful identifications seems to fall far short of the parliament's desires. Yet while the registry was a 'comparative failure' in London, as Lushington had said, elsewhere it was a total failure.⁴² In a number of major cities only one application to the registry was recorded in each year of the early 1870s. This was the case for Leeds in 1870, Birmingham and Norwich

---

³⁹ Sir Edmund Du Cane, *The Punishment and Prevention of Crime*, London: Macmillan, 1885, p. 194.
⁴⁰ Edmund Henderson, commissioner of the Metropolitan Police Force, to Godfrey Lushington, Home Office clerk, 22 Jun. 1874, TNA, MEPO 6/90/2.
⁴¹ Godfrey Lushington, Memorandum: 'Registry of Criminals', Jan. 1875, TNA, MEPO 6/90/2, pp. 8, 10.
⁴² Ibid., p. 10.

Table 3.1 The use and success of the registry in London, 1870–3

Year	Applications to Registry	Successful identifications	Percentage of applications that were successful
1870 (1 May to 31 Dec.)	145	25	17.2
1871	793	111	13.9
1872	953	188	19.7
1873	852	180	21.1

Report of the Commissioner of Police of the Metropolis, [C 358] HC 1871, xxxvi, p. 27; *Report of the Commissioner of Police of the Metropolis*, 1872, p.19; *Report of the Commissioner of Police of the Metropolis*, 1873, p. 22; *Report of the Commissioner of Police of the Metropolis*, 1874, p. 27.

in 1871, Coventry in 1872 and Bolton in 1873, and no applications at all were made by the police forces of numerous cities.[43] In investigating the neglect of the registry by forces outside London, Commissioner Henderson had been told by officers of other police forces that they were reluctant to use 'a Register kept by a local body like the Metropolitan Police', a plausible explanation that, as we will see, was accepted by the government.[44] While greater than from elsewhere, the volume of applications from members of the Metropolitan Police Force, and resulting identifications, was low. Even in these cases the benefit of the registry was questionable. Several senior police officers reported to the Home Office that 'save in few cases, the identifications would have been made without the help of the register', through other means such as the inspection of remand prisoners by police officers and warders.[45] Leon Radzinowicz and Roger Hood only slightly exaggerated, therefore, when they said that before 1876 the registry 'proved useless as a means of identification'.[46]

Ultimately Benjamin Disraeli's Conservative government acted in an effort to increase the registry's effectiveness. In March 1875 the registry was relocated from Scotland Yard to the Home Office, from which copies of the habitual criminals' register were then annually sent to all police forces. This was done in order to encourage greater usage of the registry's information by forces beyond

---

[43] See *Report of the Commissioner of Police of the Metropolis*, 1872, p. 19; *Report of the Commissioner of Police of the Metropolis*, 1873, p. 22; *Report of the Commissioner of Police of the Metropolis*, 1874, pp. 3–4, 27.
[44] Edmund Henderson to Home Office, 22 Jun. 1874, TNA, HO 45/9518/22208.
[45] Lushington, Memorandum: 'Registry of Criminals', p. 10.
[46] Radzinowicz and Hood, *Incapacitating the Habitual Criminal*, p. 1348.

London.⁴⁷ The issue of the registers' bulk required a legislative response: the passage of the *Prevention of Crimes Amendment Bill* through the parliament in 1876. This legislation, which consisted of one page, gave discretionary powers to the home secretary to stipulate who should appear in the registers. Sir Henry Selwin-Ibbetson, Undersecretary of State for the Home Department in Disraeli's government, told the Commons that the bill's object was to 'simplify' registration. He noted that the names of 169,521 offenders appeared in the habitual criminals' register, many of whom had committed only 'trifling offences', making searches for serious repeat offenders 'cumbrous'.⁴⁸ The bill elicited little discussion, no opposition, and was passed on 30 June 1876. On 15 March of the next year, a Home Office circular informed magistrates and judges that henceforth the registry would include only the details of those 'convicted on indictment of crime, a previous conviction having been proved against' them and those who had been discharged from a sentence of penal servitude.⁴⁹ The government hoped that these provisions would reduce the number of petty offenders listed in the pages of the registers, making searches quicker and more likely to lead to successful identifications of serious criminals.⁵⁰

These alterations, which had bipartisan support, led to a small amount of positive commentary. In a leading article in 1879 *The Times* argued that the 1876 legislation had remedied the registry's prior faults as the condensed registers were easier to search and more likely to facilitate the identification of serious criminals. The registry was now an 'invaluable apparatus'.⁵¹ Du Cane, perhaps predictably given that he had been placed in overall charge of the registry in 1875 following its relocation to Scotland Yard, also spoke very positively about it. Writing in 1885 he said that the registers took a convenient and useful form, meaning that evidence pertaining to suspects was able to be sourced 'at once'.⁵² How effective were these changes? And what was the impact of a new body established in 1880?

*

---

⁴⁷ Henderson to Home Office, 22 Jun. 1874; Lushington, Memorandum: 'Registry of Criminals', p. 10; Home Office circular to governors of prisons and chief officers of police, 1 Mar. 1875, TNA, HO 45/9518/22208.
⁴⁸ 229 *Parliamentary Debates*, HC (3rd ser.), col. 1597 (8 Jun. 1876).
⁴⁹ Metropolitan Police Orders, 15 Mar. 1877, TNA, MEPO 3/88.
⁵⁰ Sir Henry Selwin-Ibbetson (Conservative), 229 *Parliamentary Debates*, HC (3rd ser.), col. 1597 (8 Jun. 1876).
⁵¹ *Times*, 3 Apr. 1879, p. 9.
⁵² Du Cane, *The Punishment and Prevention of Crime*, p. 195.

Further to the legislation of 1876, in 1880 a new apparatus was established in London, the Convict Supervision Office (CSO), which also contained registers of criminals in the capital. This section will assess whether these further changes to registration in London facilitated more identifications of repeat offenders and, as a consequence, closer monitoring by members of the Metropolitan Police Force and punishment by London's magistrates and judges.

A significant change to the system of registration in London was made in 1880 with the creation of the CSO. This office, with a small staff of plain-clothes police, was charged with carrying out the various duties associated with the supervision of 'habitual criminals' in London.[53] The office was established in response to a recommendation of an 1879 inquiry into the *Penal Servitude Acts*, which was instituted following revelations of the poor conditions that those undergoing sentences of penal servitude were subjected to in prison.[54] The bipartisan committee consisted of four members of parliament and two medical doctors.[55] These commissioners heard some objections to police supervision, especially from the Royal Society for the Assistance of Discharged Prisoners. The organization criticized the 'supervision of convicts by the police, on the ground that it has been occasionally the cause of men losing their employment', as a police presence outside an individual's workplace had, it claimed, led to the discovery of some people's criminal past.[56] This charitable society sought to aid the reintegration of prisoners into society and, in particular, employment.[57] Because of the society's evidence, the commissioners came to the view that 'the best remedy as regards the metropolis … will be found in appointing special police officers to be employed exclusively' in supervising licence-holders and other supervisees.[58] The government acted on this recommendation by establishing the CSO.[59]

---

[53] *Report of the Commissioner of Police of the Metropolis: For the Year 1880*, [C 2969] HC 1881, lvi, p. 7.
[54] *Report of the Commissioners Appointed to Inquire into the Working of the Penal Servitude Acts. Vol. I – Commissions and Report*, [C 2368] HC and HL 1878–9, xxxvii, p. 358; Michael Davitt, *The Prison Life of Michael Davitt as Related by Himself*, London: n.p., 1878, pp. 1–40.
[55] *Report of the Commissioners Appointed to Inquire into the Working of the Penal Servitude Acts*, pp. iii, vi.
[56] Ibid., p. xxxv.
[57] Sean McConville, *English Local Prisons 1860–1900: Next Only to Death*, London: Routledge, 1995, p. 325.
[58] *Report of the Commissioners Appointed to Inquire into the Working of the Penal Servitude Acts*, p. xxxv.
[59] In 1886 James Monro, assistant commissioner of the Metropolitan Police Force, confirmed that it was 'upon the above recommendation [that] the Convict Supervision Department was established' to support and oversee the work of police supervision. See James Monro, 'A Report of the History of the Department of the Metropolitan Police Known as the Convict Supervision Office: Detailing System, and Showing Results and Effects Generally on the Habitual Criminal Population', 1886, TNA, HO 144/184/A45507, pp. 6–8.

Under the leadership of Chief Inspector Neame, the CSO established its own registers and processes for making information available to the police. This was made possible through the wealth of information that the CSO received from prisons and the Metropolitan Police Force. From its inception the office received descriptions of all those convicted of crime in London from the various divisions of the Metropolitan Police Force. The governors of London's various jails also forwarded descriptions, including photographs, of all prisoners about to be released following periods of penal servitude and those who had been sentenced to police supervision. This information was then used to compile numerous registers. These included books, arranged alphabetically, containing the names of all prisoners released from penal servitude and those subject to police supervision, with brief descriptions; albums of photographs; a register of tattoos; volumes of criminals who were thought to be addicted to certain specific types of crime, such as stealing bicycles; and a register of distinctive marks.[60] Therefore, the office, as a Home Office inquiry noted, sought to contain 'the whole of the records of crime and habitual criminals' in London.[61] Members of the Metropolitan Police Force could access the information contained at the CSO by filing search forms. Such a form, containing a physical description, could be submitted to the office following the arrest of an alleged criminal who the police believed may have offended previously, precipitating a search by staff of the CSO, and members of the Metropolitan Police Force could also attend the office to personally carry out searches. In addition, information was routinely disseminated. Albums containing photographs of the most serious criminals, who, according to the Metropolitan Police Force, included violent burglars, were sent to all divisions thrice yearly, information was sent daily to all metropolitan police stations containing the details of those in custody, and the *Police Gazette*, issued biweekly, also furnished descriptions of 'habitual criminals' who were about to be discharged from custody and those who had failed to report themselves to the police on release.[62] In short, the CSO, like the registry, sought to aid the police in identifying members of the criminal class.

There is some evidence from police sources that the records held at the CSO aided identification, despite the fact that consulting them could be very time-consuming. In his memoirs, which were published in 1932, Wensley recounted a number of examples of the registers' usefulness. He reported that he regularly

---

[60] Ibid., pp. 9–10.
[61] Ibid.
[62] Ibid., p. 10.

utilized the registers when he was still a constable, with some success. Two examples are recounted in his memoirs in which information was found at the CSO that enabled him to prove that individuals were repeat offenders.[63] However, in both cases the searches were 'prolonged'.[64] Journalists Charles Clarkson, a former officer in the Metropolitan Police Force, and J. Hall Richardson argued that experiences like Wensley's were not uncommon. In their book *Police!*, published in 1889, they said one would regularly 'see detectives poring over the "black books" with a view to the identification of suspected persons'.[65] According to the authors, these volumes of photographs were a 'terror to the evil doers', presumably because they were such an aid to identification.[66] This evidence must be treated with caution. As Terence Stanford has said, when assessing the writing of former police officers 'care has to be taken as they frequently project a favourable view of their actions which might not necessarily be correct', in this case emphasizing, as Wensley does, their own efforts to identify repeat offenders.[67] Moreover, the assertion by Clarkson and Richardson that the office was widely used by members of the Metropolitan Police Force requires testing.

The little data that exists shows that these authors overstated the case, at least in the first decade of the office's operation. In the first case, the number of visits to the office by members of the Metropolitan Police Force was quite low. James Monro, assistant commissioner of the Metropolitan Police Force, wrote an internal evaluation of the office in 1886 in which he admitted that there had only been 250 visits in 1880, albeit rising to 525 in 1885.[68] Most importantly, the number of successful identifications as a result of these visits and search forms received was low. In 1890, the first year for which this data is available, a total of 176 identifications were made.[69] To put this into context, in the same year 1,797 successful identifications were made through the ongoing mechanism of viewing those remanded at Holloway prison. Any person committed for trial in London or remanded in custody by a police magistrate was sent to Holloway prison to be viewed by members of the Metropolitan Police Force and warders in order to identify repeat offenders. Yet of the 1,797 identifications at Holloway

---

[63] Wensley, *Forty Years of Scotland Yard*, pp. 15–6, 73.
[64] Ibid., p. 73.
[65] Charles Clarkson and J. Hall Richardson, *Police!*, New York and London: Garland Publishing, 1984 (first published 1889), pp. 359–60.
[66] Ibid., p. 360.
[67] Terence Stanford, *The Metropolitan Police 1850-1914: Targeting, Harassment and the Creation of a Criminal Class*, unpublished doctoral thesis, University of Huddersfield, 2007, p. 100.
[68] Monro, 'A Report of the History of the Department of the Metropolitan Police Known as the Convict Supervision Office', appendix.
[69] *Report of the Commissioner of Police of the Metropolis: For the Year 1890*, [C 6472] HC 1891, xlii, p. 6.

in 1890, only 244 were made by policemen, with the remainder being made by prison warders.[70] The reasons for the low proportion of identifications by police at Holloway prison will be discussed below. The available evidence regarding the effectiveness of the registers is incomplete. Nonetheless, what survives shows that the CSO, like the registry, was only of limited use and, throughout the 1880s, prison inspections remained the main means by which repeat offenders were identified.

However, a change to the way criminals were registered at the CSO in 1890 led to greater use of the office by members of the Metropolitan Police Force. Section 7 of the *Prevention of Crime Act 1871* gave broad and unprecedented powers to police and magistrates in order to check the activities of repeat offenders.[71] 'Habitual criminals' could be sentenced to no more than one year's imprisonment for a range of 'special offences', which included appearing to gain a livelihood through dishonest means, being about to commit a crime and being in numerous places (including in a building, yard, dwelling house, orchard or garden) without a plausible explanation.[72] Until 1890 the CSO had kept lists of all those 'coming within the provisions of the 7th section of the Prevention of Crimes Act'.[73] In 1890 1,226 people were registered under that section. The legislature had been clear that the 'special offences' in section 7 only applied to registered 'habitual criminals'. But in 1890 a decision was made by the Metropolitan Police Force to compile information regarding Londoners suspected of these offences 'to an extent not hitherto attempted'.[74] This was done in order to enable a more 'vigilant inquiry' into those whose criminal history was unknown, but who were likely – in the view of the police – to have been previously convicted.[75] According to the commissioner, until this point many 'habitual criminals', 'being apparently "first offenders"', had 'been unregistered'.[76] The change resulted in a 75 per cent increase in those registered under section 7 in one year alone, from 1,226 in 1890 to 2,144 in 1891.[77] In the following year, 1892, this figure jumped by a further 170 per cent to 5,799.[78] The Metropolitan

---

[70] *Report of a Committee Appointed by the Secretary of State to Inquire into the Best Means Available for Identifying Habitual Criminals*, pp. 9–10.
[71] *Prevention of Crime Act*, s. 7.
[72] Ibid.
[73] *Report of the Commissioner of Police of the Metropolis*, 1891, p. 6.
[74] *Prevention of Crime Act*, s. 7; *Report of the Commissioner of Police of the Metropolis*, 1891, p. 6.
[75] *Report of the Commissioner of Police of the Metropolis*, 1891, p. 6.
[76] *Report of the Commissioner of Police of the Metropolis: For the Year 1891*, [C 6732] HC 1892, xli, p. 5.
[77] Ibid.
[78] *Report of the Commissioner of Police of the Metropolis: For the Year 1892*, [C 7173] HC 1893-4, xlv, p. 5.

Police Force was attempting to better target those it believed were members of a criminal class.

This change preceded, yet may not have entirely caused, a significant increase in the usage of the registers kept at the CSO and substantial growth in the number of successful identifications. In 1890, before the change was affected, there were 1,573 'attendances' by members of the Metropolitan Police Force to use the registers.[79] Attendances increased significantly in 1891, doing so again in the following years.

The number of search forms received by the office also increased. While no figure is recorded for 1890, in 1891 the 'number of search forms received from the divisions' was 2,665. This figure rose significantly in each of the next three years.

Importantly, the number of successful identifications made as a result of attendances and the receipt of search forms also climbed. As noted above this figure was only 176 in 1890, yet it rose to almost 3,000 in 1894.[80]

Table 3.2 Attendances at the Convict Supervision Office, 1890–4

Year	1890	1891	1892	1893	1894
Attendances	1,573	2,617	4,000	4,853	4,669
Percentage increase on previous year	–	66.4	52.8	21.3	-3.8

Report of the Commissioner of Police of the Metropolis, 1892, p. 5; Report of the Commissioner of Police of the Metropolis, 1893–4, p. 5; Report of the Commissioner of Police of the Metropolis, 1894, p. 6; Report of the Commissioner of Police of the Metropolis: For the Year 1894, [C 7890] HC 1895, lv, pp. 5–6.

Table 3.3 Search forms filed at the Convict Supervision Office, 1891–4

Year	1891	1892	1893	1894
Search forms filed	2,665	5,582	13,140	14,422
Percentage increase on previous year	–	109.5	135.4	9.8

[79] Ibid.
[80] Report of the Commissioner of Police of the Metropolis, 1892, p. 5; Report of the Commissioner of Police of the Metropolis, 1893–4, p. 5; Report of the Commissioner of Police of the Metropolis, 1894, p. 6; Report of the Commissioner of Police of the Metropolis, 1895, pp. 5–6.

Table 3.4 Identifications made at the Convict Supervision Office, 1890–4

Year	1890	1891	1892	1893	1894
Successful identifications	176	563	1,265	2,124	2,901
Percentage increase on previous year	–	219.9	124.7	68	36.6

The commissioner said that these figures 'cannot but be considered satisfactory', despite involving 'a large expenditure of time and labour'.[81] They demonstrate that by the last decade of the century the registers at the CSO were used on a considerable scale and that many licence-holders and repeat offenders were identified as a result. The increase in the usage of the registers at the CSO was due, according to the leadership of the Metropolitan Police Force, to the change that had been made in 1890. In 1891 the commissioner noted that the inclusion of details regarding suspected repeat offenders was 'bearing fruit'.[82] He went further the following year, labelling the change 'one of the most important enactments of the Criminal Law'.[83] Petrow and Christopher Harding have also said – with some justification – that the change led to greater usage of the registers, as they became easier for the police to use.[84] The alteration to the way the registers were compiled in 1890, to include those suspected, but not proven, to be repeat offenders, was one reason for the increase in the number of police attendances and use of search forms. This was because policemen believed that information concerning the subject of their search was more likely to be found in the registers than had previously been the case.

But it is hard to believe that this one change led to such a significant increase in the usage of the resources compiled by the CSO. It is highly probable that greater interest in the problem of recidivism in the late 1880s and 1890s at least partly precipitated the increased usage of the registers at the CSO. The late Victorian period saw the rise of views that linked crime, and recidivism, to heredity. The so-called Italian school of positivist criminology, pioneered by psychiatrist Cesare Lombroso, denied the role of free choice in crime, which had hitherto been widely accepted, and instead popularized the idea of the born

---

[81] *Report of the Commissioner of Police of the Metropolis*, 1894, p. 6.
[82] *Report of the Commissioner of Police of the Metropolis*, 1892, p. 5.
[83] *Report of the Commissioner of Police of the Metropolis*, 1893–4, p. 5.
[84] Petrow, *Policing Morals*, p. 55; Harding, '"The Inevitable End of a Discredited System"?', p. 599.

criminal.⁸⁵ Lombroso's conception, articulated in his popular work of 1876, *Criminal Man*, was that as a result of bad heredity criminals were not 'normal', but a kind of 'savage', predisposed to lawbreaking.⁸⁶ Importantly, according to Lombroso, criminals were readily identifiable by their physical features, such as a large forehead.⁸⁷ These ideas influenced many British commentators. David Taylor has quoted numerous late nineteenth-century writers who believed, as the Reverend Osborne Jay of East London did, that there was a 'submerged and semi-criminal class', which displayed 'inherited defects'.⁸⁸ Taylor has therefore argued that late Victorian social commentators increasingly referred to and accepted Lombrosian ideas.⁸⁹ Indeed, Mary Gibson and Nicole Hahn Rafter have claimed that by the time of the first International Congress of Criminal Anthropology in 1885, Lombroso's work linking recidivism to heredity 'went practically uncontested' across Western Europe.⁹⁰ This was probably one reason why, as Charles Troup, an undersecretary at the Home Office, told an 1895 select committee that had been established to investigate how the prison system could better combat recidivism, the 'police have been paying more attention in tracing habitual criminals in the last few years'.⁹¹ Given the prevalence of the idea that criminals could be discerned by their physical features, it is likely that members of the Metropolitan Police Force, and other forces, consequently made greater use of registers of habitual criminals and volumes of photographs that provided information regarding criminals' appearance.

Further significant evidence regarding the efficacy of the system of registration in London, including both the registry and the CSO, is contained in a Home Office committee report from 1895, which considered the best means to identify repeat offenders. In 1887 the Home Office had been alerted

---

⁸⁵ Daniel Pick, *Faces of Degeneration: A European Disorder, c. 1848–c. 1918*, Cambridge: Cambridge University Press, 1989, p. 17. For information regarding crime as a free choice see J. J. Tobias, *Crime and Industrial Society in the Nineteenth Century*, London: B. T. Batsford, 1967, p. 59; Edward Cox, *The Principles of Punishment: As Applied in the Administration of the Criminal Law by Judges and Magistrates*, London: Law Times Office, 1877, p. 142; *Times*, 17 Dec. 1894, p. 9.
⁸⁶ Pick, *Faces of Degeneration*, p. 17.
⁸⁷ Cesare Lombroso, *Criminal Man*, Mary Gibson and Nicole Hahn Rafter (trans. and ed.), London: Duke University Press, 2006 (first published 1876), p. 51.
⁸⁸ David Taylor, 'Beyond the Bounds of Respectable Society: The "Dangerous Classes" in Victorian and Edwardian England', in Judith Rowbotham and Kim Stevenson (eds.), *Criminal Conversations: Victorian Crimes, Social Panic and Moral Outrage*, Columbus: Ohio State University Press, p. 47; Rev. Osborne Jay, 'The East End and Crime', *Public Opinion*, 26 Oct. 1894, p. 517. Also see the comments of Reverend G. Merrick, chaplain of London's Holloway and Newgate gaols in *Prisons Committee: Report from the Departmental Committee on Prisons*, [C 7702] HC 1895, lvi, p. 58.
⁸⁹ Taylor, 'Beyond the Bounds of Respectable Society', p. 16.
⁹⁰ Lombroso, *Criminal Man*, p. 29. Garland has also noted increased focus on the issue of recidivism in the early 1890s. See *Punishment and Welfare*, pp. 59–61.
⁹¹ *Prisons Committee*, p. 409.

to the so-called anthropological system of identification developed by the Parisian police officer Alphonse Bertillon, based on measuring and recording the lengths of numerous bones. Edmund Spearman, a former civil servant, advised officials that the system was simple, accurate and economical.[92] The case for the anthropological system was taken up by the British Association for the Advancement of Science and eventually, as Radzinowicz and Hood have noted, the government 'bow[ed] to pressure' and put in place an inquiry.[93] A committee of Troup, including the prisons inspector Arthur Griffiths and Melville Macnaghten, a chief constable in the Metropolitan Police Force, was appointed by the Liberal Home Secretary Herbert Asquith to inquire into the 'best means available for identifying habitual criminals'.[94]

Notwithstanding the changes of 1876 to the compilation of the two key volumes housed at the registry, the committee justifiably found that the registry was still very little used by members of the Metropolitan Police Force and other forces for that matter. The committee argued that this was primarily because of the inexact nature of the information contained therein, which made searches long and often fruitless. Firstly, the use of aliases was widespread. My analysis of the surviving registers shows that of those criminals whose names appeared in the pages of the register of habitual criminals, 83 per cent had previously used either an alias or an alternate spelling of their own name.[95] This necessitated detailed cross-referencing, often in various copies of the register, which was compiled annually. As the committee said, this meant that the amount of 'time and labour which the searches' involved was prohibitive, which was one of the reasons why the registry was 'so little used by the police'.[96]

The committee also said that members of the Metropolitan Police Force did not often refer to the register of distinctive marks, predominantly due to the imprecise information it contained. Du Cane argued strongly to the contrary believing that the police could often 'trace' the 'antecedents' of repeat offenders due to 'the fact that, in a vast proportion of cases, the habitual criminal carries

---

[92] 'Anthropometric System', TNA, HO 144/530-532/A46508, p. 1.
[93] Leon Radzinowicz and Roger Hood, *A History of the English Criminal Law and Its Administration from 1750*, vol. 5. *The Emergence of Penal Policy*, London: Stevens and Sons, 1990, p. 263.
[94] *Report of a Committee Appointed by the Secretary of State to Inquire into the Best Means Available for Identifying Habitual Criminals*, p. 4.
[95] 'Alphabetical Register of Habitual Criminals Who Have Been Liberated, Subject to the Penalties of the 8th Clause of "The Habitual Criminals Act, 1869;" or of the 7th or 8th Clauses of "The Prevention of Crimes Act, 1871"'.
[96] *Report of a Committee Appointed by the Secretary of State to Inquire into the Best Means Available for Identifying Habitual Criminals*, p. 18.

on his person marks which afford a certain clue to his identity'.[97] However, the committee heard opposing evidence, notably from Mr Grace, the Home Office clerk who compiled the registers under the direction of Du Cane. He conceded that many entries in the register were 'vague', resulting in very few successful identifications being made. Indeed, less than 10 per cent of applications based on an offender's scars led to an identification in the register of distinctive marks. Grace concluded that 'it would be better to define the marks very closely'.[98] As this was not done, the register was used only as a 'last resort'.[99] The committee accepted the clerk's evidence, noting that a large number of convicted criminals had similar tattoos and no other marks registered. By way of example, in the 1892 register twenty-eight entries listed a tattooed ring on the second finger of the left hand. In only three cases was a further distinctive mark listed, meaning that searches based on this information would be very unlikely to lead to a successful identification.[100] The committee agreed with Grace that 'this difficulty could to a large extent be overcome by more minute descriptions' yet found that the inclusion of further information would make the register 'almost unmanageable' based on its increased size and complexity.[101] There was thus an inherent difficulty in compiling data both detailed enough to identify criminals and concise enough to make the register usable.[102] As this difficulty had not been overcome, the register was little used, and even then with limited success.

A further issue that made successful searches of the registers unlikely was the fact that the information contained in them was not up to date. The registers covered each calendar year, but they were not made available until between July and December in the following year. For instance, the register of habitual criminals for 1890 was not printed until 7 October 1891 and the register of distinctive marks for the same year was not made available until 9 December 1891. Between 1869 and 1895 the details of repeat offenders were not available until at least eight, and at the most twenty-three, months after their release from prison, due to the huge task of compiling such large documents. It is possible that over such a lengthy period some criminals with one previous conviction would have committed further crimes. Due to the delay in printing

---

[97] Du Cane, *The Punishment and Prevention of Crime*, p. 195.
[98] *Report of a Committee Appointed by the Secretary of State to Inquire into the Best Means Available for Identifying Habitual Criminals*, p. 43.
[99] Ibid.
[100] Ibid., p. 8.
[101] Ibid.
[102] Ibid.

and circulating the registers these individuals would not be registered as habitual criminals for some time. Officers at the registry were aware that the late circulation of the registers was far from desirable. Grace admitted, 'A large number [of criminals] will be reconvicted before the register comes out', meaning time spent searching the registers for such individuals was bound to be wasted. Consequently, Grace was of a view that 'the registers should be published monthly'.[103] The committee agreed that the belated availability of the registers was a 'drawback'.[104]

The outcome of these various deficiencies, which persisted after the changes of 1876, was that the police rarely used the registry. The committee received a return from the registry itself showing that on average fewer than 220 enquiries were received each year from all police forces across England.[105] And Commissioner Henderson admitted that members of the Metropolitan Police Force did not find the registry of much value in 'its present form'.[106] Clarkson and Richardson also claim that the registry was rarely visited by policemen.[107] The registry was, as the committee noted, the 'only agency specially established by Parliament' for 'identifying old offenders'.[108] It is clear that the registry, and therefore the Gladstone government's habitual criminals' legislation that precipitated its establishment, largely failed to achieve this purpose.

Nevertheless, the CSO was also established as a result of the *Prevention of Crime Act 1871*. Despite the increase in the use of the office in the early 1890s, which has already been discussed, the committee argued with justification that the CSO was not as effective as pre-existing methods of identification in London. The long-standing practice of viewing prisoners while in jail was far more successful. Those remanded at Holloway prison were viewed by both policemen and warders to ascertain whether they were recidivists. Data regarding the number of prisoners identified as having been previously convicted is available for the period from 1883 to 1893 and was tabulated in the report of the Troup committee.

---

[103] Ibid., p. 43.
[104] Ibid., p. 8.
[105] Ibid., p. 44.
[106] Ibid., p. 68.
[107] Clarkson and Richardson, *Police!*, p. 8.
[108] *Report of a Committee Appointed by the Secretary of State to Inquire into the Best Means Available for Identifying Habitual Criminals*, p. 6.

Table 3.5 Prisoners identified in Holloway by Criminal Investigations Officers and Warders as having been previously convicted, 1883–93

Year	Identifications	By Warders	By Police
1883	1,826	1,427	399
1884	1,986	1,730	256
1885	2,081	1,834	247
1886	1,913	1,727	186
1887	1,594	1,367	227
1888	1,711	1,495	216
1889	1,462	1,188	274
1890	1,797	1,553	244
1891	1,671	1,485	185
1892	1,964	1,765	199
1893	1,949	1,759	190

Report of a Committee Appointed by the Secretary of State to Inquire into the Best Means Available for Identifying Habitual Criminals, p. 11.

The results of this method of identification far exceeded those accomplished as a result of the numerous registers, both at the registry and the CSO, for all years other than 1893.[109] Yet warders identified vastly more repeat offenders in prison than policemen. Warders identified 78 per cent of repeat offenders in 1883, rising to 90 per cent in 1890. The discrepancy is not entirely surprising given that warders had far greater opportunity than policemen to study the features of repeat offenders in person, and at close quarters, during their periods of incarceration. A comparison of these figures with those above regarding successful identifications made at the CSO shows that from 1891 onwards the registers actually facilitated more identifications by the police. Presumably the changes to the way the registers were compiled in 1890, along with the popularity of Lombrosian criminology, caused policemen to devote more energy to efforts to identify criminals at the CSO than at Holloway, as from that year identifications from the registers rose dramatically while those by the police at prison fell significantly. The available data concerning identifications by the police shows that, on the whole, they were able to use neither the system at Holloway nor the registers with much success. The task of recognizing repeat offenders was one London policemen clearly found inherently difficult, which is one reason for the

[109] Ibid., p. 10.

failure of the registers to fully achieve the aims of the government. The reasons why policemen failed to identify more repeat offenders will be discussed in the coming pages. Despite the limited success of the police in identifying repeat offenders at Holloway prison, the Troup committee was correct to conclude that the viewing of prisoners was still the 'most effective' method of identification in London.[110]

The committee further criticized registration in London by asserting that more repeat offenders escaped recognition in the capital than anywhere else in the UK. It is, of course, impossible to ascertain exactly how many of those registered as habitual criminals escaped recognition as such, but individual cases can be cited. The committee asked the prison department of the Home Office if any prisoners were recognized as repeat offenders only after being sentenced during the twelve months preceding 31 October 1893, and three examples in London were provided.[111] Charles Murdoch, head of the criminal department of the Home Office, provided three further examples of failures in London between 1888 and 1893 and presented some statistics, albeit that did not solely relate to London. He asked his clerks to examine seventy-two cases in which licence-holders were convicted in magistrates' courts in 1893. In only thirty-four cases, or 47 per cent, could it be proved that the individual was known to be a licence-holder before sentencing. In the remaining thirty-six cases Murdoch presumed that the licence-holder's identity was unknown, as in these cases the clerk of the court did not report the conviction of a licence-holder to the Home Office, which was a legal requirement.[112] While this data was not specific to London, it seems likely that comparatively more registered habitual criminals escaped recognition in the capital, for reasons that will be discussed below. Cecil Douglas, justices' clerk at the mansion house, and Grace both argued that more recidivists in London went unidentified. This was also the view of the commissioner of the Metropolitan Police Force and his senior officers, despite the fact, which was noted by the committee, that their 'bias would naturally be to minimise the proportion who escape'.[113] The committee was provided with some data to support this position.[114] The Home Office prepared a comparative table of persons tried on indictment, meaning at a higher court than the magistrates', in London and three other large population centres. During the first three months

---

[110] Ibid.
[111] Ibid., p. 17.
[112] Ibid., p. 64.
[113] Ibid., p. 16.
[114] Ibid., pp. 43–6.

of 1893 the courts in Lancashire recorded previous convictions against 70 per cent of defendants. In Liverpool the figure was 79 per cent, and in Norfolk and Suffolk it was 61 per cent. However, in London only 47 per cent of those tried at the higher court were recorded as having committed earlier offences.[115] As the committee noted, it seems unlikely that significantly fewer repeat offenders operated in London than elsewhere.[116] Rather, it appears that in London, more so than elsewhere, many of those registered as habitual criminals were able to keep the courts in ignorance of their criminal histories.[117]

The committee heard that there were several reasons for the ongoing failure of identification in London, some of which were specific to the capital and some were not. To start with, a successful identification was not a guarantee of a conviction recognizing past crimes. A long-standing concern of the police was the refusal of some prison warders to go to court in order to testify that an individual on trial had previously been a prisoner, meaning that some recidivists were sentenced as first offenders despite the fact that the police believed they had uncovered evidence of past crimes in the registers.[118] In 1863 George Everest, the principal clerk for criminal business at the Home Office, told a select committee that there was a 'great unwillingness' on the part of prison officers to give evidence regarding the identity of a prisoner, due to the 'low rate of remuneration to witnesses'.[119] As the Troup committee said, identification was 'always dependent on personal recognition by police or prison officers. This is the means by which identity is *proved* in criminal courts'.[120] While he did not provide any data, in 1889 the commissioner of the Metropolitan Police Force claimed that the number of identifications leading to convictions had declined over the previous six years in London due to the low 'number of warders attending'.[121] This was the case, he believed, because of the time involved, and travel and accommodation expenses for warders from beyond London.[122] It is possible that a less tangible impact was on the behaviour of police in utilizing

---

[115] Ibid., p. 72. The total number of persons convicted was as follows: London, 653; Lancashire, 343; Liverpool, 177; Norfolk and Suffolk, 36.
[116] Ibid., p. 18.
[117] Ibid.
[118] *Report from the Select Committee of the House of Lords, on the Present State of Discipline in Gaols and Houses of Correction; Together with the Proceedings of the Committee, Minutes of Evidence, Appendix and Index*, [C 499] HC 1863, ix, p. 221.
[119] *Report of the Commissioners Appointed to Inquire into the Operation of the Acts Relating to Transportation and Penal Servitude*, p. 136.
[120] *Report of a Committee Appointed by the Secretary of State to Inquire into the Best Means Available for Identifying Habitual Criminals*, p. 14.
[121] *Report of the Commissioner of Police of the Metropolis: For the Year 1888*, [C 1059] HC 1889, xl, p. 22.
[122] Ibid.

the registers. If a conviction was not assured as a result of a long and laborious search of the registers, even when successful, then some police would rationally have used them less than if this had not been the case.

The key reason why many London recidivists were not identified, according to the committee, was the size and nature of the city itself. Its report said that identifying repeat offenders was very difficult in large cities, and 'especially ... in London', which was, of course, the largest city in the UK, and one in which the committee believed criminals were prone to move between different police divisions for the purpose of evading recognition. The committee said that 'the problem of identification is far more difficult and complex' in London than elsewhere.[123] Some commentators disagreed with this assessment and argued that London's criminal class lived in clearly defined areas – often called rookeries – and were, as a result, easily monitored by the police.[124] However, as S. J. Stevenson has noted, many other mid- and late Victorian commentators claimed that 'habitual criminals' in London were highly mobile, thereby using the size of the city to escape the gaze of the police.[125] Some scholarship contradicts this discourse, providing compelling evidence that the poorest members of London's working class, from whom it was often argued that the criminal class emanated, were largely immobile.[126] This work has implications for our assessment of whether the committee, the Metropolitan Police Force and the Home Office were correct in asserting that the principal reason for the especial failure of the registers in London was the ability of repeat offenders to evade recognition by the police in such a large city. David Green and Alan Parton claim that, despite the increasing capacity of many members of society to travel (in particular by train), the inner-city poor lived their lives within a very small area. They write that the poor lived, worked and enjoyed leisure pursuits within 'tightly circumscribed spatial limits'.[127] And Lynn Lees has undertaken work tracking the movements of poor Irish families (believed by some commentators at the time to

---

[123] *Report of a Committee Appointed by the Secretary of State to Inquire into the Best Means Available for Identifying Habitual Criminals*, pp. 6, 9. Also see the evidence of Cecil Douglas, justices' clerk at the Mansion House, and Grace, pp. 43–6, to this effect.

[124] Cox, *The Principles of Punishment*, p. 131; Peter Quennell (ed.), *London's Underworld: Being Selections from 'Those That Will Not Work', the Fourth Volume of 'London Labour and the London Poor' by Henry Mayhew*, vol. 7, London: Hamlyn, 1969, pp. 58, 138, 207–8.

[125] S. J. Stevenson, 'The "Habitual Criminal" in Nineteenth-Century England: Some Observations on the Figures', *Urban History*, vol. 13 (May 1986), p. 42.

[126] Harriet Martineau, 'Life in the Criminal Class', *Edinburgh Review*, vol. 122, no. 250 (Oct. 1865), p. 337; Mary Carpenter, *Our Convicts*, vol. 1, London: Longman, Green, Longman, Roberts and Green, 1864, p. 11.

[127] D. Green and A. Parton, 'Slums and Slum Life in Victorian England: London and Birmingham at Mid-Century', in M. Gaskell (ed.), *Slums*, Leicester: Leicester University Press, 1990, p. 31.

constitute a large element of the criminal class) in London around mid-century in which she finds very little evidence of significant changes of location.[128] While several families moved between areas that were close to one another, notably Southwark and Bermondsey, their new abode was always no more than half a mile from their previous home.[129] This immobility, it is argued, was caused by various factors, including the need to live close to places of employment, and the grouping together of dwellings with affordable rents.[130] Finally, and most importantly, Stevenson has carried out an analysis of the location of registered habitual criminals in London between 1869 and 1871. He found that the positive correlation between the criminal's stated address on release from prison and that of their next of kin was .911, and that in London's East End there was a correlation of .898 between the address of the next of kin and the destination of letters sent by the prisoner while incarcerated.[131] This evidence suggests that much of the lives of those registered as habitual criminals in London were confined to a small area. As Stevenson has argued, it therefore appears the idea that 'habitual criminals' were mobile was a 'myth' and that few regularly moved about in order to conceal their identity from the police.[132]

Given the immobility of London's working class, another reason must be found for the particular failure of registration in the capital. As was the case from 1869–71, the attitudes and actions of London's police magistrates were major factors that contributed to the legislation's ineffectiveness. Many members of the police believed magistrates and judges refused to take a criminal's record into consideration in sentencing.[133] The actual extent to which the Gladstone government's habitual criminals' legislation led to longer sentences for repeat offenders will be discussed at length in a following chapter. Yet it can be demonstrated that many policemen, along with some prison officials, believed past convictions were not taken into account in sentencing. While Petrow has argued strongly that police and magistrates worked together to oppress those believed to be part of a criminal class, between 1869 and 1871 senior members

---

[128] Quennell (ed.), *London's Underworld*, p. 79.
[129] L. Lees, *Social Change and Social Stability among the London Irish, 1830–1870*, unpublished doctoral thesis, Harvard University, 1969, p. 36.
[130] Ibid.
[131] S. J. Stevenson, 'The "Criminal Class" in the Mid-Victorian City: A Study of Policy Conducted with Special Reference to Those Made Subject to the Provisions of 34 & 35 Vict., c.112 (1871) in Birmingham and East London in the Early Years of Registration and Supervision', unpublished doctoral thesis, the University of Oxford, 1983, pp. 315–17.
[132] Stevenson, 'The "Habitual Criminal" in Nineteenth-Century England', p. 42.
[133] For the ubiquitous nature of this view see *Judicial Statistics, England and Wales, 1893. Part 1 – Criminal Statistics*, [C 7725] HC 1895, cviii, p. 78.

of the Metropolitan Police Force justifiably believed that London's police magistrates were actively working against their efforts to enforce the Liberal's habitual criminals' legislation, and this continued to be the case.[134] Similar views were expressed later in the century. J. B. Manning, the governor of London's Pentonville prison, denounced the sentencing practices of many magistrates and judges in 1894.[135] When testifying before the Troup committee Manning said that magistrates and judges in London disregarded past convictions, 'to a very large extent'.[136] Indeed, the committee said that it had 'repeatedly' heard policemen complain that '[i]t is in vain for us to exert ourselves to discover the history of offenders, if no difference is to be made between a hardened criminal and a first offender' in sentencing.[137] The committee accepted this evidence and believed that the police relaxed their efforts to provide the court with accurate histories of a defendant's convictions as a result.[138] Given the fact that senior London police officers so frequently criticized the sentencing practices of magistrates and judges, it is not altogether surprising that the committee concluded that police were discouraged from pursuing time-consuming searches for records of prior convictions.

It remains to be demonstrated that London magistrates were particularly averse to punishing offenders based on evidence garnered from the various registers. As quoted above, Henry, London's chief magistrate, made his view clear to the Home Office that photographs and registers did not prove identity and could give rise to cases of mistaken identity.[139] It is possible that other magistrates and judges in London held this view and that this influenced the behaviour of the police. Stevenson has extracted data regarding prosecution rates of those registered as habitual criminals from a range of sources.

Based on the comparatively low rate of both arrests and prosecution in London, despite its relatively large police presence and the tendency of many members of the working class in major cities to live their lives within a small area, Stevenson is right to label London an 'exceptional case'.[140] The key reason for the low rate of prosecution in London, according to Stevenson, is that many magistrates refused to fully implement the Gladstone government's habitual

---

[134] Petrow, *Policing Morals*, p. 51.
[135] *Report of a Committee Appointed by the Secretary of State to Inquire into the Best Means Available for Identifying Habitual Criminals*, p. 42.
[136] Ibid., p. 44.
[137] Ibid., p. 15.
[138] Ibid., p. 16.
[139] Henry to Liddell, 13 Mar. 1869.
[140] Ibid., p. 47.

Table 3.6 The rate of prosecution of habitual criminals in various English cities, 1871–90

City	Population in thousands (1871)	Population per police constable (1871)	Average prosecutions of habitual criminals per 10,000 p.a. (1871–90)
London	3,254.3	339	2.01
Liverpool	489.5	582	8.54
Manchester	351.2	456	12.47
Birmingham	343.8	661	1.58
Leeds	259.2	762	2.78
Sheffield	239.9	750	0.51
Bristol	182.5	506	2.98
Bradford	145.8	729	3.05
Newcastle-on-Tyne	128.2	642	4.30
Hull	121.6	767	4.02

The sources used by Stevenson in extracting this data were the annual reports of H. M. inspector of constabulary, the commissioner of police of the metropolis, poor law commissioners and the local government board, and the annual volumes of judicial statistics. See Stevenson, 'The "Habitual Criminal" in Nineteenth-Century England', p. 52.

criminals' legislation.[141] Their antipathy towards the act was known to the police. They therefore arrested relatively few repeat offenders as they believed magistrates were unlikely to convict. This explanation, as we will see, is a plausible one.

Some evidence of magistrates' opposition to the *Prevention of Crime Act 1871*, although not restricted to London, can be found in Home Office papers. In 1886 a Home Office memorandum was penned by Lushington regarding 'irregular sentences under section[s] 5 and 7 of the *Prevention of Crime Act 1871*'.[142] The paper said that sentencing irregularities were 'frequent occurrence[s]'. A term of imprisonment of less than one year was often the punishment for a breach of the 'special offences' that were listed in section 7 and discussed earlier in this chapter.[143] Such a breach contravened the conditions outlined on tickets-of-leave. Under section 5 magistrates could revoke the licence, thereby returning the

[141] Ibid., pp. 46–8.
[142] Godfrey Lushington, Memorandum: 'Irregular Sentences under Section 5 and 7 of the *Prevention of Crime Act 1871*', 25 Oct. 1886, TNA HO 45/9658/A41414/1, p. 1.
[143] *Prevention of Crime Act*, s. 7.

defendant to prison for the remainder of their initial term of penal servitude.[144] But the Home Office asserted that it was 'the rule' that magistrates, eager to avoid such a harsh punishment for a minor offence, were 'not revoking the licence'. When challenged by Home Office officials about instances of this broader failure to properly enforce the legislation, magistrates had – in every case – requested that 'the prisoner should be discharged' rather than face a lengthy term of penal servitude. In the end, the Home Office had to send a circular to all magistrates urging them to fully enforce section 7 of the act.[145] Contrary to the view of Petrow, therefore, breaches of the Liberal government's habitual criminals' legislation by those registered as habitual criminals did not necessarily lead to lengthy periods in prison or even a further conviction.[146] London's police magistrates took their role as advisers to the poor very seriously and, as a consequence, often acted in the interests of their working-class clientele and against positions that appeared to be widely held within the middle class.[147] As Stevenson has said, 'the politics of the judiciary' should be taken into consideration as a 'factor operating to control' the number of registered habitual criminals who were 'punished'.[148]

*

In London the various registers of habitual criminals were of limited use in identifying criminals until the 1890s. In part this was because of technical limitations. Before more sophisticated means of identifying repeat offenders were developed late in the century, any registers were bound to be lengthy, inexact, cumbersome and time-consuming to utilize. Yet problems with the legislation itself also contributed significantly to the failure of the system of registration to live up to politicians' expectations. The legislation's definition of crime, which included all felonies and several misdemeanours, led to the registration of huge numbers of petty offenders. Searches of the registers were therefore time-consuming and rarely led to a successful identification. Even after this defect was remedied in 1876 and then the CSO was established in 1880, the numerous registers available to members of the Metropolitan Police Force remained large and contained information that was often unhelpfully broad.

---

[144] Lushington, Memorandum: 'Irregular Sentences under Section 5 and 7 of the *Prevention of Crime Act 1871*', p. 1.
[145] Circular, 10 Jan. 1887, TNA HO45/9658/A41414/2, p. 1.
[146] Petrow, *Policing Morals*, p. 51.
[147] This was discussed at length in the previous chapter. Also see Ellis and Ellis, solicitors, to Edmund Henderson, 11 Nov. 1869, TNA, MEPO 3/88; Adolphus Liddell to Edmund Henderson, 14 Jan. 1870, TNA, MEPO 3/88; Draft circular, 6 May 1870, TNA, HO 12/184/85459A/40; Superintendent of F division to Edmund Henderson, 18 May 1870, TNA, MEPO 3/88.
[148] Stevenson, 'The "Habitual Criminal" in Nineteenth-Century England', p. 46.

It was predominantly for these reasons that the Troup committee found the registers were so little used.

Registration had the potential to brand individuals as criminal in the eyes of the police, magistrates and judges. This is a point that numerous historians have made.[149] However, the impact of registration upon those believed to be part of a criminal class was much more limited in London than the Gladstone government had hoped. The dominant position in the relevant literature is that, despite their deficiencies, the various registers of habitual criminals were oppressive instruments of control that enabled the monitoring and even creation of a criminal class. Politicians, the police, and magistrates and judges were, it is argued, participants in this project.[150] In this chapter it has been shown that, at least in London, this thesis is plainly incorrect. Nonetheless, the Gladstone government's habitual criminals' legislation introduced other measures designed to control elements of the working class, such as the supervision of some registered habitual criminals. Whether police surveillance in London met with more success will be the subject of the next chapter.

---

[149] Petrow, *Policing Morals*, p. 51; Martin Wiener, *Reconstructing the Criminal: Culture, Law and Policy in England, 1830–1914*, Cambridge: Cambridge University Press, 1990, p. 149; Godfrey, Cox and Farrall, *Serious Offenders*, p. 205.

[150] Godfrey, Cox and Farrall, *Serious Offenders*, p. xii; Emsley, *Crime and Society in England*, pp. 172–4; Johnston, *Crime in England*, p. 36; Petrow, *Policing Morals*, p. 51.

4

Police Supervision of the Criminal Class: A Spy System

> His [Robert Audley's] generous nature revolted from the office into which he had found himself drawn – the office of spy, the collector of damning facts that led to horrible deductions.[1]
>
> (Lady Audley's Secret, 1862)

A further objective of the Gladstone government's habitual criminals' legislation was the establishment of a thorough system of police supervision. The *Prevention of Crime Act 1871* allowed magistrates and judges throughout the UK to impose a period of police supervision in the community of up to seven years upon anyone convicted of crime, who had previously been found guilty of an indictable offence.[2] Supervision, which was also extended to all those whose sentences of penal servitude had been remitted and were at large in Britain subject to the conditions of a licence, which was commonly called a ticket-of-leave, entailed monthly reporting to a local police station – by male criminals – and surveillance by the police. Women were excused from reporting as the government presumably believed they did not pose as great a risk to society as male offenders.[3] Under the 1869 act licence-holders and those sentenced to supervision were not required to report themselves each month and the courts were obliged to sentence all those guilty of multiple crimes, as defined by the

---

[1] Mary Elizabeth Braddon, *Lady Audley's Secret*, London: Penguin Books, 2013 (first published 1862), p. 197.
[2] The act defined crime as all felonies and the misdemeanours of obtaining money by false pretences, conspiracy to defraud and being at large at night with the intent of committing a crime with either housebreaking instruments or a disguised face. See *Prevention of Crime Act*, 34 & 35 Vict., c. 112, 1871, s. 6, 8, 20.
[3] For the greater threat that male criminals were believed to represent, see Martin Wiener, *Men of Blood: Violence, Manliness and Criminal Justice in Victorian England*, Cambridge: Cambridge University Press, 2004, pp. 123–69.

legislation, to supervision. However, under the 1871 act magistrates and judges were given the discretion not to impose supervision upon repeat offenders. This greater discretion was intended to ensure that petty offenders were no longer sentenced to supervision, thereby reducing the number of people subject to police supervision and making the task of monitoring criminals who posed a significant danger to society more manageable for the police.[4] Meanwhile, monthly reporting was introduced in response to criticisms that the police had little knowledge, such as a residential address, of those they sought to supervise. The government and the opposition hoped that the new legislation would lead to a closer monitoring of repeat offenders than had occurred between 1869 and 1871.[5] The Conservative position, articulated by the Earl of Carnarvon, was that supervision would be transformed from a 'sham into a reality' as, the party believed, those subject to it would now be closely watched and, therefore, deterred from committing further crimes.[6] The extent to which police supervision achieved this objective in London will be assessed in this chapter. The chapter will begin with an explanation of how police supervision operated in London, and will then analyse the effectiveness of supervision until 1880. A new Convict Supervision Office (CSO) was created in 1880 to coordinate police supervision in London.[7] The system of police supervision was also altered through new legislation that came into force in September 1879. Consequently, the second section will analyse the effectiveness of supervision in London from 1880 to 1895.

Police supervision of licence-holders and repeat offenders, so numerous historians have claimed, was carried out in a heavy-handed manner, which forced those under surveillance to turn, once more, to crime.[8] For example, Helen Johnston – whose research is primarily provincially focused – has said that police supervision led to employers, landlords and associates becoming

---

[4] The Earl of Morley (Liberal), 207 *Parl. Deb.*, HL (3rd ser.), cols. 1082–6 (4 Jul. 1871).
[5] Ibid., cols. 1084–5.
[6] Ibid., col. 1087.
[7] *Report of a Committee Appointed by the Secretary of State to Inquire into the Best Means Available for Identifying Habitual Criminals; with Minutes of Evidence and Appendices*, [C 7263] HC and HL 1894, lxxii, pp. 1–16.
[8] Barbara Weinberger, 'The Criminal Class and the Ecology of Crime', *Historical Social Research*, vol. 15, no. 4 (1990), p. 129; Clive Emsley, *Crime and Society in England, 1750–1900*, 2nd ed., London: Longman, 1996, p. 174; Martin Wiener, *Reconstructing the Criminal: Culture, Law and Policy in England, 1830–1914*, Cambridge: Cambridge University Press, 1990, p. 149; Barry Godfrey, David Cox and Stephen Farrall, *Serious Offenders: An Historical Study of Habitual Criminals*, London: Oxford University Press, 2010, p. 205; Stefan Petrow, *Policing Morals: The Metropolitan Police and the Home Office 1870–1914*, Oxford: Clarendon Press, 1995, p. 51; Jennifer Davis, 'From "Rookeries" to "Communities": Race, Poverty and Policing in London, 1850–1985', *History Workshop*, no. 27 (Spring 1989), pp. 68, 71.

aware of an individual's criminal history. Johnston argues that this served to 'reproduce' criminality, as opportunities for honest employment, in particular, were denied.[9] There is a consensus among the historians who have assessed the system of police supervision that it was highly flawed in its early years, with many under supervision able to escape the gaze of the police altogether.[10] Nonetheless, most historians who have analysed the operation of police supervision believe that, as refinements were made over time, the police were increasingly able to monitor so-called habitual criminals in a manner that endangered employment and, consequently, left them with little option but to commit further crimes.[11] As Barry Godfrey, David Cox and Stephen Farrall have said, based on their research focused in the north of England, police 'attention must have fallen heavily on ... those who were thought dangerous enough to be sentenced to police supervision'.[12] The consequence of this attention, according to Stefan Petrow, was that the police were able to 'manufacture a criminal class'.[13] However, as Mary Elizabeth Braddon implied in *Lady Audley's Secret*, her best-selling novel of 1862, spies and spying were widely regarded with hostility in mid- and late Victorian Britain.[14] We will see that, influenced by this public sentiment, London's police, and the courts, did not support and implement a system of supervision in such a way as to aid the creation of a criminal class.

*

The Liberal government and the Conservative opposition anticipated that the supervision of licence-holders and repeat offenders would entail the close monitoring of this cohort of offenders. Such supervision, it was hoped, would deter 'habitual criminals' from committing further crime due to the increased likelihood of detection.[15] This was not achieved in London between 1869 and 1871 due, primarily, to the huge numbers subject to supervision and the absence

---

[9] Helen Johnston, *Crime in England 1815–1880: Experiencing the Criminal Justice System*, Abingdon: Routledge, 2015, p. 36.
[10] Godfrey, Cox and Farrall, *Serious Offenders*, p. 67; Leon Radzinowicz and Roger Hood, 'Incapacitating the Habitual Criminal: The English Experience', *Michigan Law Review*, vol. 78, no. 8 (Aug. 1980), p. 1345; Petrow, *Policing Morals*, p. 82; S. J. Stevenson, 'The "Habitual Criminal" in Nineteenth-Century England: Some Observations on the Figures', *Urban History*, vol. 13 (May 1986), pp. 47–8.
[11] Weinberger, 'The Criminal Class and the Ecology of Crime', p. 129; Emsley, *Crime and Society in England*, p. 174; Wiener, *Reconstructing the Criminal*, p. 149; Godfrey, Cox and Farrall, *Serious Offenders*, p. 205; Petrow, *Policing Morals*, p. 151; Davis, 'From "Rookeries" to "Communities"', pp. 68, 71.
[12] Godfrey, Cox and Farrall, *Serious Offenders*, p. 186.
[13] Petrow, *Policing Morals*, p. 82.
[14] Braddon, *Lady Audley's Secret*, p. 197.
[15] Douglas Straight (Conservative), 208 *Parl. Deb.*, HC (3rd ser.), cols. 1756–9 (16 Aug. 1871).

of any mechanism to compel those under supervision to report themselves to the police.[16] New legislation was introduced in 1871 with the intention of remedying these shortcomings.[17] This section will analyse the extent to which supervision was effective up to 1880, at which time the CSO was established.

There were two elements to the system of supervision: monthly reporting by the licence-holder or repeat offender and regular surveillance of that person by the police. Monthly reporting was seen as vital to the system of police supervision in London. Twice a week a detective from the criminal investigation department of every Metropolitan Police Force division, along with one inspector, would attend Millbank and Brixton prisons: the institutions from which, respectively, male and female licence-holders were released. These policemen met with all those about to be released from prison subject to the conditions of a ticket-of-leave and gave male prisoners a form that specified their obligation to report themselves monthly to their nearest police station, and also to report any change of address. The penalty for non-compliance, they were informed, was up to one year's imprisonment with hard labour.[18] Men released into police supervision and not in receipt of a ticket-of-leave were given the same form, but by prison officials and not the police. All licence-holders and repeat offenders under supervision, both male and female, were then required to report themselves to their nearest police station within forty-eight hours of release, at which time the requirement to report monthly was stressed once again to the men.[19] Men subject to police supervision were therefore clearly informed of the primary importance of monthly reporting.

Secondly, the police were to monitor licence-holders and repeat offenders sentenced to police supervision in the community. To aid them in this endeavour, policemen were given written information about those under supervision and how surveillance was to be carried out. Brief information regarding every person sentenced to supervision within the Metropolitan Police District, including their age, address and any distinctive marks, was communicated weekly to all police stations in the district in order to aid police in monitoring them.[20] The commissioner informed all policemen that, while carrying out this task, every

---

[16] The Earl of Morley (Liberal), 207 *Parl. Deb.*, HL (3rd ser.), cols. 1082–6 (4 Jul. 1871).
[17] *Prevention of Crime Act*, 1871, s. 6, 8, 20.
[18] For a copy of this form see the *Report of the Commissioners Appointed to Inquire into the Working of the Penal Servitude Acts. Vol. I – Commissions and Report*, [C 2368] HC and HL 1878–9, xxxvii, p. 394.
[19] William Harris, chief inspector, executive division, Metropolitan Police Department, *Report of the Commissioners Appointed to Inquire into the Working of the Penal Servitude Acts*, pp. 394–5.
[20] Ibid., p. 395.

effort must be made to guard against the repeat offender's criminal history being made known, 'improperly or injuriously', to his or her employer or other acquaintances. To this end the police were told to only carry out surveillance while out of uniform.[21] It is not surprising that policemen were so instructed. Evidence suggests that many members of the working class strongly opposed the growing power of police forces in the nineteenth century, and their focus on policing spaces such as streets and music halls in poor communities.[22] In particular, the notion that the police would surreptitiously monitor working-class activity met with fierce animosity from the working class, and many within the middle and upper classes also. Long-standing respect for the liberty of the subject meant that spying by the police, or other representatives of the state, was strongly opposed in nineteenth-century Britain.[23] The leadership of the Metropolitan Police Force was cognizant of this widespread sentiment. This meant that it often opposed, or sought to lessen the severity of, measures that were unpopular with working-class communities.[24] The Metropolitan Police Force was, from its inception, a tool of the middle and upper classes that clearly served their interests through a focus, in particular, on theft and other property crime.[25] Nevertheless, the force was not a completely willing element in a broader apparatus of social control, as some historians suggest.[26] And as we will see, instructions to take great care when monitoring licence-holders and repeat offenders, which were often issued to policemen in London and were in keeping with other communications from the leadership of the Metropolitan Police Force, did not bode well for the close surveillance of members of the so-called criminal class.

---

[21] Metropolitan Police Order, 23 Jan. 1872, TNA, MEPO 7/34.
[22] Robert D. Storch, 'The Plague of Blue Locusts', *International Review of Social History*, vol. 20, no. 1 (Apr. 1975), pp. 67, 77; A. P. Donajgrodzki, "Social Police' and the Bureaucratic Elite: A Vision of Order in the Age of Reform', in A. P. Donajgrodzki (ed.), *Social Control in Nineteenth Century Britain*, London: Croom Helm, 1977, pp. 54–5; Robert D. Storch, 'The Policeman as Domestic Missionary: Urban Discipline and Popular Culture in Northern England, 1850–1880', *Journal of Social History*, vol. 9, no. 4 (1976), pp. 481–2.
[23] Bernard Porter, *The Origins of the Vigilant State; the London Metropolitan Police Special Branch before the First World War*, London: Weidenfeld and Nicolson, 1987, pp. 1, 4; *Times*, 16 Apr. 1870, p. 9.
[24] Stephen Inwood, 'Policing London's Morals: The Metropolitan Police and Popular Culture, 1829–1850', *London Journal*, vol. 15, no. 2 (1990), p. 134; A. L. Beier, 'Identity, Language, and Resistance in the Making of the Victorian "Criminal Class": Mayhew's Convict Revisited', *Journal of British Studies*, vol. 44, no. 3 (Jul. 2005), p. 515; Howard Taylor, 'Rationing Crime: The Political Economy of Criminal Statistics since the 1850s', *Economic History Review*, vol. 51, no. 3 (Aug. 1998), pp. 578–90.
[25] Storch, 'The Plague of Blue Locusts', pp. 67, 77; Donajgrodzki, '"Social Police" and the Bureaucratic Elite', pp. 54–5; Storch, 'The Policeman as Domestic Missionary', pp. 481–2; David Ascoli, *The Queen's Peace: The Origins and Development of the Metropolitan Police, 1829–1979*, London: Hamish Hamilton, 1979, pp. 1–8.
[26] Storch, 'The Plague of Blue Locusts', pp. 67, 77; Donajgrodzki, '"Social Police" and the Bureaucratic Elite', pp. 54–5; Storch, 'The Policeman as Domestic Missionary', pp. 481–2.

Yet some sources commended the system of police supervision that had been augmented by the *Prevention of Crime Act 1871*. In their contributions to the annual reports of the commissioner of the Metropolitan Police Force two superintendents argued that supervision would be strengthened by the legislation. In 1871 the superintendent of Clapham division wrote that the 'criminal classes' would now be able to be 'kept under a more effectual supervision'. The superintendent of Wandsworth division echoed this sentiment.[27] For reasons that will become apparent, no other senior members of the Metropolitan Police Force praised police supervision in the 1870s. Indeed, there is much evidence to suggest that supervision was most ineffective in London between 1871 and 1880, due primarily, as with registration, to the actions of the police magistrates. Section 20 of the *Prevention of Crime Act 1871* stated that all those reporting monthly to the police must do so to the chief officer of police or an individual nominated by him.[28] By May 1872 London's chief magistrate, Sir Thomas Henry, had informed the Metropolitan Police Force that the capital's police magistrates interpreted this section as meaning that reports had to be made to the commissioner himself, or to someone specifically chosen by him. So, London's magistrates would refuse to convict for failure to report unless the commissioner personally took the stand to provide sworn information as to the infringement.[29] This, as Henry was presumably well aware, was impossible. However, this situation persisted throughout the 1870s. In 1879 Chief Inspector William Harris noted that as a result of the way in which London's police magistrates interpreted section 20 of the *Prevention of Crime Act 1871*, the Metropolitan Police Force had 'not proceeded against anyone' for failure to report 'since 1871'.[30] The reporting requirement, which, as discussed, was central to the system of police supervision, was not interpreted so strictly anywhere else in the UK. In all other areas courts accepted the officer on duty as the nominee of the chief officer, and were happy to receive his evidence of a failure to report.[31] Given the negative attitude of London's police magistrates to the Gladstone government's habitual criminals' legislation, it is not surprising that, as with registration, they acted to undermine supervision. In their view

---

[27] *Report of the Commissioner of Police of the Metropolis*, [C 652] HC 1872, xxx, pp. 68–9.
[28] *Prevention of Crime Act*, 1871, s. 20.
[29] Douglas Labalmondiere, assistant commissioner of the Metropolitan Police Force, to the Home Office, 6 May 1872, TNA, HO 45/9320/16629A.
[30] *Report of the Commissioners Appointed to Inquire into the Working of the Penal Servitude Acts*, p. 395.
[31] Stevenson, 'The "Habitual Criminal" in Nineteenth-Century England', pp. 47–8; Thomas Barwick Lloyd Baker, *War with Crime: Being a Selection of Reprinted Papers on Crime, Reformatories, Etc.*, London: Longmans, 1889, p. 116.

it inappropriately targeted their working-class clientele, with whom they were eager to maintain good relations.³²

The manner in which London's police magistrates interpreted section 20 of the *Prevention of Crime Act 1871* meant that those subject to police supervision could easily avoid being watched by the police. Without any way to compel licence-holders and those sentenced to supervision to report themselves, many were lost track of in London. This point was made in evidence to a parliamentary committee, the genesis of which was discussed in the previous chapter, in 1879 by Edmund Henderson, commissioner of the Metropolitan Police Force, William Hardman, the chairman of the Surrey quarter sessions, and Chief Inspector Harris.³³ Hardman said that supervision was 'entirely futile' in London because 'it is so easily avoided', and the commissioner produced evidence showing many did avoid surveillance.³⁴ Of the 4,316 prisoners who had been released into the Metropolitan Police District between 1875 and 1879 with an obligation to report themselves, 987 had failed to do so, or 23 per cent.³⁵ Henderson plausibly asserted that those who evaded the police were probably those most in need of supervision, as those who were committing further crimes were more likely to seek to avoid being monitored by the police than those living honestly.³⁶ This was certainly sometimes the case. In his memoirs Arthur Harding, a leading figure within an East End gang in the late nineteenth century, said that the Eastern European burglar Steinie Morrison had been wanted by the police for failure to report, before ultimately being convicted of murder.³⁷ As the majority of male licence-holders and those sentenced to supervision in London reported themselves regularly, the measure was not futile as Hardman claimed. Surveillance was, however, very easy to evade.

The surveillance of those subject to police supervision in London was made more difficult as their residential addresses were often unknown. Many of those

---

³² For the hostility of police magistrates to the legislation, see Thomas Henry, chief magistrate of London, to Adolphus Liddell, permanent undersecretary at the Home Office, 13 Mar. 1869, TNA, HO 12/184. For the importance that police magistrates placed on maintaining good relations with the working class, see Jennifer Davis, 'A Poor Man's System of Justice: The London Police Courts in the Second Half of the Nineteenth Century', *Historical Journal*, vol. 27, no. 2 (Jun. 1984), pp. 262–3; H. T. Waddy, *The Police Court and Its Work*, London: Butterworth and Co., 1925, p. 1; Lydia Murdoch, *Imagined Orphans: Poor Families, Child Welfare, and Contested Citizenship in London*, New Jersey and London: Rutgers University Press, 2006, pp. 105–6; Alfred Plowden, *Grain or Chaff?: The Autobiography of a Police Magistrate*, London: T.F. Unwin, 1903, p. 266.
³³ *Report of the Commissioners Appointed to Inquire into the Working of the Penal Servitude Acts*, pp. 360, 395–6, 1012–3.
³⁴ Ibid., p. 1012.
³⁵ Ibid., p. 360.
³⁶ Ibid.
³⁷ Raphael Samuel, *East End Underworld: The Life of Arthur Harding*, London: Routledge and Kegan Paul, 1981, pp. 143–4.

about to be released from a period of incarceration under police supervision refused to disclose their intended place of residence. The *Prevention of Crime Act 1871* stated that those subject to supervision must inform the police of any change of address, but not their initial address on leaving prison.[38] In October 1872 Colonel Cobbe, the inspector of constabulary for the Midlands, who was responsible for reporting to parliament on the efficiency of police forces in that part of England, informed the Home Office of this problem. He attached a copy of the most recent *Police Gazette*, which included details regarding fourteen prisoners in England and Wales who were about to be released into police supervision. For their 'intended residence after liberation' five prisoners had provided a specific street address, seven had only stated the town in which they would live and two gave no information.[39] This meant, according to Cobbe, that: 'the worst and most dangerous class' of criminals 'have all opening to evade the law by giving no destination'.[40] It is likely that this was not problematic for local police forces in many villages and smaller towns, as their size would have made locating those under supervision relatively straightforward. Yet in the UK's most populous city the failure of many of those subject to supervision to state an address meant they could effectively disappear, compounding the problems that beset monthly reporting in London. In 1872 the Home Office also received correspondence from Commissioner Henderson, which informed it that the inability to oblige those sentenced to supervision to provide a residential address was a particular problem in London. He stated that, when coupled with the incapacity to enforce monthly reporting in London, police supervision was 'a dead letter' as the criminals believed by the police to be most at risk of reoffending could evade surveillance.[41] In short, before 1880 the ease with which supervision could be avoided meant the provision was particularly ineffective in London.

To make matters worse, many of London's repeat offenders were not being sentenced to police supervision. Data contained in the annual reports of the commissioner of the Metropolitan Police Force show that in each of the years 1872 and 1873, which are the last years in which these data are available, fewer than 350 people were sentenced to police supervision in the Metropolitan Police District.

---

[38] *Prevention of Crime Act*, 1871, s. 8.
[39] *Police Gazette*, 4 Oct. 1872, p. 4.
[40] Colonel Cobbe, inspector of constabulary, to the Home Office, 16 Oct. 1872, TNA, HO 45/9320/16629D.
[41] Edmund Henderson, commissioner of the Metropolitan Police Force, to the Home Office, 12 Nov. 1872, TNA, HO 45/9320/16629D.

Table 4.1 People convicted within the Metropolitan Police District and sentenced to a period of police supervision, 1870–3

1870	1871	1872	1873
764	755	306	337

Report of the Commissioner of Police of the Metropolis, [C 358] HC 1871, xxxvi, p. 26; *Report of the Commissioner of Police of the Metropolis*, [C 652] HC 1872, xxx, p. 18; *Report of the Commissioner of Police of the Metropolis: For the Year 1872*, [C 839] HC 1874, xxxi, p. 21; *Report of the Commissioner of Police of the Metropolis: For the Year 1873*, [C 1059] HC 1874, xxxvii, p. 26.

These figures, which decreased statistically significantly by 56 per cent from 1870 to 1873, show that London's magistrates and judges utilized the discretion afforded them by the *Prevention of Crime Act 1871* to submit fewer repeat offenders to supervision. While under the *Habitual Criminals Act 1869* all 'habitual criminals' were to be sentenced to supervision, the *Prevention of Crime Act 1871* gave magistrates and judges discretion to impose supervision or not.[42] Given the attitude of London's magistrates towards this legislation it is hardly surprising that in 1872 and 1873 they, along with London's judges – whose, often similar, views will be addressed in the next chapter – used their discretion to limit the impact of supervision.[43] While this data only covers the period from 1870 to 1873, it shows that police supervision, which, in any case, was easily avoided in London, was imposed upon fewer than half the number of repeat-offenders in both of these years than it had been before the legislative change of 1871.

Action was eventually taken in an effort to enable police supervision to be more effectively administered in London. In 1879 a parliamentary committee accepted evidence that it was 'practically impossible in the metropolis' to 'enforce the law which requires convicts on licence and other persons under supervision to report themselves'. Consequently, the committee recommended an immediate amendment to the *Prevention of Crime Act 1871*.[44] This recommendation was accepted and the Conservative home secretary, Richard Assheton Cross, hurriedly prepared a short bill designed to make monthly reporting enforceable in London and to compel licence-holders and those sentenced to police supervision to provide the address of their place of residence or face up to one

---

[42] *Prevention of Crime Act*, 1871, s. 8.
[43] Thomas Henry, chief magistrate of London, to Adolphus Liddell, 13 Mar. 1869, TNA, HO 12/184; Murdoch, *Imagined Orphans*, pp. 105–6; Waddy, *The Police Court and Its Work*, p. 1; Plowden, *Grain or Chaff?* p. 266; Davis, 'A Poor Man's System of Justice', pp. 262–3.
[44] *Report of the Commissioners Appointed to Inquire into the Working of the Penal Servitude Acts*, p. lxiv.

year's imprisonment. Concerning monthly reporting the legislation stated that: 'The power of a chief officer of a police district to direct that the reports required' by the *Prevention of Crime Act 1871* 'shall be made by some other person and shall extend to authorise him to direct such reports to the constable or person in charge of any particular police station or office without naming the individual person'.[45] So the government acted in response to the London police magistrates' unique interpretation of the reporting provisions of the *Prevention of Crime Act 1871*, that only the chief officer of police could provide evidence of a failure to report. The bill was presented to parliament, debated and passed – with bipartisan support – in August 1879, receiving royal assent on the 15th. It came into force on 1 September 1879 and gave parliamentary sanction to the notion that, to a large extent, supervision in London had hitherto been a failure.[46]

Although police supervision was especially ineffective in London in the 1870s, members of the Metropolitan Police Force were persistently accused of abusing their new powers. According to numerous historians, these accusations demonstrate that the police vigorously and inappropriately enforced supervision in a manner that created a 'criminal class'.[47] But, as we will see, claims of undue interference in London were largely unfounded. It was alleged that policemen hounded those under supervision by overtly monitoring them while at or nearby their place of work, or – more damaging still – by directly informing their employers of their criminal pasts, resulting in the loss of their jobs. The police supposedly acted in this way in order to achieve a reputation for being thorough in the performance of their duties and to gain promotion.[48] William Ranken and Lawrence Cave both put this argument to the penal servitude acts commission in 1879. These men were the honorary secretaries of London's Royal Society for the Assistance of Discharged Prisoners, which was a charitable society seeking to aid the reintegration of prisoners into society and, in particular, employment.[49] The former said that numerous cases of men losing their employment as a result of the actions of police had come to his notice and called for the introduction

---

[45] *Prevention of Crime Act*, 42 & 43 Vict., 1879, c. 55, s. 2.
[46] 249 *Parl. Deb.*, HL (3rd ser.), col. 1029 (15 Aug. 1879).
[47] Emsley, *Crime and Society in England*, p. 174; Wiener, *Reconstructing the Criminal*, p. 149; Petrow, *Policing Morals*, p. 51.
[48] *Report of the Commissioners Appointed to Inquire into the Working of the Penal Servitude Acts*, p. xxxvii; Anonymous, *Five Years' Penal Servitude by One Who Has Endured It*, London: Richard Bentley and Son, 1877, p. 269; Anonymous, *Convict Life, or, Revelations Concerning Convicts and Convict Prisons, by a Ticket-of-Leave Man*, London: Wyman, 1879, pp. 214–5.
[49] Sean McConville, *English Local Prisons 1860–1900: Next Only to Death*, London: Routledge, 1995, p. 325.

of a system similar to Dublin's, where supervision was carried out by civilians.⁵⁰ Supervision, according to Ranken, was a 'constant source of difference' between the society and the Metropolitan Police Force, due to the high volume of complaints.⁵¹ Cave also said that he was aware of some cases of improper interference.⁵² The Metropolitan Police Force admitted that accusations of this kind were consistently levelled against its members. For instance, in a review of the CSO that was conducted in 1886 Assistant Commissioner James Monro said that prior to the establishment of that office in 1880 many repeat offenders had, when brought before the courts, claimed that police interference had prevented them from securing employment. The Metropolitan Police Force had been continually frustrated by the 'numerous complaints' from those under supervision that they had been 'prevented from earning an honest living'. 'There was scarcely an assize, sessions or police court', Monro complained, 'at which these pleas were not put forward.'⁵³

Several of these pleas survive. The Irish republican Michael Davitt said that the harassment of those under supervision was a widespread problem and that policemen acted in this way 'in order to get promotion and a character for vigilance'.⁵⁴ Davitt, who had been arrested in London and convicted of conspiring against the crown, presumably came to this conclusion following discussions with other prisoners, given that his numerous lectures and publications on prison reform included much evidence from prisoners themselves.⁵⁵ Davitt's account, and those mentioned above, was in keeping with views published anonymously in 1877 and 1880 by men claiming to have been imprisoned. In 1877 the author of *Five Years' Penal Servitude by One Who Has Endured It* claimed, based on conversations with prisoners who had been subject to supervision, that the police intentionally pointed out those under supervision to their employers, causing their dismissal.⁵⁶ The author of this work was the London stockbroker Edward Callow, who had been sentenced to five years' penal servitude in 1868

---

⁵⁰ This system was discussed in Chapter 1. Also see Patrick Carroll-Burke, *Colonial Discipline: The Making of the Irish Convict System*, Dublin: Four Courts Press, 2000, pp. 102–3.
⁵¹ *Report of the Commissioners Appointed to Inquire into the Working of the Penal Servitude Acts*, pp. 1083–4.
⁵² Ibid., p. 1119.
⁵³ James Monro, 'A Report of the History of the Department of the Metropolitan Police known as the Convict Supervision Office: Detailing System, and Showing Results and Effects Generally on the Habitual Criminal Population', 1886, TNA, HO 144/184/A5507, p. 8.
⁵⁴ *Report of the Commissioners Appointed to Inquire into the Working of the Penal Servitude Acts*, p. 393.
⁵⁵ See Michael Davitt, *Leaves from a Prison Diary, or, Lectures to a 'Solitary' Audience*, vol. 1, London: Chapman and Hall, 1885, pp. 169–82.
⁵⁶ Anonymous, *Five Years' Penal Servitude by One Who Has Endured It*, p. 269.

for defrauding his employer by issuing false cheques worth up to 700 pounds.[57] Then in 1880 a London 'ticket-of-leave' man who claimed to have personal experience of police supervision made the same point. He said that 'policemen are naturally anxious to show their acuteness and activity to their superiors and the man with honest intentions is often foiled in his attempts to gain an honest living by the assiduity of the police'.[58] Thus, in the 1870s it was regularly alleged that members of the Metropolitan Police Force zealously used their supervisory powers to target repeat offenders, endangering their employment.

Notwithstanding these complaints, it seems probable that inappropriate conduct by the police towards those under supervision was relatively rare. As discussed, police supervision in London could be easily avoided and, in the years for which data is available, it affected less than half of those repeat offenders convicted in London who were eligible to be sentenced to the punishment. In addition, the Metropolitan Police Force vigorously denied wrongdoing. Commissioner Henderson said that the police carefully investigated all allegations of undue interference. Based on the findings of these investigations he asserted that there had only been two confirmed cases of improper behaviour by a member of the Metropolitan Police Force towards an individual under supervision. He believed the figure was so low because the leadership of the force was 'always trying to impress upon the police the great care' that must be shown in undertaking these duties.[59] Such directions had indeed been given. Following the passage of the *Habitual Criminals Act 1869*, the home secretary penned a circular, which was distributed to police forces, stating that care should be taken regarding how supervision was enacted 'so as not to interfere with but as far as possible to assist the efforts of those who evince a desire to return to an honest life by earning an honest livelihood'.[60] Furthermore, in 1872 Metropolitan Police Force rule number 372 was put in place, which articulated how carefully supervision should be undertaken.

It said that:

When the divisional police are directed to make inquiries respecting licence holders or supervisees, the greatest care must be taken not to injure them

---

[57] Samuel Halkett and John Laing, *Dictionary of Anonymous and Pseudonymous Literature of Great Britain: Including the Works of Foreigners Written in, or Translated into the English Language*, vol. 4, Edinburgh: n.p., 1888, p. 107; 'Miscellaneous Cases', *Railway Times and Joint-Stock Chronicle*, vol. 31, no. 28 (11 Jul. 1868), p. 727.
[58] Anonymous, *Convict Life*, pp. 214–5.
[59] *Report of the Commissioners Appointed to Inquire into the Working of the Penal Servitude Acts*, p. 361.
[60] Henry Bruce, home secretary, Circular, 8 Nov. 1869, TNA, HO 12/184/85.

directly or indirectly either with their employers or landlords. Officers should be employed on this duty who are not well known in the locality immediately in the neighbourhood in which they live, and on no account is a man in uniform ever to be employed on such duty.[61]

Similar directives had also been given in the 1840s and 1850s.[62] Several scholars argue convincingly that members of the Metropolitan Police Force were well aware of the need to maintain good relations with working-class communities, not appearing heavy-handed in their application of the law.[63] For instance, Arthur Harding said that policemen were always kind to working-class children. Speaking of London's Kingsland Road police station, he said that:

> They used to make a fuss of you there. They knew that you was hungry. And so they'd give you a slice of bread and jam. Sometimes the policeman would carry you, sometimes he would walk you back home.[64]

Therefore, Henderson's assertion that very few constables defied express instructions and acted inappropriately is a reasonable one. The discrepancy between the very numerous claims and the number of substantiated cases was due, he argued, to a belief among offenders that magistrates might take pity on someone who alleged that their offending was necessary after having been hounded out of honest employment by the police. As Henderson said, surely with some justification, 'of course they are all ready to say that the police' harass them.[65] The social commentator Charles Booth echoed this view in 1902.[66]

The penal servitude acts commission was certainly not convinced by reports that those under supervision were regularly interfered with. It noted that the evidence it had received was conflicting and found that any 'interference' from members of the Metropolitan Police Force was 'comparatively rare'.[67] Yet the commissioners agreed with Ranken that it was potentially problematic for supervisory duties to ever be carried out by local policemen who may be

---

[61] See *Prisons Committee: Report from the Departmental Committee on Prisons*, [C 7702] HC 1895, lvi, p. 393.

[62] See Metropolitan Police Orders, 10 Jul. 1845, TNA, MEPO 7/131 and Metropolitan Police Orders, 20 Mar. 1856, reproduced in the *Report of the Commissioners Appointed to Inquire into the Operation of the Acts Relating to Transportation and Penal Servitude. Vol. 2. Minutes of Evidence*, [C 3190] HC 1863, xxi, p. 150.

[63] Inwood, 'Policing London's Morals', p. 134; Beier, 'Identity, Language, and Resistance in the Making of the Victorian "Criminal Class"', p. 515; Taylor, 'Rationing Crime', pp. 578–90.

[64] Samuel, *East End Underworld*, p. 36.

[65] *Report of the Commissioners Appointed to Inquire into the Working of the Penal Servitude Acts*, pp. 360–2.

[66] Charles Booth, *Life and Labour of the People of London*, vol. 17, London: Macmillan, 1902, p. 138.

[67] *Report of the Commissioners Appointed to Inquire into the Working of the Penal Servitude Acts*, p. xxxv.

known in the community. The committee accepted that the criminal past of those under supervision might be uncovered as a result of this surveillance. So, the commission recommended that plain-clothes policemen specially selected for their discretion and with no other duties should carry out supervision in London.[68] This recommendation was accepted and led directly to the establishment of the CSO in 1880.[69] A major change to the manner in which supervision was carried out was about to be made.

*

Primarily because of the way London's police magistrates interpreted the *Prevention of Crime Act 1871*, police supervision had initially been very ineffective as a means of monitoring those designated as habitual criminals in London. In 1879 a legislative change was made in order to enable those required to report themselves to the police each month to do so to the police officer on duty at a particular station without that person being specifically chosen for the task by the chief officer of police.[70] Then, in 1880 the CSO was established in London with a staff of plain-clothes policemen whose sole duties concerned supervision. This section will analyse whether these alterations enabled police supervision to become more effective in London.

From its foundation the CSO adopted a new conception of police supervision in keeping with the views of its founder, Howard Vincent, who was the director of criminal investigation within the Metropolitan Police Force. As a result, those under supervision were unlikely to be closely monitored in the manner the parliament had intended when passing the Liberal government's habitual criminals' legislation. In April 1880 Vincent proposed the establishment of the CSO as a response to the report of the penal servitude acts commissioners.[71] Commissioner Henderson accepted the proposal, and Vincent oversaw the establishment of the new office.[72] Vincent strongly believed that the key function of the police with regard to repeat offenders should be to aid their efforts to reform. Most, he asserted, were keenly desirous to return to the ranks of respectable society after having initially fallen into crime through circumstance

---

[68] Ibid., p. lxiv.
[69] Monro, 'A Report of the History of the Department of the Metropolitan Police Known as the Convict Supervision Office', p. 9.
[70] *Prevention of Crime Act*, 1879, s. 2.
[71] Howard Vincent, director of criminal investigation, to Edmund Henderson, 28 Apr. 1880, TNA, HO 45/9570/76871.
[72] Monro, 'A Report of the History of the Department of the Metropolitan Police Known as the Convict Supervision Office', pp. 1–8.

rather than choice. However, as he wrote in 1883, the 'prison taint' often prevented repeat offenders from gaining employment, leading to a 'relapse' into crime. Consequently, he believed that the key aim of the police concerning repeat offenders should be to enable their return to honest employment.[73] When it was first introduced both the Liberal government and the Conservative opposition conceived of supervision as a way to deter further offending by members of a 'criminal class', who freely chose a life of crime.[74] The founder of the CSO had a very different view.

Vincent's ideas informed the practice of the CSO. The regulations that guided the actions of staff at the CSO, along with the department's stated objectives, clearly embraced the notion that reformation, rather than deterrence, was the chief aim of the policing of this group of offenders. The department's regulations, which cautioned that the 'greatest tact and discretion' must be taken when carrying out supervision, compelled staff 'to assist by all means in their power all those who desire or appear to desire to lead an honest life' and also to make 'every effort' to work 'in harmony' with London's Discharged Prisoners' Aid Societies.[75] These regulations were intended to aid staff in the attainment of the department's two objectives. The first 'object' was 'the reformation, or restitution to honest labour, of old offenders, thereby preventing fresh crime', and the second was 'the prosecution and punishment of habitual criminals'. But this second objective was qualified. The staff of the CSO was told to only proceed against 'habitual criminals' who 'wilfully and persistently break the law'.[76] This new system only applied to male licence-holders and repeat offenders. Two civilian female 'visitors', who were appointed by the home secretary, carried out the supervision of women in London. London's Discharged Prisoners' Aid Societies for women approved of this arrangement, which was modelled on the system that operated in Dublin for both men and women. The emphasis of the visitors was, again, upon finding work for female repeat offenders.[77] As several historians have noted, the primary aim of police work concerning those categorized as habitual criminals in London changed. For example, Martin Weiner has said, referring to increased cooperation between prisoners' aid societies and the police in order

---

[73] Howard Vincent, 'Discharged Prisoners: How to Aid Them', *Contemporary Review*, vol. 43 (Mar. 1883), pp. 325–31; Howard Vincent, 'Repression of Crime', *Transactions of the National Association for the Promotion of Social Science 1883*, London: Longmans, Green and Co., 1884, p. 199.
[74] The Earl of Morley (Liberal), 207 *Parl. Deb.*, HL (3rd ser.), cols. 1082–6 (4 Jul. 1871); Douglas Straight (Conservative), 208 *Parl. Deb.*, HC (3rd ser.), cols. 1756–9 (16 Aug. 1871).
[75] Monro, 'A Report of the History of the Department of the Metropolitan Police Known as the Convict Supervision Office', pp. 8–9.
[76] Ibid., p. 9.
[77] Ibid., pp. 11, 12.

to help criminals integrate back into society, that the aim of supervision shifted from a deterrent surveillance to what he called 'social aid'.[78]

In 1886 the Metropolitan Police Force carried out a review of the workings of the CSO. At the review's completion Assistant Commissioner Monro, who had been placed in charge of the CSO, compiled a report, which was provided to the Home Office. While, as we will see, the document was flawed, it was unequivocal in its view that supervision was now effective in London.[79] Those under supervision were well known to the police, it argued, because of monthly reporting and regular communication between police forces. The result was a 'considerable diminution in crime'.[80] In referring to the findings of this report, Assistant Commissioner Robert Anderson claimed that supervision was now 'a powerful engine for the punishment of the hopelessly depraved' in London.[81] There is some evidence that the staff of the CSO worked hard, and with some success, alongside London's eleven discharged prisoners' aid societies in an effort to achieve the new objective of reformation.[82] In 1880 Vincent had sent a circular to many London businesses asking if they would be willing to employ men who had been placed under supervision. From the positive responses a list of 1,000 businesses was compiled and passed to London's discharged prisoners' aid societies, which ensured that if a vacancy arose suitable candidates were provided.[83] Candidates had often been trained in various trades, including shoe and chair mending, and plumbing, by William Wheatley and his staff at the Mission Refuge.[84] Monro claimed that 'several thousand persons' had been led back to honest employment as a result of this system in the first six years of the CSO's operation, meaning that 'in very numerous instances' they had 'retrieved their character'.[85] Vincent had a far more conservative figure, which

---

[78] Wiener, *Reconstructing the Criminal*, pp. 304–5; Leon Radzinowicz and Roger Hood, *A History of the English Criminal Law and Its Administration from 1750*, vol. 5. *The Emergence of Penal Policy*, London: Stevens and Sons, 1990, pp. 258–60; Petrow, *Policing Morals*, pp. 78–9.

[79] Monro, 'A Report of the History of the Department of the Metropolitan Police Known as the Convict Supervision Office', pp. 10–13.

[80] Ibid., pp. 14, 19.

[81] Robert Anderson, 'Morality by Act of Parliament', *Contemporary Review*, vol. 59 (1891), p. 86.

[82] The discharged prisoners' aid societies in London were the Royal Society for the Assistance of Discharged Prisoners, Westminster Memorial Refuge, Metropolitan Discharged Prisoners' Aid Society, St Giles Christian Mission, Sheriff's Fund, Surrey Society for the Employment and Reformation of Discharged Prisoners, Elizabeth Fry Refuge for the Reception of Female Prisoners, British Ladies' Society for Promoting the Reformation of Female Prisoners, Prison Mission, Dalston Refuge, Royal Female Philanthropic Society. See Vincent, 'Discharged Prisoners', p. 327.

[83] S. H. Jeyes, *The Life of Sir Howard Vincent*, London: George Allen, 1912, p. 99; Vincent, 'Discharged Prisoners', p. 330.

[84] Monro, 'A Report of the History of the Department of the Metropolitan Police Known as the Convict Supervision Office', p. 10.

[85] Ibid.

was, therefore, perhaps more accurate. He said that by the end of 1883 the CSO had been 'instrumental' in the successful employment of 300 men who had been under supervision.[86] In practice the primary focus of police work in London regarding those under supervision therefore changed fundamentally as the staff of the CSO worked, not without success, to bring about the reformation of licence-holders and repeat offenders.

Nonetheless, several sources believed that the CSO also successfully deterred those subject to police supervision from committing further crimes. In 1880 Sir Walter Crofton, a key proponent of police supervision whose influence in the framing of the *Habitual Criminals Act 1869* has been discussed in an earlier chapter, asserted that the legislative change of 1879, coupled with the establishment of the CSO, meant that those subject to supervision in London were now closely watched and brought to justice when they offended.[87] *The Times*, in a leading article, mounted a similar argument in 1886.[88] Finally, in 1889 Charles Clarkson, a former member of the Metropolitan Police Force, and journalist J. Hall Richardson, provided fulsome praise for the system of supervision in London in a book about policing. They asserted that surveillance, while carried out carefully and, therefore, not injurious to an individual's employment, was a real check on offending due to the high probability of arrest in the event of a crime being committed. They said that for those who were 'well-disposed', the system had 'no draw-backs' and that supervision 'exercised a wholesome influence upon many clever thieves who ostensibly lived in London' as the 'risk of recognition is now too great' to contemplate committing further crimes.[89] Numerous sources said that the changes to police supervision in London that had been made in 1879 and 1880 meant that licence-holders and repeat offenders were now subject to thorough surveillance.[90]

Meanwhile, senior police officers differed in their analysis of the effectiveness of supervision in London. According to Monro, thorough communication between different districts of the Metropolitan Police Force, and with other forces, meant that there was no escape from surveillance for those under supervision who meant to commit further crimes. He said that, as a consequence

---

[86] Vincent, 'Repression of Crime', p. 220; Vincent, 'Discharged Prisoners', p. 330.
[87] Sir Walter Crofton, 'Address on the Repression of Crime', *Transactions 1880*, London: Longman, 1881, p. 278.
[88] *Times*, 2 Dec. 1886, p. 9.
[89] Charles Clarkson and J. Hall Richardson, *Police!*, New York and London: Garland Publishing, 1984 (first published 1889), p. 356.
[90] Anderson, 'Morality by Act of Parliament', p. 86; Jeyes, *The Life of Sir Howard Vincent*, p. 99; Crofton, 'Address on the Repression of Crime', p. 278; Clarkson and Richardson, *Police!*, p. 356.

of this information sharing, criminals now 'dread supervision more than actual imprisonment'.[91] It is possible that Monro, whose report was made available to the press, was exaggerating the effectiveness of the department that he himself oversaw. Even after the changes that were brought about by the *Prevention of Crime Act 1879*, others argued that supervision was able to be evaded with little difficulty. This was the view of Vincent, who – in direct contrast to Monro – bemoaned a lack of communication between different police forces. This enabled, he argued, the 'worst offenders' to move about unnoticed.[92] Sir James Fraser, the head of the City Police until 1890, shared this view. He said, with obvious exaggeration, that police supervision 'was the most absurd measure that ever was passed' and that those who wished to avoid surveillance simply 'disappeared' by failing to report.[93] Vincent also claimed that close supervision was 'the exception rather than the rule'.[94] In other words, knowledgeable sources made very different assessments of police supervision in London in the 1880s and 1890s.

The available data is also open to differing interpretations. By 1891 21,388 people were subject to police supervision in London.[95] According to the available police statistics, which are reproduced below, members of the Metropolitan Police Force apprehended a small proportion of these people between 1888 and 1894.

These data show that less than 1 per cent of those subject to police supervision in London were apprehended each year for failing to report themselves, while only around 2 per cent either currently or previously under supervision were

Table 4.2 Habitual criminals apprehended in the Metropolitan Police District for failure to report, 1888–94

1888	1889	1892	1893	1894
119	101	63	81	71

Report of the Commissioner of Police of the Metropolis: For the Year 1888, [C 5761] HC 1889, xl, p. 5; *Report of the Commissioner of Police of the Metropolis: For the Year 1889*, [C 6237] HC 1890–1, xlii, p. 5; *Report of the Commissioner of Police of the Metropolis, 1893–4*, p. 6; *Report of the Commissioner of Police of the Metropolis, 1895*, p. 5.

[91] Monro, 'A Report of the History of the Department of the Metropolitan Police Known as the Convict Supervision Office', p. 14.
[92] Vincent, 'Discharged Prisoners', pp. 290, 331.
[93] *Prisons Committee*, p. 334.
[94] Vincent, 'Discharged Prisoners', pp. 290, 331.
[95] *Report of the Commissioner of Police of the Metropolis: For the Year 1890*, [C 6472] HC 1891, xlii, p. 6.

Table 4.3 Licence-holders, supervisees and expirees apprehended for fresh offences, 1888–94

Year	Number convicted	Number discharged	Total apprehended	Total number of licence-holders, supervisees and expirees registered
1888	647	99	746	36,778
1889	820	126	946	38,862
1890	627	74	701	40,701
1892	-	-	872	44,167
1893	-	-	881	45,662
1894	-	-	926	47,464

Report of the Commissioner of Police of the Metropolis, 1889, p. 6; *Report of the Commissioner of Police of the Metropolis*, 1890–1, p. 5; *Report of the Commissioner of Police of the Metropolis*, 1893–4, p. 6; *Report of the Commissioner of Police of the Metropolis*, 1895, p. 5.

Expirees were those whose sentences of police supervision had concluded. See the *Report of the Commissioner of Police of the Metropolis*, 1889, p. 6.

apprehended for committing a new offence. One interpretation of these figures is that police supervision functioned incredibly effectively in London. The low number of arrests for failure to report could indicate that the vast majority of those under supervision were now complying with this requirement. Relatively few arrests for fresh offences could also mean that police monitoring in the community had its desired effect. But these figures could also suggest that members of the Metropolitan Police Force did not closely monitor those sentenced to police supervision in London. An annual rate of apprehension of 2 per cent appears very low. Policemen, under instruction from their superiors, sought not to alienate working-class communities that were wary of the police and strongly opposed to anything resembling a 'spy-system'.[96] The East End criminal Arthur Harding thought this was the case. In reference to a row of tenements called the Gibraltar Building, in which 'there were always fights going on' and that 'had a very bad character', he said 'the police gave the inhabitants

---

[96] Porter, *The Origins of the Vigilant State*, pp. 1, 4; Storch, 'The Plague of Blue Locusts', pp. 67, 77; Donajgrodzki, '"Social Police" and the Bureaucratic Elite', pp. 54–5; Storch, 'The Policeman as Domestic Missionary', pp. 481–2.

a wide berth'.[97] A low arrest rate could indicate that the police in London, eager not to cause the disaffection of members of the working class, did not place a high priority on watching licence-holders and repeat offenders. Given the aim of the CSO, to provide support to habitual criminals rather than to carry out surveillance, this interpretation appears most likely. It is the conclusion that Radzinowicz and Hood have come to after assessing data regarding prosecutions of those subject to supervision in the 1890s. Few prosecutions, according to these scholars, show that police forces opposed imposing supervision as spying was widely believed to be an inappropriate function of the police. Supervision was, they claim, 'too foreign to the body politic of England ever to be put into effect'.[98] Martin Wiener has also concluded that this data shows supervision was 'eventually less applied'.[99] While the evidence is inconclusive, it does appear likely that the police in London were reluctant to carry out surveillance of licence-holders and repeat offenders.

Although the CSO carried out work to aid licence-holders and repeat offenders in finding employment many complaints of undue police interference continued to be made. As previously, it was often alleged that the police hounded men out of employment in order to gain a reputation for vigilance and, consequently, a promotion. This was the view of George Bidwell, a London-based forger from America, who even argued that licence-holders were blackmailed by police who threatened to expose them to their employers. According to Bidwell the police interfered with licence-holders and repeat offenders in this way in order to gain 'fame and promotion'.[100] Four witnesses made similar points before a Home Office inquiry that had been established in 1895 to investigate how the prison system could better combat recidivism.[101] One of these, called Mr E in order to protect his identity, was a licence-holder who said his employer was told of his criminal past by police who were supervising him. He claimed that as a result his employment as a dishwasher on London's Hackney Road was terminated. His view of supervision in London was that: 'It is tyrannous. It is a terrible

---

[97] Samuel, *East End Underworld*, pp. 84–5.
[98] Radzinowicz and Hood, 'Incapacitating the Habitual Criminal: The English Experience', pp. 1346–7.
[99] Wiener, *Reconstructing the Criminal*, pp. 303–4.
[100] George Bidwell, *Forging His Chains: The Autobiography of George Bidwell*, Hartford: S.S. Scranton, 1888, pp. 552–3.
[101] Rev. G. D. Merrick, chaplain at Holloway and Newgate prisons; Mr E; Captain Henry Wilson, inspector of prisons; Michael Davitt, *Prisons Committee*, pp. 57, 322, 393, 443.

thing.' As discussed, numerous historians also argue that the police used their supervisory powers inappropriately.¹⁰²

However, other sources claimed that any improper interference with those under supervision was rare between 1880 and 1895. Several officials at the periphery of the system of police supervision argued that no persecution of licence-holders and repeat offenders occurred. In Monro's report on the CSO he included comments from numerous London judges, prison officials and staff of charitable organizations about the alleged harassment of those undergoing supervision. Many argued very strongly that this did not occur. Stephen Johnson Field, a justice of the Queen's Bench division of the high court in London, said that he had 'never once seen it [police interference with those under supervision] proved', a view that was echoed by Sir Ford North, another justice of the same division of the high court.¹⁰³ The governor of the convict prison at Wormwood Scrubs in London asserted that: 'stories of persecution … had no foundation in fact', and the chaplain of London's Clerkenwell prison, the Reverend J. W. Horsley, said he had personally investigated numerous complaints against the police and always found them to be baseless. William Wheatley, who ran the St Giles Christian Mission in London, which sought to aid the reformation of criminals, also stated categorically that there was 'not an atom of truth' in allegations that police hounded habitual criminals out of employment.¹⁰⁴ Even the leadership of the Royal Society for the Assistance of Discharged Prisoners, which had previously been so critical of police supervision, said that it was 'comparatively rare' for surveillance to lead to the loss of employment, and that there was no desire by the 'police to injure individual convicts'.¹⁰⁵ Numerous knowledgeable parties therefore articulated strong and contradictory views regarding police interference with those they sought to supervise in London.

Nevertheless, it appears more likely that policemen did not regularly hound those under supervision. The leadership of the Metropolitan Police Force was very eager to avoid any appearance that licence-holders and repeat offenders received attention from the police that would be detrimental to them pursuing

---

¹⁰² Weinberger, 'The Criminal Class and the Ecology of Crime', p. 129; Emsley, *Crime and Society in England*, p. 174; Wiener, *Reconstructing the Criminal*, p. 149; Godfrey, Cox and Farrall, *Serious Offenders*, p. 205; Petrow, *Policing Morals*, p. 151; Davis, 'From "Rookeries" to "Communities"', pp. 68, 71.
¹⁰³ Monro, 'A Report of the History of the Department of the Metropolitan Police Known as the Convict Supervision Office', p. 19.
¹⁰⁴ Ibid., pp. 19, 20.
¹⁰⁵ Ibid., p. 6.

honest lives in the future.¹⁰⁶ Then, with the establishment of the CSO, the focus of police work regarding those designated as habitual criminals shifted from deterrence to the provision of support, especially for employment. As a result, the staff of the CSO was explicitly warned that great care was needed when carrying out surveillance. They were forbidden from allowing the 'dissemination of any information to employers and others' of the 'antecedents' of those under supervision.¹⁰⁷ In their memoirs two former members of the Metropolitan Police Force argued that the rank and file acted upon these directives. Writing in 1910, Richard Quinton said that the 'hunting' of those under supervision did not occur because such conduct was 'officially discountenanced'.¹⁰⁸ Meanwhile, Frederick Wensley, who was a constable in Whitechapel from 1888 to 1895, said that orders from the commissioner regarding how supervision should be carried out were obeyed as to do otherwise could result in a policeman losing his employment.¹⁰⁹ As Terence Stanford has found, members of the Metropolitan Police Force were repeatedly warned about the need for discretion when dealing with repeat offenders and a failure to heed these warnings could lead to policemen being 'disciplined'.¹¹⁰ There is contradictory evidence regarding police treatment of those subject to supervision, and what data exists is open to differing conclusions. However, given the clarity with which policemen were cautioned against improper treatment of licence-holders and repeat offenders it appears probable police action that was likely to precipitate the discovery of a criminal's past offending was rare.¹¹¹ Police orders and other directives urging policemen to be cautious when dealing with those under supervision have not been considered by the historians who claim that the supervisory power of the police was an oppressive tool, which was deliberately used to hound repeat

---

[106] Metropolitan Police Orders, 10 Jul. 1845, TNA, MEPO 7/131; Metropolitan Police Orders, 20 Mar. 1856, reproduced in *Report of the Commissioners Appointed to Inquire into the Operation of the Acts Relating to Transportation and Penal Servitude*, p. 150; Bruce, Circular, 8 Nov. 1869; *Prisons Committee*, p. 393.

[107] Monro, 'A Report of the History of the Department of the Metropolitan Police Known as the Convict Supervision Office', p. 9.

[108] R. F. Quinton, *Crime and Criminals: 1876–1910*, London: Garland Publishing, 1984 (first published 1910), p. 204.

[109] Frederick Wensley, *Forty Years of Scotland Yard: The Record of a Lifetime's Service in the Criminal Investigation Department*, New York: Garden City Publishing Co., 1930, p. 72.

[110] Terence Stanford, *The Metropolitan Police 1850-1914: Targeting, Harassment and the Creation of a Criminal Class*, unpublished doctoral thesis, University of Huddersfield, 2007, pp. 187, 221.

[111] Weinberger, 'The Criminal Class and the Ecology of Crime', p. 129; Emsley, *Crime and Society in England*, p. 174; Wiener, *Reconstructing the Criminal*, p. 149; Godfrey, Cox and Farrall, *Serious Offenders*, p. 205; Petrow, *Policing Morals*, p. 151; Davis, 'From "Rookeries" to "Communities"', pp. 68, 71.

offenders out of employment, thereby creating a criminal class.[112] The existence of these instructions, and evidence that they were heeded by policemen, renders the conclusion of these historians unlikely in the case of London.

*

Police supervision was largely ineffective in London from 1871 to 1895. Up until 1880 this was primarily the case due to the way in which London's police magistrates interpreted the reporting provisions of the *Prevention of Crime Act 1871*. Because they insisted on the commissioner of the Metropolitan Police Force himself taking the stand to provide evidence of a failure to report, no one in London was convicted of not reporting between 1871 and 1879, when further legislation was passed. As a result, 23 per cent of licence-holders and repeat offenders did not report each month and avoided supervision altogether. While the *Prevention of Crime Act 1879* enabled monthly reporting to be enforced in London, it appears probable that those subject to police supervision were, in most cases, not monitored closely. The leadership of the Metropolitan Police Force was anxious not to sour relations with working-class communities and urged policemen to exercise great caution when carrying out surveillance, lest the employment of the individual being watched be endangered by the discovery of their criminal past. Furthermore, with the establishment of the CSO the focus of supervision shifted from a deterrent surveillance to rehabilitation. Assistant Commissioner Anderson referred to this situation when he wrote in 1891 that there was a 'morbid sympathy for hardened offenders'. He was reduced to 'pleading for a due administration of the existing law respecting police supervision'.[113] The monitoring of designated offenders in the community, which was a key aim of the Gladstone government, was never fully embraced by the leadership of the Metropolitan Police Force, who instructed policemen accordingly.

As discussed in the Introduction to this work, the oppressive potentiality of police supervision greatly unsettled many mid- and late Victorians of all social classes. It was widely believed that greatly increasing the power of the police could lead to the liberties of many within working-class communities being infringed.[114] And several historians assert that this is exactly what occurred.

---

[112] Johnston, *Crime in England*, p. 36; Weinberger, 'The Criminal Class and the Ecology of Crime', p. 129; Emsley, *Crime and Society in England*, p. 174; Wiener, *Reconstructing the Criminal*, p. 149; Godfrey, Cox and Farrall, *Serious Offenders*, p. 205; Petrow, *Policing Morals*, p. 151; Davis, 'From "Rookeries" to "Communities"', pp. 68, 71.

[113] Anderson, 'Morality by Act of Parliament', pp. 85–6.

[114] Porter, *The Origins of the Vigilant State*, pp. 1, 4.

It has been argued that, notwithstanding early problems of implementation in London, supervision enabled the police to target the poorest elements of the working class for arrest, therefore creating a criminal class.[115] However, as was the case with registration, this chapter has shown that neither police magistrates nor the Metropolitan Police Force were uncritical and willing actors in a project to control the working class, as several historians allege.[116] The Gladstone government's habitual criminals' legislation had one further objective: the imposition of lengthy sentences upon repeat offenders. While both registration and supervision were, to a large extent, ineffective in London, the next chapter will analyse the sentencing of repeat offenders in order to determine whether this final aim was achieved.

---

[115] Weinberger, 'The Criminal Class and the Ecology of Crime', p. 129; Emsley, *Crime and Society in England*, p. 174; Wiener, *Reconstructing the Criminal*, p. 149; Godfrey, Cox and Farrall, *Serious Offenders*, p. 205; Petrow, *Policing Morals*, p. 151; Davis, 'From "Rookeries" to "Communities"', pp. 68, 71.

[116] Emsley, *Crime and Society in England*, pp. 172–4; Petrow, *Policing Morals*, p. 51.

5

Sentencing Repeat Offenders: Leniency and Severity in the Late Nineteenth Century

It is of the greatest importance that those offenders who are commencing a course of crime should be made aware that each repetition of it, duly recorded and proved, will involve a material increase of punishment, pain, and inconvenience to them.[1]

(Select Committee Report, 1863)

The Gladstone Liberal government, along with the Conservative opposition, hoped that its habitual criminals' legislation would lead to lengthier sentences for repeat offenders. During the period in which transportation was ceasing to be a penal option, there was much criticism of sentences for repeat offenders that were perceived to be too short either to act as a deterrent or to provide enough time for an individual to be reformed while imprisoned.[2] In particular, members of the influential Social Science Association (SSA), which had played a vital role in the drafting of the habitual criminals' legislation of 1869 and 1871, argued that now repeat offenders could not be sent abroad, from whence they had rarely returned, long sentences of incarceration should be imposed instead in order to act as a deterrent to crime and protect society.[3] As quoted above, the

---

[1] *Report from the Select Committee of the House of Lords, on the Present State of Discipline in Gaols and Houses of Correction; Together with the Proceedings of the Committee, Minutes of Evidence, Appendix and Index*, [C 499] HC 1863, ix, p. xvi.

[2] *Second Report from the Select Committee of the House of Commons on Transportation; Together with the Minutes of Evidence, and Appendix*, [C 296] HC 1856, xvii, pp. 17, 106, 128; *Report of the Commissioners Appointed to Inquire into the Operation of the Acts Relating to Transportation and Penal Servitude. Vol. 2. Minutes of Evidence*, [C 3190] HC 1863, xxi, pp. 77, 134, 150, 154–6; The Earl of Carnarvon (Conservative) quoted in the *Daily News*, 9 Jan. 1863, p. 4.

[3] *The Transportation of Criminals: Being a Report of a Discussion at a Special Meeting of the Association Held at Burlington House, on the 17th February, 1863*, London: Emily Faithfull, 1863, pp. 1–3; Thomas Barwick Lloyd Baker, 'On the Theory and Practice of Sentences for Crime', letter to the editor of the *Gloucestershire Chronicle*, 20 Jun. 1863, reproduced in Thomas Barwick Lloyd Baker, *War with Crime: Being a Selection of Reprinted Papers on Crime, Reformatories, Etc.*, London: Longmans, 1889, p. 32.

report of a select committee from 1863 shows that members of parliament largely agreed.[4] A clause of the *Habitual Criminals Bill 1869* stipulating that a minimum period of seven years' penal servitude must be imposed upon an offender after a third conviction for a felony was removed in the committee stage due largely to its perceived harshness.[5] This was discussed in Chapter 2. However, the legislation contained other mechanisms that, the government and the opposition still hoped, would remedy, in the Liberal Duke of Cleveland's words, the 'admitted and increasing evil' of short sentences.[6] One intended function of the registers was to ensure that magistrates and judges had full information before them regarding a defendant's criminal past, hopefully resulting in the application of longer sentences as fewer repeat offenders would be able to escape recognition as such.[7] Meanwhile, supervision was, in part, intended to ensure offending behaviour was detected and then punished. As Stefan Petrow has said, 'refinements of the system of supervision, registration, and identification were essential steps towards singling out for special punishment habitual offenders'.[8]

Were longer sentences of incarceration imposed upon repeat offenders in London as a consequence of this legislation? In seeking to answer this question this chapter will firstly analyse the sentencing of recidivists in the capital between 1871 and 1879, at which point relevant legislative and operational changes were made. The *Prevention of Crime Act 1879* enhanced judicial discretion by removing the minimum period of seven years' penal servitude for previously convicted felons. As will be discussed, the government accepted the finding of a select committee that this measure had been perceived to be overly harsh by judges.[9] Then the creation of the Convict Supervision Office (CSO) in London in 1880 significantly altered the process of registration in the capital in an effort, in part, to ensure lengthier sentences were imparted upon members of the criminal class. Because of these changes, the second section of the chapter will examine the sentencing of those designated as habitual criminals in London from 1880 to 1895.

---

[4] *Report from the Select Committee of the House of Lords, on the Present State of Discipline in Gaols and Houses of Correction*, p. xvi.
[5] For the debate regarding the omission of the mandatory minimum period of seven years' penal servitude see 198 *Parl. Deb.*, HC (3rd ser.), cols. 1278–9 (4 Aug. 1869).
[6] Lord Cleveland (Liberal), 194 *Parl. Deb.*, HL (3rd ser.), col. 712 (5 Mar. 1869); Henry Bruce (Liberal), 198 *Parliamentary Debates*, HC (3rd ser.), cols. 1251–60, 1276–8 (4 Aug. 1869) and 200 *Parl. Deb.*, HC (3rd ser.), col. 2134 (29 Apr. 1870); The Earl of Shaftesbury (Conservative), 194 *Parl. Deb.*, HL (3rd ser.), col. 1326 (15 Mar. 1869).
[7] *Prevention of Crime Act*, 34 & 35 Vict., c. 112, 1871, s. 6.
[8] Stefan Petrow, *Policing Morals: The Metropolitan Police and the Home Office 1870–1914*, Oxford: Clarendon Press, 1995, p. 101.
[9] *Report of the Commissioners Appointed to Inquire into the Working of the Penal Servitude Acts. Vol. I – Commissions and Report*, [C 2368] HC and HL 1878–9, xxxvii, pp. xxxi–ii.

As with registration and supervision, there is agreement among the small group of scholars who have scrutinized the elements of the Gladstone government's habitual criminals' legislation intended to precipitate longer sentences that this objective was achieved. The general view is that not only were those subject to the legislation targeted for arrest by the police but that they were then dealt with severely when brought before magistrates and judges.[10] Petrow believes that magistrates, judges, the police and the parliament were united in their aspiration to repress members of the criminal class.[11] He has found that 'in court police testimony largely determined whether a convict deserved rescue from or was consigned to a life of crime'. According to Petrow, this was because an adverse report from the police would inevitably lead to a conviction, regardless of other evidence.[12] Barry Godfrey, David Cox and Stephen Farrall, whose work concentrates largely on the north of England, but nonetheless does cite numerous examples from London, have also said that habitual criminals' legislation led to severe sentences for repeat offenders.[13] They argue that the 'application of the acts' of 1869 and 1871 led to 'life trashing' sentences, even for those who had committed 'relatively minor offences'.[14] Whether this was the case in London is the subject of this chapter, which highlights, once again, sharp divisions between different elements of the Victorian state.

*

An increase in the length of sentences passed upon repeat offenders was a clear aim of the parliament in passing the Gladstone government's habitual criminals' legislation. In this section the effectiveness of the legislation in bringing about such a change before 1880 will be assessed.

Prior to the introduction of the habitual criminals' legislation of 1869 and 1871 strong views were often expressed against the great 'evil' of short sentences for repeat offenders, which, allegedly, were increasingly replacing longer terms of transportation.[15] There is some evidence that the lengths of sentences

---

[10] Barry Godfrey, David Cox and Stephen Farrall, *Serious Offenders: An Historical Study of Habitual Criminals*, London: Oxford University Press, 2010, p. xii; Helen Johnston, *Crime in England 1815–1880: Experiencing the Criminal Justice System*, Abingdon: Routledge, 2015, p. 36.
[11] Petrow, *Policing Morals*, p. 51.
[12] Ibid.
[13] Godfrey, Cox and Farrall, *Serious Offenders*, pp. 161–77.
[14] Ibid., p. 177.
[15] This was discussed in Chapter 1. Also see *Second Report from the Select Committee of the House of Commons on Transportation*, p. 17; Thomas Barwick Lloyd Baker, 'Prevention of Crime', read at the Bradford meeting of the SSA, 1859, reproduced in Baker, *War with Crime*, p. 5; Thomas Barwick Lloyd Baker, 'On the Sentences Passed on Criminals', read at the York meeting of the SSA, 1864, reproduced in Baker, *War with Crime*, p. 38.

passed upon London's repeat offenders were, in general, decreasing in the years before 1869. Data from London's central criminal court, which throughout the nineteenth century heard London's most serious criminal cases, showed that as transportation was ceasing shorter periods of detention were being imposed upon repeat offenders in the capital. Figures regarding the sentencing of repeat offenders following convictions for robbery, burglary, forgery and larceny between 1838–42 and 1858–62 show that while 83 per cent of those convicted for these crimes were sentenced to transportation for seven years or more in the five years from 1838, only 50 per cent were incarcerated for three years or more in the same period commencing in 1858, with the remainder undergoing periods of imprisonment of up to two years.[16] Many repeat offenders in London were therefore not receiving periods of incarceration that were as lengthy as former sentences of transportation. While further data regarding the sentencing of repeat offenders is hard to come by, the annual volumes of judicial statistics showed that across England and Wales the length of sentences for all offenders was decreasing. For example, between 1857 and 1868 the proportion of long sentences of three years' penal servitude or more fell from 17 per cent to 13 per cent.[17] The Home Office and many members of parliament bemoaned this trend. In 1864 Horatio Waddington, undersecretary at the Home Office, criticized 'the shortness of punishment generally inflicted upon convicts', by which he meant criminals who had previously been convicted.[18] An 1863 select committee also found that there had been a 'remarkable diminution' in the length of sentences over the last '20 or 30 years', which was the result of an 'increasing leniency' on the part 'of the courts of law'.[19] While the evidence regarding repeat offenders is incomplete, that which exists shows that the duration of sentences they received decreased in the years before 1869. The legislation of 1869 and 1871 was intended to rectify this perceived problem.

It is necessary, at the outset, to explain the scope of discretion enjoyed by London's magistrates and judges in sentencing repeat offenders between 1871 and 1880. In short, while not entirely unfettered, they enjoyed great freedom in sentencing despite the desire of parliament to see longer sentences imposed.

---

[16] *Report of the Commissioners Appointed to Inquire into the Operation of the Acts Relating to Transportation and Penal Servitude. Vol. 1. Report and Appendix*, [C 3190] HC 1863, xxi, p. 190.

[17] *Judicial Statistics, England and Wales, 1869. Part I – Criminal Statistics*, [C 4196] HC 1869, lviii, p. xxv.

[18] *Correspondence between the Secretary of State for the Home Department and the Directors of Convict Prisons, on the Subject of the Recommendations of the Royal Commission on the Penal Servitude Acts*, [C 61] HC 1864, xlix, p. 1.

[19] *Report of the Commissioners Appointed to Inquire into the Operation of the Acts Relating to Transportation and Penal Servitude. Vol. 2*, pp. 23–4.

Anyone convicted of a felony, which was a crime that had at one point been a capital offence, could receive a sentence as lenient as one day's imprisonment in a local jail or as harsh as a maximum term of penal servitude, which, for many offences, was life.[20] As discussed in Chapter 1, sentences of penal servitude had been introduced as a substitute for transportation and were carried out in specially constructed penitentiaries. All those arrested by the police in London, either for a felony or a less serious misdemeanour, were first taken before a police magistrate. He could hear the matter himself and, upon conviction, sentence the offender to a period of no more than two years' imprisonment, or refer those charged with felonies for trial at a higher court.[21] The two criminal courts in the nineteenth century were the quarter sessions and the assizes, the latter dealing with the most serious cases. In London those committed for trial were dealt with at either the Middlesex sessions or the central criminal court, which was London's court of assize. Judges at these higher courts could, if the jury found the offender guilty, impose a penalty of up to two years' imprisonment in a local jail or a period of penal servitude of five years or more for first offenders or seven years or more upon someone who had previously been convicted of a felony. Two proposed mechanisms to ensure some uniformity in sentencing were debated in the second half of the nineteenth century: a sentencing code and a court of appeal.[22] Yet neither was adopted before 1895, probably, as Leon Radzinowicz and Roger Hood have found, as they were believed to pose a threat to judicial discretion, which was a cherished element of the British judicial system.[23] Consequently, as Sir William Erle, a judge of the court of the Queen's Bench, told a parliamentary committee in 1856, the law left 'an almost absolute discretion in the judge after conviction'.[24] In 1863 the commissioner of the Metropolitan Police Force, Sir Richard Mayne, also correctly noted that judges 'have almost unlimited discretion whether they will pass a very long sentence of penal servitude, or a very short sentence of imprisonment'.[25] While the parliament

---

[20] D. A. Thomas, *Constraints on Judgement: The Search for Structured Discretion in Sentencing, 1860–1910*, Cambridge: Institute of Criminology Occasional Series No. 4, 1979, p. 1.

[21] Regarding the scope of magisterial discretion see Drew D. Gray, *Crime, Prosecution and Social Relations: the Summary Courts of the City of London in the Late Eighteenth Century*, Basingstoke: Palgrave Macmillan, 2009, p. 8.

[22] Thomas, *Constraints on Judgement*, pp. 47–92; Richard Harris (ed.), *The Reminiscences of Sir Henry Hawkins (Baron Brampton)*, London and New York: Thomas Nelson and Sons, 1904, pp. 367–8.

[23] Leon Radzinowicz and Roger Hood, 'Judicial Discretion and Sentencing Standards: Victorian Attempts to Solve a Perennial Problem', *University of Pennsylvania Law Review*, vol. 127, no. 5 (1978–1979), pp. 1291, 1301.

[24] *Second Report from the Select Committee of the House of Commons on Transportation*, p. 131.

[25] *Report of the Commissioners Appointed to Inquire into the Operation of the Acts Relating to Transportation and Penal Servitude. Vol. 2*, p. 134.

hoped the legislation of 1869 and 1871 would lead to the imposition of longer sentences, magistrates and judges retained great discretion in sentencing.

Although the legislation received some support, based on its perceived potential to precipitate longer sentences for repeat offenders, the *Prevention of Crime Act 1871* did not quell criticism of the sentencing of recidivists in London, which persisted through the 1870s. Initially, the *Standard*, a conservative newspaper, had argued that the 'best' element of the *Habitual Criminals Act 1869* was that it would lead to 'tougher sentences' for members of the so-called criminal class.[26] *The Times* also believed the legislation would end the imposition of 'short sentences' upon 'well-known and inveterate offenders'.[27] However, numerous London newspapers quickly found that this eventuality had not come to pass and that the capital's magistrates and judges, despite the desire of the parliament in passing the *Habitual Criminals Act 1869* and the *Prevention of Crime Act 1871*, continued to utilize their discretion to pass sentences upon those with previous convictions that were deemed overly lenient. In 1871 a leading article appeared in the conservative *Pall Mall Gazette* denouncing the leniency shown to London's recidivists. Repeat offenders, the newspaper claimed, could expect a 'gentle caution' from a magistrate or a sentence so light 'that they themselves are tickled with the fun of the proceedings'.[28] The *Standard*, despite its early optimism, also wrote in 1871 that recidivists continued to receive sentences that were too short. It said that magistrates were to blame for sentencing so many repeat offenders summarily rather than referring them to higher courts where a long period of penal servitude could be imposed.[29] A further leading article in the following year, which discussed violence by trade union members in London, criticized what the newspaper thought were very lenient sentences for recidivists.[30] The article said that the sentencing of repeat offenders in London was 'a great scandal'.[31] In the pages of other London newspapers in the early 1870s senior officials, such as Barwick Baker, the Gloucestershire magistrate and SSA member, and Sir John Pakington, the chair of the international prison congress and a Conservative member of parliament, also denounced the manner in which those with many previous convictions often received 'repeated short sentences'.[32] Much criticism of sentencing in London continued in the 1870s.

[26] *Standard*, 24 Aug. 1869, p. 6.
[27] *Times*, 21 Aug. 1869, p. 9.
[28] *Pall Mall Gazette*, 9 Sept. 1871, p. 4.
[29] *Standard*, 20 Sept. 1871, p. 4.
[30] *Standard*, 30 Aug. 1872, p. 4.
[31] *Standard*, 8 Mar. 1877, p. 3; 7 Nov. 1881, p. 2.
[32] *Daily News*, 13 Jul. 1872, p. 6; *Morning Post*, 6 Oct. 1873, p. 2.

In the late 1870s numerous senior London judges also argued that sentences for repeat offenders were, if anything, becoming increasingly lenient. This was largely due, they plausibly claimed, to the significant gap between the maximum period of imprisonment in a local jail and the minimum term of penal servitude for repeat offenders.[33] Following the tabling of a parliamentary report in 1863 the Palmerston Whig/Liberal government had introduced legislation that increased the minimum sentence of penal servitude. After 1863, a felony conviction attracted a minimum sentence of five years for a first-time offender and seven years for a repeat offender.[34] It was hoped that increasing the minimum term of penal servitude would lead to more long sentences being passed, especially upon repeat offenders, who, the government believed, were part of a dangerous 'criminal class'.[35] However, magistrates and judges retained the discretion to sentence repeat offenders to a period of less than two years' imprisonment in a local prison. Numerous judges claimed that the long minimum period of penal servitude for repeat offenders unintentionally led to a general lessening in the severity of punishments inflicted upon recidivists. When faced with the choice of inflicting a sentence of seven years or more in a penitentiary, or up to two years in a local jail, many judges, it was said, opted for the latter in order to avoid imposing a punishment that, they believed, was unduly severe.[36] Edward Cox was a London judge who advocated the imposition of harsh penalties for habitual criminals.[37] He believed that many of his colleagues were often reluctant to impose a sentence of seven years' penal servitude.[38] He criticized the *Penal Servitude Act 1864* for forcing judges to inflict an 'inadequate penalty of imprisonment where the proper sentence would have been three or four years penal servitude'.[39] Therefore, 'by aiming at excessive severity', he found that 'the law has practically driven reluctant Judges to excessive leniency'.[40]

Similar views were also expressed by a group of judges to a select committee in 1879, the genesis of which has been discussed in previous chapters. In 1878 Richard Assheton Cross, the Conservative home secretary, appointed four legal

---

[33] Edward Cox, *The Principles of Punishment: As Applied in the Administration of Criminal Law, by Judges and Magistrates*, London: Law Times Office, 1877, p. 147; *Report of the Commissioners Appointed to Inquire into the Working of the Penal Servitude Acts*, pp. xxxi–ii.
[34] *Penal Servitude Act*, 27 & 28 Vict., c. 47, 1864, s. 2.
[35] *Report of the Commissioners Appointed to Inquire into the Operation of the Acts Relating to Transportation and Penal Servitude. Vol. 1*, p. 23.
[36] Cox, *The Principles of Punishment*, pp. 130–48; *Report of the Commissioners Appointed to Inquire into the Working of the Penal Servitude Acts*, pp. xxxi–ii.
[37] Cox, *The Principles of Punishment*, pp. 130–48.
[38] Ibid., p. xvii.
[39] Ibid., p. 147.
[40] Ibid.

experts to inquire into a draft code relating to indictable offences. They, like Cox, believed that the seven-year minimum period of penal servitude for previously convicted felons had achieved the opposite of its objective: a decrease in the duration of sentences passed upon repeat offenders. Sir Robert Lush, a judge of the high court and a visiting justice at London's central criminal court, gave evidence on behalf of the commission and explained that, given the significant difference between the maximum period of two years' imprisonment and the seven-year minimum period of penal servitude, 'there must be an error on one side or the other' and it was rarely 'on the side of excess'. Lush said that many short sentences were passed, even though they were felt to be inadequate by the judges who imposed them.[41] According to Lush, these views were widely held by members of the judiciary. Indeed, he said that 'every judge I am acquainted with' believed the seven-year minimum led to more short sentences being imposed, and the select committee accepted Lush's evidence that this was indeed the case.[42] Three historians have also argued that many sentences of imprisonment were imposed following the legislative change of 1863 as the minimum period of penal servitude was often deemed overly harsh. David Garland has said that the 'ironic effect' of the seven-year minimum was to 'make imprisonment in local prisons the mainstay of the whole system', ensuring 'a very large number of short sentences'.[43] Radzinowicz and Hood have also found that the measure led to increased leniency, thereby mirroring the views of many informed contemporaries.[44]

The surviving data relating to the sentencing of London recidivists during the early 1870s also points to a decline rather than an increase in the length of sentences. The annual reports of the commissioner of the Metropolitan Police Force contained data regarding the sentencing of all those found guilty of crime, as defined by the legislation 1871. The legislation's definition of crime included all felonies, and the misdemeanours of obtaining money by false pretences, conspiracy to defraud, and being at large at night, intent of committing a crime, with either housebreaking instruments or a disguised face.[45] The data, which is reproduced below, shows that penal servitude came to be used slightly less between 1870 and 1873 as a penal option in London.

---

[41] *Report of the Commissioners Appointed to Inquire into the Working of the Penal Servitude Acts*, pp. xxxi–ii.
[42] Ibid., p. xxxii.
[43] David Garland, *Punishment and Welfare*, London: Gower, 1985, pp. 7, 63.
[44] Leon Radzinowicz and Roger Hood, 'Incapacitating the Habitual Criminal: The English Experience', *Michigan Law Review*, vol. 78, no. 8 (Aug. 1980), p. 1335.
[45] *Prevention of Crime Act*, 1871, s. 20.

Table 5.1 Persons convicted within the Metropolitan and City of London Police Districts of crime, with sentences and proportion of all convictions, 1870-3

	1870	1871	1872	1873
Number of persons convicted in all courts	7,160	6,183	6,134[a]	6,047[b]
Sentenced to 10 years or over	87 (1.2)	84 (1.4)	78 (1.3)	96 (1.6)
Between 7 and 10 years	359 (5)	297 (4.8)	243 (4)	216 (3.6)
Between 5 and 7 years	157 (2.2)	129 (2.1)	120 (2)	139 (2.3)
Between 12 months and 2 years	900 (12.6)	867 (14)	712 (11.6)	752 (12.4)
Between 6 and 12 months	1,169 (16.3)	1,085 (17.6)	1,062 (17.3)	1,084 (17.9)
Between 3 and 6 months	1,715 (24)	1,401 (22.7)	1,245 (20.3)	1,439 (23.8)
Under 3 months	2,567 (35.9)	2,174 (35.2)	2,251 (36.7)	2,116 (35)
Fined, or sentenced to a period in a reformatory school	206 (2.9)	146 (2.4)	423 (6.9)	205 (3.4)

Report of the Commissioner of Police of the Metropolis, [C 358] HC 1871, xxxvi, p. 26; Report of the Commissioner of Police of the Metropolis, [C 652] HC 1872, xxx, p. 18; Report of the Commissioner of Police of the Metropolis: For the Year 1872, [C 839] HC 1873, xxxi, p. 21; Report of the Commissioner of Police of the Metropolis: For the Year 1873, [C 1059] HC 1874, xxxvii, p. 26.

a The sum of all recorded convictions in 1872 is 6,134. However, 5,716 is the total figure that is stated in the report. The reason for this discrepancy is unclear. See the Report of the Commissioner of Police of the Metropolis, 1873, p. 21.

b The sum of all recorded convictions in 1873 is 6,047. However, 5,882 is the total figure that is stated in the report. Again, the reason for this discrepancy is unclear. See the Report of the Commissioner of Police of the Metropolis, 1874, p. 26.

This data shows that the proportion of sentences of five years or more decreased slightly, albeit statistically significantly, from 8.4 per cent in 1870 down to 7.5 per cent in 1873. The greatest decrease was in the imposition of sentences of seven years or more, which dropped from 6.2 per cent to 5.2 per cent over this period. There was also an increase in the percentage of sentences of between six and twelve months' imprisonment, from 16.3 per cent in 1870 to 17.9 per cent in 1873, while the proportion of sentences of imprisonment for other periods remained relatively stable. Thus, in London in these years there was a slight shift away from the use of long sentences of penal servitude for criminals guilty of these offences. It should be noted that this data is not confined to repeat offenders. However, data from the early 1890s shows that in London only 47 per cent of those tried at the higher courts were recorded as having committed earlier offences and the Home Office committee that was presented with this statistic believed that it significantly underestimated the true figure.[46] Furthermore, newspaper reports of London trials at the higher courts in the 1870s show that over half of defendants were repeat offenders.[47] For offenders convicted in London during 1870–3, sentences of penal servitude did not rise as a proportion of total sentences passed, but instead fell slightly. Although the figures do not allow us to identify recidivists, it seems safe to assume that the same sentencing pattern applied to them as well.

There were several reasons, in addition to the minimum period of seven years' penal servitude, for the failure of the habitual criminals' legislation of 1869 and 1871 to precipitate longer sentences for repeat offenders in London in the 1870s. The attitude of London's police magistrates was one. As noted in earlier chapters, in 1869 Sir Thomas Henry, London's chief magistrate, informed Adolphus Liddell, the permanent undersecretary at the Home Office, that he and his fellow magistrates would not take evidence of recidivism garnered from the registers into account. Neither descriptive returns nor photographs could definitively prove identity, he claimed, and both types of evidence could lead to cases of mistaken identity.[48] Numerous examples of London magistrates seemingly disregarding evidence of prior convictions in sentencing could be cited.[49] For instance, in October 1885 Michael Hayes was convicted of assaulting James Sedler in the Little Wonder beer shop on Commercial Road, punching him in the head and then kicking him once he had fallen to the ground. The magistrate, Thomas Saunders, said the attack, which lasted half an hour and led to Sedler's hospitalization, was 'most cruel and brutal'. Despite this, and the fact that Hayes was known to be a repeat offender, he received one month's imprisonment.[50] Then in September 1889 Robert Curtis, a striking dock worker, was convicted on four charges of assaulting numerous men working at the London docks. On one occasion he led a group of fifteen or sixteen men in an unprovoked attack

---

[46] *Report of a Committee Appointed by the Secretary of State to Inquire into the Best Means Available for Identifying Habitual Criminals; with Minutes of Evidence and Appendices*, [C 7263] HC and HL 1894, lxxii, p. 72.

[47] For example see *Reynolds's Newspaper*, 3 Oct. 1869, p. 6; 13 Oct. 1872, p. 6; 24 Mar. 1874, p. 4; *Standard*, 7 Jan. 1875, p. 6; *Times*, 20 Jan. 1875, p. 11; 19 Aug. 1876, p. 11; 23 Apr. 1877, p. 11; *Lloyd's Weekly Newspaper*, 26 Jan. 1873, p. 4.

[48] Thomas Henry, chief magistrate of London, to Adolphus Liddell, 13 Mar. 1869, TNA, HO 12/184.

[49] For example see *The Times*, 29 Apr. 1872, p. 13; 22 Oct. 1881, p. 11; 17 Apr. 1881, p. 12; 2 Jan. 1884, p. 3; 7 Oct. 1885, p. 4; 25 Dec. 1885, p. 10; 7 Sept. 1889, p. 3; 28 Apr. 1889, p. 6; 29 Apr. 1890, p. 4; 23 Jan. 1891, p. 14.

[50] *Times*, 7 Oct. 1885, p. 4.

upon one William Woodhouse, a dock labourer. In court a constable proved a previous conviction against Curtis. Yet the Thames police court magistrate, Frederick Lushington, said that he 'should not take into account what the constable had said' and sentenced Curtis to three months' imprisonment for each offence.[51] London's police magistrates had a dim view of the Gladstone government's habitual criminals' legislation on the basis that it unreasonably targeted their working-class clientele. So they actively worked to mitigate its severity.[52] During the mid- and late Victorian period the overwhelming majority of offenders in London were dealt with by magistrates, with only between 4 and 8 per cent annually committed for trial at a higher court.[53] The attitude of London's magistrates towards the habitual criminals' legislation, therefore, was a further factor that worked against the parliament's objective of ensuring repeat offenders received lengthier sentences.

The failure of police supervision to ensure all designated criminals were closely monitored was another reason why a general increase in the length of sentences for recidivists was not achieved. Police supervision was largely ineffective in London from 1871 to 1895, which meant that magistrates and judges often did not have access to fulsome information regarding the criminal behaviour of defendants who had been under surveillance when sentencing them. Before 1880 London's police magistrates interpreted the monthly reporting provisions of the *Prevention of Crime Act 1871* to mean that the commissioner of the Metropolitan Police Force himself must testify concerning a failure to report.[54] Thus, no one in London was convicted of not reporting between 1871 and 1879, when further legislation was passed, and many repeat offenders avoided supervision altogether by failing to report.[55] The police believed, quite justifiably, that the most dangerous and persistent criminals were those who sought to avoid the gaze of the police in London by failing to report.[56] A close supervision

---

[51] *Times*, 7 Sept. 1889, p. 3.
[52] Ellis and Ellis to Edmund Henderson, 11 Nov. 1869, TNA, MEPO 3/88; Adolphus Liddell to Edmund Henderson, 14 Jan. 1870, TNA., MEPO 3/88; Draft circular, 6 May 1870, TNA, HO 12/184/85459A/40; Superintendent of F division to Edmund Henderson, 18 May 1870, TNA, MEPO 3/88; Jennifer Davis, 'A Poor Man's System of Justice: The London Police Courts in the Second Half of the Nineteenth Century', *Historical Journal*, vol. 27, no. 2 (Jun. 1984), p. 326; Thomas Henry to Adolphus Liddell, 13 Mar. 1869, TNA, HO 12/184; *Judicial Statistics, England and Wales, 1893. Part 1 – Criminal Statistics*, [C 7725] HC 1895, cviii, p. 78; J. B. Manning, governor of London's Pentonville prison, *Report of a Committee Appointed by the Secretary of State to Inquire into the Best Means Available for Identifying Habitual Criminals*, p. 42.
[53] *Judicial Statistics, England and Wales, 1895. Part I – Criminal Statistics*, [C 8616] HC 1897, c, p. 32.
[54] Edmund Henderson to the Home Office, 12 Nov. 1872, TNA, HO 45/9320/16629D.
[55] Edmund Henderson, *Report of the Commissioners Appointed to Inquire into the Working of the Penal Servitude Acts*, p. 360.
[56] Ibid.

of these criminals may have provided police with incriminating evidence that, in turn, could have led to longer sentences at trial. However, as demonstrated in the previous chapter, many of those subject to police supervision were not closely monitored.

Disagreement among London's judges regarding appropriate punishment was yet another reason why the sentencing of repeat offenders did not increase in severity. London's judges did not share the police magistrates' animosity towards the legislation of 1869 and 1871, presumably because the higher courts, unlike the police courts, had not been established explicitly as a resource for the use of the working class.[57] In fact, several openly advocated the imposition of longer sentences for repeat offenders.[58] However, as we will see, they nonetheless did not universally accept that evidence of recidivism should lead to increasingly lengthy sentences. As Sir Henry Hawkins, a judge of the high court, noted, a 'diversity of opinion' was inevitable among any large group of people.[59] Virtually all judges, of course, were middle-aged or elderly, middle-class, public school- and Oxbridge-educated men, who had practised for many years as barristers in the same courts, while based in the London inns of court.[60] Nonetheless, while judges had few major class or ideological differences, those of personality and prejudice were only natural. Given the significant discretion they enjoyed, and the lack of a sentencing code or court of appeal, it is 'no matter for wonder' that the various opinions of judges concerning the punishment of repeat offenders translated into very different sentencing practices.[61]

Between 1871 and 1879 three judges presided at the Middlesex sessions: Edward Cox, for the duration of the period, William Bodkin, until 1874, and Peter Edlin, from 1874 onwards. Meanwhile, until 1878 the two permanent judges at the central criminal court, the recorder and the common sergeant, were Russell Gurney and Thomas Chambers. These judges had quite different views regarding the punishment of repeat offenders. Cox and Bodkin both advocated the imposition of long sentences of penal servitude for repeat offenders. In 1877 Cox wrote that 'penal servitude should be inflexibly awarded' to 'professional criminals', even if the most recent offence was not a serious one.[62]

---

[57] Davis, 'A Poor Man's System of Justice', p. 326.
[58] Sir Thomas Chambers, 'An Address on Punishment and Reformation', in *Transactions of the National Association for the Promotion of Social Science 1862*, London: John W. Parker and Son, 1863, pp. 45–58; Cox, *The Principles of Punishment*, p. 136.
[59] Harris (ed.), *The Reminiscences of Sir Henry Hawkins*, p. 367.
[60] D. Duman, *The Judicial Bench in England 1727–1875: The Reshaping of a Professional Elite*, London: Royal Historical Society, 1982, p. 80.
[61] Cox, *The Principles of Punishment*, p. 368.
[62] Ibid., p. 136.

This was because, in Cox's view, those who lived by crime were not capable of rehabilitation.[63] Newspaper reports, which often contained significantly more information than court records, show that Cox was true to his word.[64] In January 1875 Henry Duce came before him, charged with wounding two police constables. It was alleged that Duce had been acting in a disorderly fashion before being asked to move on from the City road by constable John King. He disobeyed this instruction and said, 'I will do for you,' before attacking King and then assaulting another constable. After several other convictions were proven against Duce he was sentenced to five years' penal servitude.[65] Press reports of the Middlesex sessions also demonstrate that Bodkin believed repeat offenders should often be given lengthy sentences of penal servitude. For example, in 1872 he sentenced William Jones to ten years' penal servitude for stealing a chest of tea worth 5 pounds. He did so after the police had proved several previous convictions.[66] In numerous other cases he imposed long sentences of penal servitude upon repeat offenders for seemingly minor crimes.[67] Peter Edlin took a different approach. While not entirely averse to imposing sentences of penal servitude, he did not rigidly hold that recidivists should be punished thus.[68] In 1875 one previously convicted thief was so happy at being sentenced to six months' imprisonment for the theft of a watch that she said, 'I can do that little lot upon my head.'[69] In addition, in 1876 Edlin sentenced Abraham Isaacson to twelve months' imprisonment for receiving stolen goods. The judge noted that Isaacson was 'guilty of a serious offence' and that he had been a receiver 'for some time'. Yet he accepted that the prisoner was contrite and, therefore, did not impose a sentence of penal servitude.[70] Given the perceived seriousness of the offence it is hard to believe that either Cox or Bodkin would have done likewise.[71]

---

[63] Ibid., pp. 135–48.
[64] Regarding the limited usefulness of English court records see J. M. Beattie, *Crime and the Courts in England, 1660–1800*, Oxford: Clarendon Press, 1986, p. 611.
[65] *Standard*, 7 Jan. 1875, p. 6.
[66] *Times*, 5 Nov. 1872, p. 9.
[67] See *Reynolds's Newspaper*, 22 Jan. 1871, p. 6; 13 Oct. 1872, p. 6; 24 Mar. 1874, p. 4; *Lloyd's Weekly Newspaper*, 26 Jan. 1873, p. 4.
[68] For examples of Edlin sentencing repeat offenders to penal servitude see *The Times*, 23 Apr. 1877, p. 11; 9 Mar. 1880, p. 4; 21 Dec. 1887, p. 6. For examples of repeat offenders being sentenced to periods of imprisonment see *Reynolds's Newspaper*, 9 Jan. 1887, p. 4; 27 Nov. 1887, p. 4; 9 Dec. 1888, p. 4; *Times*, 20 Jan. 1875, p. 11.
[69] *Times*, 20 Jan. 1875, p. 11.
[70] *Times*, 19 Aug. 1876, p. 11.
[71] For the seriousness with which receiving stolen goods was generally viewed see The Earl of Kimberley (Liberal), 194 *Parl. Deb.*, HL (3rd ser.), cols. 345–6 (26 February 1869); Arthur Morrison, *Child of the Jago*, 3rd ed., Woodbridge: The Boydell Press, 1982 (first published 1896), p. 124; *Standard*, 12 Oct. 1870, p. 4.

Judges at London's central criminal court, which heard London's most serious criminal cases – usually involving violence – also did not inflexibly believe that repeat offenders should receive increasingly lengthy sentences.[72] Gurney and Chambers held the two permanent judicial positions at the court until 1878. Both these men were members of parliament when the habitual criminals' legislation was debated, and both supported it. Chambers had also previously supported the notion that repeat offenders should receive harsher penalties than first offenders.[73] However, they also both spoke out against the clause in the *Habitual Criminals Bill 1869* that mandated a seven-year minimum sentence for repeat offenders on the grounds that it was overly harsh. Gurney, a Conservative, said that 'there would be many cases where … seven years would be too severe a sentence'.[74] Chambers, a Liberal and a member of the SSA, agreed with Gurney and presented parliament with a hypothetical case in which a young boy, due to poverty, stole several pieces of food over a period of years. Judges and juries, he believed, would 'shudder at the consequences' of convicting in such a case.[75] A survey of the sentences handed down by Gurney and Chambers in the 1870s confirms that they often imposed periods of penal servitude upon repeat offenders. They also often took circumstances into account, as Gurney had explained to the parliament in 1869, and passed shorter sentences of imprisonment upon recidivists.[76] Consequently, as Cox said, there was a marked diversity of opinion regarding the sentencing of repeat offenders: some judges held 'leniency, others severity, to be the best policy'.[77] A variety of opinion as to the value of long mandatory sentences was not unique to judges.[78] They were simply reflecting differing public and expert opinion. But, of course, judges were the ones who actually had to impose sentences. The different views of judges regarding

---

[72] For information regarding the sort of cases heard at the central criminal court see David Bentley, *English Criminal Justice in the Nineteenth Century*, London and Rio Grande: The Hambledon Press, 1988, pp. 55–6.
[73] Chambers, 'An Address on Punishment and Reformation', pp. 45–58.
[74] 198 *Parliamentary Debates*, HC (3rd ser.), col. 1278, 1276–8 (4 Aug. 1869).
[75] Ibid., col. 1262.
[76] For examples of sentences of penal servitude for repeat offenders see *The Times*, 21 Jan. 1871, p. 9; 2 May 1871, p. 1; 10 Jul. 1872, p. 11; 12 Jul. 1872, p. 11. For examples of sentences of imprisonment for repeat offenders see *The Times*, 27 Oct. 1871, p. 9; 24 Nov. 1871, p. 11.
[77] Cox, *The Principles of Punishment*, p. xii.
[78] For examples of those seeking harsher sentences see Lord Cleveland (Liberal), 194 *Parl. Deb.*, HL (3rd ser.), col. 712 (5 Mar. 1869); Henry Bruce (Liberal), 198 *Parliamentary Debates*, HC (3rd ser.), cols. 1251–60, 1276–8 (4 Aug. 1869) and 200 *Parl. Deb.*, HC (3rd ser.), col. 2134 (29 Apr. 1870); The Earl of Shaftesbury(Conservative), 194 *Parl. Deb.*, HL (3rd ser.), col. 1326 (15 Mar. 1869); *The Transportation of Criminals*, pp. 1–3; Baker, 'On the Theory and Practice of Sentences for Crime', p. 32. For examples of those who opposed long mandatory sentences see 'The Habitual Criminals Act', *Law Times*, vol. 47 (May–Oct. 1869), p. 323.

sentencing, which could be acted upon due to the wide discretion they enjoyed, presented an obstacle to the achievement of longer sentences for recidivists in London.

There were numerous reasons for the failure of the legislation of 1871 to effect a general increase in the severity of sentences for repeat offenders in London. The penal servitude acts commissioners, who reported to parliament in 1879, accepted that the sentencing of repeat offenders was not becoming more severe. In particular, they justifiably found that the seven-year minimum period of penal servitude for repeat offenders, 'although sound in principle, in so far as it aimed at securing that a severer punishment should be inflicted on persons convicted a second time of a serious crime, has failed in obtaining the object in view'.[79] Because of this finding the Conservative Home Secretary, Richard A. Cross, prepared a short bill that repealed the section of the *Penal Servitude Act 1864* that had stipulated a minimum period of seven years' penal servitude upon a second conviction for a felony.[80] Repeat offenders, like other criminals, could now be sentenced to either a period of two years or less in a local prison or five years or more in a penitentiary. This change was made in order to encourage judges to impose more sentences of penal servitude upon recidivists. It passed with bipartisan support in August 1879 and came into force on 1 September 1879. The next section will assess whether this change, along with the establishment of the CSO, led to longer sentences for repeat offenders in London.

*

There is no evidence that the sentences inflicted upon repeat offenders in London before 1880 had increased in length as the parliament had hoped. Indeed, sentences – in general – decreased in severity slightly. In 1879 a legislative change was made that reduced the gap between the maximum period of imprisonment and the minimum term of penal servitude. Did this provision achieve what the *Prevention of Crime Act 1871* had, hitherto, been unable to?

Firstly, there is evidence that magistrates continued to find ways to lessen the severity of the 1871 legislation even after the amendments that were made in 1879. In 1886 a Home Office memorandum was written by Godfrey Lushington, the permanent undersecretary, regarding the sentences imposed upon those

---

[79] *Report of the Commissioners Appointed to Inquire into the Working of the Penal Servitude Acts*, pp. xxxi–ii.
[80] *Prevention of Crime Act*, 42 & 43 Vict., 1879, c. 55, s. 1.

designated as habitual criminals.[81] His inquiries found that magistrates regularly acted to reduce the severity of the legislation when sentencing recidivists. For instance, a term of imprisonment of less than one year was normally the punishment for those found guilty of one of several offences listed in section 7.[82] These offences included gaining a livelihood by dishonest means, giving a false name to a magistrate and being found in any place 'about to commit … any offence'.[83] The commission of any of these offences violated the conditions outlined on tickets-of-leave, which were given to criminals when a portion of their sentence of penal servitude was remitted. So magistrates could revoke a criminal's licence upon conviction for any of these offences, which would result in their return to prison for the remainder of their initial term of penal servitude.[84] Nonetheless, the Home Office found that magistrates never sent criminals back to penal servitude for committing these offences.[85] As they had done regarding both registration and supervision, magistrates therefore acted to reduce the harshness of the law, sentencing those in receipt of a licence to lesser periods of incarceration than the *Prevention of Crime Act 1871* allowed.

There is also much anecdotal evidence that repeat offenders in London, far more often than not, continued to be sentenced to periods of imprisonment rather than lengthier terms of penal servitude. Many members of the Metropolitan Police Force and numerous London prison officials expressed this view in the 1890s. Discussion of the sentencing practices of judges and the proper extent of judicial discretion increased in the 1890s as a result of the controversial statements and sentences of Charles Hopwood, the recorder of Liverpool since 1886, who advocated short periods of imprisonment for repeat offenders.[86] Both houses of parliament, in 1889 and then 1890, debated Hopwood's approach and the broader issue of inequality in sentencing.[87] Then in 1892 the council of judges, which had been established through the *Judicature Act 1873* to investigate defects in the administration of the law, was asked by Lord Herschell, the Lord Chancellor in the new Gladstone government and the instigator of the debate in the Lords in 1890, to inquire into how inequality in sentencing might

---

[81] Godfrey Lushington, Memorandum: 'Irregular Sentences under Section 5 and 7 of the *Prevention of Crime Act 1871*', 25 Oct. 1886, TNA, HO 45/9658/A41414/1, p. 1.
[82] *Prevention of Crime Act*, 1871, s. 7.
[83] Ibid.
[84] Ibid., s. 5; Lushington, Memorandum: 'Irregular Sentences under Section 5 and 7 of the *Prevention of Crime Act 1871*', p. 1.
[85] Circular, 10 Jan. 1887, TNA, HO 45/9658/A41414/2, p. 1.
[86] Thomas, *Constraints on Judgement*, p. 67.
[87] 336 *Parl. Deb.*, HC (3rd ser.), cols. 1002–56 (24 May 1889); 343 *Parl. Deb.*, HL (3rd ser.), cols. 924–55 (21 Apr. 1890).

be reduced.[88] The council reported in 1894, acknowledging 'a great diversity in the sentences passed by different Courts in respect of sentences of the same kind', and recommended the establishment of a court of appeal.[89] These debates and the inquiry, which came about as a consequence of the sentencing practices of Hopwood, gave, as D. A. Thomas has said, 'a renewed vigour to the discussion of disparity of sentences throughout the 1890s'.[90] The assertion that magistrates and judges rarely took previous convictions into account in sentencing featured heavily in this discussion. As noted in Chapter 3, in 1895 a parliamentary committee that had been established to inquire into the state of Britain's prisons reported that it had 'repeatedly' heard police officers complain that '[i]t is in vain for us to exert ourselves to discover the history of offenders, if no difference is to be made between a hardened criminal and a first offender' in sentencing.[91] Several prison officials in London made similar objections to the sentencing practices of the police magistrates. J. B. Manning, the governor of London's Pentonville prison, said that magistrates did not 'trouble about previous convictions'. When asked directly if they 'ignore previous convictions', he agreed that they often did.[92] Given the attitude of London's police magistrates to the habitual criminals' legislation it seems that Manning's statement was correct. Captain Helby, the governor of London's Wandsworth prison, and Colonel Garcia, the Home Office's prisons inspector, also argued that previous convictions were generally not taken into consideration by magistrates and judges. The latter said that 'the present system of giving short sentences to habitual criminals works ... very badly'.[93] This was the case, these officials argued, as short sentences did not deter or reform recidivists, who simply emerged from jail after a short period to commit further crimes.[94] In short, many policemen and prison officials in London were convinced that short sentences of imprisonment were the usual punishment for the capital's repeat offenders due to the failure of magistrates and judges to take evidence of previous convictions into account.

Numerous other informed sources also bemoaned the purported failure of magistrates and judges to ensure that those with former convictions were sentenced to periods of penal servitude. In 1890 the central committee of

---

[88] Thomas, *Constraints on Judgement*, p. 67.
[89] Quoted in *The Times*, 6 Aug. 1892, p. 10.
[90] Thomas, *Constraints on Judgement*, p. 67.
[91] *Prisons Committee: Report from the Departmental Committee on Prisons*, [C 7702] HC 1895, lvi, p. 15.
[92] Ibid., p. 44.
[93] Ibid., pp. 142, 217.
[94] Ibid., pp. 15, 44, 142, 217.

discharged prisoners' aid societies said that short sentences for recidivists were 'a public scandal'.[95] This committee had been established in 1863 in order to coordinate the activities of London's prisoners' aid societies and liaise with government.[96] In a letter to the editor of *The Times* the honorary chairman of the committee, Thomas Murray Browne, who was Barwick Baker's nephew, argued that there was a 'mass of evidence' that repeat offenders 'received repeated short sentences'.[97] Instead, Browne called for progressively lengthy periods of penal servitude for recidivists, as his uncle had done previously. The leadership of London's Elizabeth Fry women's refuge, the Howard Association and the St. Giles' Christian mission shared similar sentiments.[98] It was claimed that repeat offenders were routinely given short sentences, which neither enabled the reformation of the offender nor the deterrence of others. Long sentences of penal servitude, these sources claimed, enabled criminals the time to reflect upon their previous misdeeds and to develop a Christian faith, leading to their rehabilitation. Lengthy periods of incarceration were also dreaded by criminals. They therefore acted, claimed the sources, as a deterrent to crime. Consequently, the consistent imposition of long sentences of penal servitude was sought.[99] In the 1890s numerous letter writers to *The Times* also criticized the perceived leniency of sentences for repeat offenders. Many sentences, it was argued, were so short that they caused 'astonishment' among the police and left criminals 'laughing'.[100] This 'craze' for short sentences was thought to be due either to the despair of magistrates, who felt all options had already been tried and failed, or to significant differences of opinion on the bench regarding the sentencing of recidivists.[101] In 1892 Sir Walter Crofton, the director of Irish prisons who had been so influential in the drafting of the 1869 legislation, urged magistrates and judges to 'protect society' by inflicting lengthier 'punishment for persistence in crime'.[102] Finally, some London magistrates and judges criticized their colleagues for not giving due weight to previous convictions in their sentencing. Ralph Littler, a judge of the Middlesex sessions, and Westminster magistrate John Sheil

---

[95] *Times*, 4 Feb. 1890, p. 14.
[96] Sean McConville, *English Local Prisons, 1860–1900: Next Only to Death*, London: Routledge, 1995, p. 322.
[97] *Times*, 4 Feb. 1890, p. 14.
[98] See the comments of Miss Fry, William Wheatley and William Tallack in the report of the *Prisons Committee*, pp. 183, 233, 245.
[99] Ibid., pp. 183, 233, 245; *Times*, 4 Feb. 1890, p. 14.
[100] F. C. Pawle, letter to the editor of *The Times*, 6 Dec. 1892, p. 3.
[101] A. C. P., letter to the editor of *The Times*, 1 Nov. 1892, p. 13; Sir Walter Crofton, letter to the editor of *The Times*, 10 Nov. 1892, p. 3; Quarter Sess., letter to the editor of *The Times*, 25 Jan. 1890, p. 7.
[102] Sir Walter Crofton, letter to the editor of *The Times*, 10 Nov. 1892, p. 3.

Table 5.2 Sentences of penal servitude in London, including as a percentage of all those convicted, 1870–3 and 1893–5

	1870	1871	1872	1873	1893	1894	1895
Total convictions	46,193	48,265	54,928	52,851	60,528	62,372	60,858
Sentences of five years to life imprisonment	603 (1.3)	510 (1.1)	441 (0.8)	451 (0.9)	383 (0.6)	379 (0.6)	340 (0.6)
Sentences of seven years or more	446 (1.0)	381 (0.8)	321 (0.6)	312 (0.6)	62 (0.1)	49 (0.01)	29 (0.01)

Report of the Commissioner of Police of the Metropolis, 1871, p. 26; *Report of the Commissioner of Police of the Metropolis*, 1872, p. 18; *Report of the Commissioner of Police of the Metropolis, 1872*, 1874, p. 21; *Report of the Commissioner of Police of the Metropolis, 1873*, 1874, p. 26; *Report of the Commissioner of Police of the Metropolis: For the Year 1893*, [C 7556] HC 1894, xlii, pp. 58–9; *Report of the Commissioner of Police of the Metropolis: For the Year 1894*, [C 7890] HC 1895, lv, pp. 56–7; *Report of the Commissioner of Police of the Metropolis: For the Year 1895*, [C 8199] HC 1896, xlii, pp. 44, 58–9.

both did so in the 1890s, with the former objecting to what he believed was the norm of imposing 'short sentences' upon repeat offenders.[103] Therefore, of those with a knowledge of sentencing practices there was a consensus that a short period of imprisonment, rather than a lengthy term of penal servitude, remained the usual punishment for repeat offenders in London.

The available data suggests that the views expressed above were well founded and that, in fact, fewer repeat offenders in London were being sentenced to long periods of incarceration between 1880 and 1895 than had previously been the case. Figures regarding the types of sentences imposed upon those convicted were included in the annual reports of the commissioner of the Metropolitan Police Force for the years 1893, 1894 and 1895, and are tabulated below, along with the available figures from the 1870s.

This data shows that London's judges were imposing far fewer long sentences than they had in the first years following the passage of the Gladstone government's habitual criminals' legislation. In 1870, 603 convicted criminals in London received sentences of penal servitude, of which five years was the minimum. By the 1890s both the number and proportion of sentences of five years or more had dropped significantly. Despite significant growth in the total number of convictions, the number of sentences of five years or more decreased to 340 in 1895. The number of offenders being sentenced to long periods of seven years' penal servitude or more also decreased markedly, from 446 in 1870 to only

[103] *Reynolds's Newspaper*, 8 Jan. 1893, p. 8; 28 Jan. 1894, p. 8.

29 in 1895. This data does not solely relate to repeat offenders. However, other data shows that around 50 per cent of those who came before London's higher courts in the late nineteenth century were repeat offenders.[104] Therefore, such a large decrease in the imposition of long sentences of penal servitude in general clearly indicates a significant reduction in the use of this punishment upon London's recidivists. One reason for the declining use of long sentences was that proportionally fewer criminals charged with serious crimes were being brought before the courts. For example, the number of felonies relating to property each year, and serious crimes against the person – such as murder and manslaughter – fell significantly between 1871 and 1895 as a proportion of all convictions.[105] This was one reason why between 1871 and 1895 London's magistrates referred increasingly fewer defendants to the higher courts for trial. In 1871, of all those brought before the magistrates, 5 per cent were committed for trial. But by 1895 this figure had fallen, statistically significantly, to 3.7 per cent.[106] Defendants were being brought before the courts, convicted of less serious crimes and sentenced to shorter periods in jail. Yet sentences for crimes that were often carried out by repeat offenders decreased in duration between 1871 and 1895. Of those convicted in London of larceny from the person, which included pickpocketing, 16 per cent were sentenced to five years' penal servitude or more in 1873, falling to only 0.34 per cent in 1894. Meanwhile, in 1873, 19 per cent of receivers of stolen goods, who were widely believed to facilitate much habitual criminality, were sentenced five years' penal servitude or more, declining to 2 per cent in 1894.[107] Both these decreases are statistically significant. Habitual criminals in London were therefore being sentenced to shorter, not longer, periods of incarceration.

Evidence suggests that the decreasing severity of sentences was not confined to London. Data contained in the annual volumes of judicial statistics shows

---

[104] *Report of a Committee Appointed by the Secretary of State to Inquire into the Best Means Available for Identifying Habitual Criminals*, p. 72. Also see numerous examples of court reports in which the status of defendants, either (alleged) first offender or repeat offender, is noted. See *The Times*, 9 Mar. 1880, p. 4; 21 Dec. 1887, p. 6; *Reynolds's Newspaper*, 9 Jan. 1887, p. 4; 27 Nov. 1887, p. 4; 9 Dec. 1888, p. 4.

[105] *Report of the Commissioner of Police of the Metropolis*, 1894, pp. 4–5; *Report of the Commissioner of Police of the Metropolis*, 1895, p. 5.

[106] *Report of the Commissioner of Police of the Metropolis*, 1872, p. 11; *Report of the Commissioner of Police of the Metropolis*, 1896, p. 44.

[107] *Report of the Commissioner of Police of the Metropolis*, 1874, pp. 17, 20; *Report of the Commissioner of Police of the Metropolis*, 1895, pp. 54–8. For the linkages between picking pockets, receiving stolen goods and habitual criminality see The Earl of Kimberley (Liberal), 194 *Parl. Deb.*, HL (3rd ser.), col. 338 (26 Feb. 1869); Patrick Colquhoun, *A Treatise on the Police of the Metropolis*, London: Patterson Smith, 1795, p. 4; Morrison, *Child of the Jago*, p. 124; *Standard*, 12 Oct. 1870, p. 4.

that the proportion of longer sentences decreased significantly from 1871 to 1895 across England and Wales.[108] Statistics compiled by Gatrell also indicate that sentences became more lenient over time. He found that across Britain 12 per cent of those convicted of a felony or malicious wounding were sentenced to penal servitude in 1871. This figure fell to 9 per cent by 1895.[109] Sentences of penal servitude, while becoming less common, were also becoming less severe. Between 1883 and 1894 the proportion of those guilty of indictable offences and sentenced to a period of ten years' penal servitude or more fell from 1.5 per cent to 0.6 per cent.[110] Again, these reductions are statistically significant. Thus, the Home Office was correct in noting that 'there has been a tendency to reduction in the amount of sentence', which was most significant 'in the longer sentences of penal servitude'.[111] This 'undeniable' tendency, it was argued with good cause, was 'very marked'.[112] Increasing leniency was being shown in sentencing, not only in London, but across England and Wales.

There were other factors influencing the trend towards greater leniency in the sentencing of recidivists during 1880–95, in addition to magistrates' resistance to lengthy mandatory sentences. The rise of the so-called Italian school of criminology is one.[113] According to *The Times*, a key reason for the trend towards shorter sentences was the emergence of what it called 'modern controversies' about the causes of crime. As the newspaper said, and as noted in previous chapters, prior to the final two decades of the nineteenth century there had been a widely 'accepted opinion' that crime was primarily the result of the free choices of the criminal.[114] However, the Italian psychiatrist Cesare Lombroso was largely responsible for popularizing the notion of the born criminal, primarily through his work of 1876, *Criminal Man*.[115] He argued that those who repeatedly broke the law did not do so as a result of free choice but rather bad heredity. Repeat

---

[108] *Judicial Statistics, England and Wales, 1894. Part I – Criminal Statistics*, [C 8072] HC 1896, xciv, pp.14, 17.
[109] V. A. C. Gatrell, 'The Decline of Theft and Violence in Victorian and Edwardian England', in V. A. C. Gatrell, Bruce Lehman and Geoffrey Parker (eds.), *Crime and the Law: The Social History of Crime in Western Europe since 1500*, London: Europa Publications, 1980, p. 368.
[110] *Judicial Statistics, England and Wales*, 1896, p. 16.
[111] *Judicial Statistics, England and Wales*, 1895, p. 78.
[112] Home Office memorandum, 'Standard Sentences in Criminal Cases', 1899, quoted in Thomas, *Constraints on Judgement*, p. 34; *Judicial Statistics, England and Wales*, 1896, pp. 14, 17.
[113] Daniel Pick, *Faces of Degeneration: A European Disorder, c. 1848–c. 1918*, Cambridge: Cambridge University Press, 1989, p. 17.
[114] *Times*, 17 Dec. 1894, p. 9; Pick, *Faces of Degeneration*, p. 17; J. J. Tobias, *Crime and Industrial Society in the Nineteenth Century*, London: B. T. Batsford, 1967, p. 59; Cox, *The Principles of Punishment*, p. 142; *Times*, 17 Dec. 1894, p. 9.
[115] Cesare Lombroso, *Criminal Man*, Mary Gibson and Nicole Hahn Rafter (trans. and ed.), London: Duke University Press, 2006 (first published 1876), p. 51.

offenders could not be held fully responsible for their crimes, as they were the result of degenerate stock.[116] As shown in Chapter 3, Lombrosian ideas were highly influential in Britain, particularly in the last two decades of the nineteenth century.[117] As some magistrates and judges came to believe that recidivists were not fully responsible for their crimes, they responded by inflicting less severe punishments than had been imposed previously. Newspaper reports of some decisions by London judges, which will be discussed below, show that this was the case in certain instances.[118]

Some magistrates and judges also felt greater leniency was a rational response to a declining crime rate. The official figures show that crime rates declined significantly between 1871 and 1895, both in London and elsewhere in Britain. This trend was revealed in the annual reports of the commissioner of the Metropolitan Police Force and in the volumes of judicial statistics. In London recorded felonies relating to property fell from 4.4 per 1,000 people in 1871 to 2.9 in 1895, while offences against the person dropped from 7.5 per 100,000 people in 1871 to 7.2 in 1895.[119] The judicial statistics for England and Wales also show that during this period recorded crime per capita decreased markedly.[120] Numerous historians, while recognizing the many problems one encounters when attempting to interpret criminal statistics, believe that crime, in actual fact, did decrease in Britain during the latter half of the nineteenth century.[121] As V. A. C. Gatrell and Martin Weiner, among others, have shown, this was due to a variety of factors, including improved education levels and the declining acceptance of violence to settle disputes.[122] Some magistrates and judges responded to the decreasing crime rate by imposing more lenient sentences, as they believed it was now less important to deter criminals through the imposition of harsh punishments. This was the view of the Home Office, which, in 1895, said, 'The

---

[116] Pick, *Faces of Degeneration*, p. 17; Lombroso, *Criminal Man*, p. 51.
[117] David Taylor, 'Beyond the Bounds of Respectable Society: The "Dangerous Classes" in Victorian and Edwardian England', in Judith Rowbotham and Kim Stevenson (eds.), *Criminal Conversations: Victorian Crimes, Social Panic and Moral Outrage*, Columbus: Ohio State University Press, 2005, pp. 16, 47; Rev. Osborne Jay, 'The East End and Crime', *Public Opinion*, 26 Oct.1894, p. 517; Taylor, 'Beyond the Bounds of Respectable Society', p. 16. Also see the comments of Reverend G. Merrick, chaplain of London's Holloway and Newgate gaols in the report of the *Prisons Committee*, p. 58.
[118] *Reynolds's Newspaper*, 9 Jan. 1887, p. 4; *Times*, 3 May 1892, p. 4.
[119] *Report of the Commissioner of Police of the Metropolis*, 1896, pp. 45–6.
[120] *Judicial Statistics, England and Wales*, 1895, pp. 18–9.
[121] Phillip Smith, *Policing Victorian London*, London: Greenwood Press, 1985, p. 207; Yue-Chim Richard Wong, 'An Economic Analysis of the Crime Rate in England and Wales, 1857–1892', *Economica*, vol. 62, no. 246 (May 1995), p. 245.
[122] Gatrell, 'The Decline of Theft and Violence in Victorian and Edwardian England', pp. 238–337; Martin Wiener, *Men of Blood: Violence, Manliness and Criminal Justice in Victorian England*, Cambridge: Cambridge University Press, 2004, p. 289.

knowledge that crime is diminishing encourages judges and magistrates to deal with crime more leniently.'[123] Some judges openly admitted as much. In 1885 the lord chief justice, Lord Coleridge, said that he, and several other judges, accepted the logic that the severity of sentences should be mitigated in response to the decreasing recorded rate of crime. With the threat of crime receding, he believed sentences could be further reduced 'without detriment to the administration of the criminal law'.[124] Sir Henry Hawkins also said that judges reduced the severity of their sentences when the crime rate fell.[125] As Gatrell found regarding the end of public executions, 'humane feelings prevail when their costs in terms of security ... are bearable'.[126] J. M. Beattie has also argued that changes in the incidence of crime influenced sentencing in this way.[127] Thus, for some London magistrates and judges, 'humane feelings' towards repeat offenders prevailed as a result of the declining rate of recorded crime.[128]

As was the case in the 1870s, between 1880 and 1895 there is evidence that London's judges disagreed regarding the appropriate punishment of repeat offenders. The actions of numerous judges who did not believe that repeat offenders should routinely receive increasingly lengthy sentences also contributed to the tendency to greater leniency. From 1880 to 1895 five judges presided at the Middlesex sessions: Peter Edlin, until 1889; John Dunnington Fletcher, from 1879 to 1889; Samuel Prentice, between 1880 and 1884; and Ralph Littler and Richard Loveland Loveland, both from 1889. From 1880 onwards there is evidence that, as previously, Edlin often did not sentence repeat offenders to periods of penal servitude. In 1887 he sentenced James Davis, who had broken into a dwelling house and stolen 30 pounds worth of goods, to fourteen months' imprisonment, despite the fact that he had been 'many times convicted'.[129] The few reports of trials conducted by John Dunnington Fletcher suggest that his disposition towards repeat offenders was harsher. He sentenced John Bowen, who had previously been convicted for theft, to five years' penal servitude and three years' supervision for stealing 1 pound from a man in 1882.[130] And Mary Dawson, another repeat offender, also received five years' penal servitude

---

[123] *Judicial Statistics, England and Wales*, 1895, p. 80.
[124] Lord Coleridge, lord chief justice of England, to Lord Cairns, the Lord Chancellor, 26 Mar. 1885, reproduced in Thomas, *Constraints on Judgement*, p. 61.
[125] Harris (ed.), *The Reminiscences of Sir Henry Hawkins*, p. 369.
[126] V. A. C. Gatrell, *The Hanging Tree: Execution and the People of England, 1770–1868*, Oxford and New York: Oxford University Press, 1994, p. 12.
[127] Beattie, *Crime and the Courts in England*, p. 14.
[128] Gatrell, *The Hanging Tree*, p. 12.
[129] *Reynolds's Newspaper*, 9 Jan. 1887, p. 4.
[130] *Morning Post*, 12 Jan. 1882, p. 6.

from Fletcher, this time for stealing only 8 shillings. She clearly believed the punishment was overly harsh, as she reportedly tried to assault a warder as she was escorted from the court.[131] Prentice had a more merciful disposition towards repeat offenders. For instance, in 1880 he heard the case of Charles Downs, who had been arrested for stealing cloth from a dealer and, during the trial, was proven to have been convicted four times before, including for the very serious crime of forgery. Prentice said he 'hesitated whether it was not his duty to send Downs into penal servitude, but he would give him one more chance', and sentenced him to twenty months' imprisonment.[132] Presumably it was because of sentences such as this that the *Biograph and Review,* a short-lived biographical magazine, commended Prentice for his 'very fair' rulings.[133] Fletcher would indeed have found it his duty to sentence Downs to a period of penal servitude.

On the retirement of Fletcher and Edlin in 1889, two more judges were appointed to preside at the Middlesex sessions who, once again, had quite different views on the sentencing of repeat offenders. Ralph Littler advocated lengthy sentences of penal servitude for recidivists and was often criticized for his severity. In 1894 he informed the court that his policy was to impose 'long sentences on habitual offenders', and Littler acted on this view.[134] Arthur Harding, the leader of an East End gang, confirmed that Littler was true to his word. He said that his gang

> never used to go to Hampstead Heath. That was because it was in Middlesex and the judge at Middlesex Sessions – Sir Ralph Littler – was the hottest judge in England ... He gave a man 14 years for breaking a window and stealing a bottle of whiskey. He said he would make Middlesex so safe that a man could hang his watch and chain on a lamp post and nobody would take it.[135]

Interestingly, Harding's comments suggest that harsh sentences did in fact act as a deterrent – if not to crime in total, then at least to crime in certain areas. Littler's long sentences for repeat offenders were also criticized in parliament, and in one of his obituaries it was noted that he would often 'impose heavy sentences on habitual criminals'.[136] However, Loveland Loveland appeared to have a different view. He regularly did not impose sentences of penal servitude

---

[131] *Reynolds's Newspaper*, 11 Jan. 1885, p. 2.
[132] *Times*, 8 Jan. 1880, p. 11.
[133] 'Samuel Prentice Q.C.', *Biograph and Review*, vol. 5 (1881), p. 37.
[134] *Reynolds's Newspaper*, 8 Jul. 1894, p. 4.
[135] Raphael Samuel, *East End Underworld: The Life of Arthur Harding*, London: Routledge and Kegan Paul, 1981, p. 76.
[136] John Ward (Liberal) and Will Thorne (Labour), 194 *Parl. Deb.*, HC (3rd ser.), col. 1357 (22 Oct. 1908); 'Sir Ralph Littler', *Scots Law Times*, vol. 16, part 2 (1909), p. 138.

upon repeat offenders. In many instances he sentenced recidivists who had been convicted on multiple occasions to periods of imprisonment.[137] The judges at the Middlesex sessions therefore continued to have differing views about the sentencing of repeat offenders.

Likewise, judges at the central criminal court embraced quite different sentencing practices. From 1878 until 1891 Thomas Chambers was recorder, at which point Charles Hall was appointed, and William Thomas Charley was common sergeant until 1892, when Forrest Fulton was appointed to the position. These judges were also members of parliament, all bar Chambers as Conservatives, and Charley and Chambers were members of the SSA. Newspaper reports of cases at which they presided show that Hall and Fulton generally imposed harsher penalties upon recidivists than Charley and Chambers, whose approach to sentencing has been discussed above. Numerous examples could be cited of the former two judges punishing recidivists more harshly than first offenders.[138] In 1893 Fulton sentenced Joseph Riley and Charles Turner to ten years' penal servitude for being in possession of counterfeit coins, while Walter Closier, who was indicted along with the others, received three years. The only difference between Closier and the others, according to the newspaper report, was that they had previously been convicted.[139] Reports suggest Charley was more lenient. In 1892 Charley sentenced the convicted coiner Alfred Phillips to three years' penal servitude, even though he had previously served a sentence of five years' duration for the same offence.[140] In other cases Charley also imposed more lenient sentences upon repeat offenders than they had previously received.[141] The impression that Hall and Fulton were more severe than Charley is corroborated by some contemporary commentary regarding these judges. In its obituaries for the former two judges *The Times* said that their sentences were often overly harsh. Hall, according to the newspaper, imposed periods of penal servitude that were 'unduly severe', while Fulton also erred on the 'side of severity'.[142] Meanwhile, Charley was criticized by the *Belfast News-Letter* for passing sentences that were perceived to be too lenient. The newspaper said that his sentences made a 'mockery of justice'.[143] As was the case

---

[137] *Times*, 4 Jan. 1890, p. 12; 11 Apr. 1892, p. 4; 9 Jan. 1893, p. 13; 29 May 1893, p. 3; *Reynolds's Newspaper*, 17 Apr. 1892, p. 1.
[138] For example see *The Times*, 10 Jan. 1893, p. 11; 14 Jan. 1896, p. 9.
[139] *Times*, 11 Apr. 1893, p. 12.
[140] *Times*, 3 May 1892, p. 4.
[141] *Times*, 26 Jul. 1892, p. 12.
[142] *Times*, 10 Mar. 1900, p. 13; 27 Jun. 1925, p. 16.
[143] *Belfast News-Letter*, 1 Aug. 1892, p. 5.

at the Middlesex sessions, numerous long sentences of penal servitude were inflicted upon repeat offenders at the central criminal court between 1880 and 1895. Yet the length of these sentences generally decreased over time, at least in part, because judges had differing views regarding the sentencing of repeat offenders.

Another noteworthy factor is that from 1880 to 1895 registration and police supervision remained less effective in London than the Gladstone government had hoped. This meant that much evidence about offenders, which may have led to the imposition of lengthier sentences, was not available to magistrates and judges. The various registers of habitual criminals were lengthy, inexact, cumbersome and time-consuming to utilize.[144] Regarding police supervision, the *Prevention of Crime Act 1879* meant that monthly reporting could be enforced in London.[145] However, it remained the case that those subject to police supervision were often not monitored closely. From its inception in 1880 the CSO, which was responsible for supervision in London, focused more on the provision of employment opportunities for licence-holders and repeat offenders than their surveillance.[146] As a result, much criminal behaviour went unrecorded. It is also probable that those subject to supervision were often not monitored closely by the police for fear of enabling the discovery of the individual's criminal past by their employer or associates.[147] For these reasons registration and police supervision rarely yielded useful information to magistrates and judges about any further lawbreaking by recidivists, which may have led to longer sentences.

*

In London the habitual criminals' legislation of 1869 and 1871 did not lead to longer sentences for repeat offenders. In fact, from 1880 to 1895 the average length of sentences imposed upon recidivists in London decreased significantly. There are several reasons for this. Firstly, police magistrates in London were careful not to alienate their working-class clientele and, as a response, acted to mitigate the severity of the habitual criminals' legislation in numerous ways. Secondly, while numerous judges in London often sentenced repeat offenders

---

[144] *Report of a Committee Appointed by the Secretary of State to Inquire into the Best Means Available for Identifying Habitual Criminals*, p. 11.
[145] *Prevention of Crime Act*, 1879, s. 2.
[146] James Monro, 'A Report of the History of the Department of the Metropolitan Police Known as the Convict Supervision Office: Detailing System, and Showing Results and Effects Generally on the Habitual Criminal Population', 1886, TNA, HO 144/184/A5507, p. 9.
[147] Charles Clarkson and J. Hall Richardson, *Police!*, New York and London: Garland Publishing, 1984 (first published 1889), p. 356.

to long periods of penal servitude, others did not accept that recidivists should be subject to harsher punishments than had previously been the case and could act on their views due to the great discretion judges enjoyed. The failure of registration and police supervision to fully achieve the objectives of the parliament also meant that magistrates and judges often did not have access to full information regarding the criminal past of defendants. As a consequence, police magistrates and judges in London did not impose longer sentences on habitual criminals. Finally, the wide acceptance of Lombrosian criminology and a declining rate of recorded crime also contributed to a reduction in the severity of sentences for repeat offenders.

However, a number of historians have claimed, inaccurately, that the Gladstone government's habitual criminals' legislation led to sentences for recidivists that were increasingly harsh.[148] Most of these historians were influenced by the concept of social control.[149] This framework has not proven to be a useful analytical tool in this case. As Wiener has noted, social control interpretations of responses to crime in the nineteenth century have often asserted the existence of an 'ever-expanding "carceral archipelago"', with more and more members of the working class becoming subject to long periods of incarceration.[150] The evidence in London does not bear this notion out. In addition, the misconception that magistrates and judges consistently acted in keeping with the desires of the parliament has been allowed to persist as a feature of the literature concerning the acts of 1869 and 1871 due to limited research on sentencing practices in this period.[151] On the contrary, it is clear that these acts failed to produce longer periods of incarceration for London's repeat criminal offenders.

---

[148] Godfrey, Cox and Farrall, *Serious Offenders*, pp. 161–77; Petrow, *Policing Morals*, p. 51; Johnston, *Crime in England*, p. 36.
[149] A. P. Donajgrodzki (ed.), *Social Control in Nineteenth Century Britain*, London: Croom Helm, 1977, p. 9.
[150] Martin Wiener, 'The March of Penal Progress?' *Journal of British Studies*, vol. 26, no. 1 (Jan. 1987), p. 87.
[151] Duman, *The Judicial Bench in England 1727–1875*, p. viii; Martin Wiener, 'Judges v. Jurors: Courtroom Tension in Murder Trials and the Law of Criminal Responsibility in Nineteenth-Century England', *Law and History Review*, vol. 17, no. 3 (Aug. 1999), pp. 470–1.

Conclusion

There are few more persistent calls in debates about penal policy than those urging more severe treatment of repeat offenders. These calls are heard right around the world. At Australia's 2016 election the former radio shock jock Derryn Hinch won a seat in the Senate after forming his Justice Party shortly before the poll. His limited manifesto included policies to 'name and shame' sex offenders by making the sex offenders' register public, strengthen the supervisory powers of the state over those who had been released from prison on parole and increase the length of sentences imposed upon repeat offenders. 'Dangerous recidivist violent offenders', Hinch said, 'ought to be behind bars'. His policies gained significant public support following the brutal rape and murder of Jill Meagher by Adrian Bayley in one of Melbourne's inner suburbs in 2012. Bayley was a parolee with a long criminal record, including other convictions for rape and assault. Thus Hinch could justify his tough policies quite reasonably in the eyes of many Australians by arguing that '[i]t's just common sense'. Knowledge of the course of British penal policy in the 1850s and 1860s makes it unsurprising that support for repressive measures continues. But an understanding of legislation designed to suppress the criminal class in the mid- and late Victorian period should also lead us to be sceptical of the specific measures advocated by Hinch in Australia and countless other organs of the press, pressure groups and politicians in any number of other countries. This is despite the fact that many mid- and late Victorians undoubtedly came to think that the measures contained in the *Habitual Criminals Act 1869* and the *Prevention of Crime Act 1871* were 'just common sense'.[1]

The aim of this book has been to analyse the reasons for the introduction of the habitual criminals' legislation of 1869 and 1871 and assess its effectiveness

---

[1] 'Justice in Sentencing' and 'Parole Reform', https://www.justiceparty.com.au/our-policies/ (accessed 22 Dec. 2017).

in London before 1896. It has shown, firstly, that the Social Science Association (SSA) played a pivotal role in influencing the government to introduce the *Habitual Criminals Bill* into parliament in February 1869 and, secondly, that the impact of the acts of 1869 and 1871 was far more limited than members of parliament had hoped. Clearly, most historians who have studied these acts have misunderstood the reasons for their passage and exaggerated their impact. These findings raise serious doubts about the adequacy of our current understanding of the reasons for the introduction of other social legislation. They also bring into question prevailing views about the outcomes of other government measures introduced during the mid- and late Victorian periods that were, like the Gladstone government's habitual criminals' legislation, intended to control the working class.

The 1869 and 1871 acts resulted from major changes in Britain's penal system. The ending of transportation to the Australian colonies, which began in 1840 and was completed in 1868, precipitated alarm throughout the UK that a large body of offenders, who previously would have been deposited in Australia, were now to be released at home on the expiry of these sentences. There was fear that many of these offenders were recidivists: members of a professional criminal class who were habituated to a life of crime.[2] The *Habitual Criminals Act 1869* was, as the government acknowledged, a response to the ending of transportation and the consequent increase in the number of criminals being released into the community at home.[3]

The Gladstone government's habitual criminals' legislation was intended to regulate and restrain licence-holders and repeat offenders through registration, supervision and more severe sentencing. These acts were more than mere hasty responses to newspaper-inspired moral panics about an imagined criminal class, as some historians have suggested. On the contrary, they reflected a detailed penal reform agenda developed from the mid-1850s onwards by leading members of the SSA, an agenda that enjoyed considerable support in parliament and especially among the ranks of the Liberal Party. Since its establishment in 1857 the SSA had consistently advocated for a register of criminals, police supervision of repeat offenders, and a strict and deterrent sentencing regime for members of the criminal class.[4] These measures, due to the group's great

---

[2] *Times*, 14 Aug. 1862, p. 8; *Daily News*, 2 Dec. 1862, p. 4.
[3] The Earl of Kimberley (Liberal), 194 *Parl. Deb.*, HL (3rd ser.), cols. 335, 338 (26 Feb. 1869).
[4] For example see Matthew Davenport Hill, *Papers on the Penal Servitude Acts: And on the Regulations of the Home Department for Carrying Them into Execution*, London: Longman, Green, Longman, Roberts and Green, 1864, p. 3.

influence, formed the core of the 1869 act. As a consequence of the strong links between the government and the SSA, the association was able to influence Henry Bruce, the home secretary, to introduce the *Habitual Criminals Bill* into parliament in February 1869. The legislation, therefore, was a triumph for the SSA, demonstrating the political influence of the organization. This begs the question: has the role of pressure groups, or other extra-parliamentary groupings, in the formation of other mid- and late Victorian social measures been misunderstood and underappreciated by historians? It certainly has been in this case.

The acts did not achieve what their framers and supporters had originally hoped. There were a variety of reasons for this failure, some involving problems with the provisions of the acts themselves, but others involving those called upon to enforce the acts. Firstly, numerous amendments were made to the 1869 act, which had to be rushed through given that parliament was very shortly to rise.[5] These changes, which were significant, substantially reduced the severity of the legislation and contained several important drafting errors. Consequently, major problems became obvious shortly after the legislation came into force. In particular, amendments to the two principal provisions of the legislation, registration and police supervision, reduced the effectiveness of the act in London. London's police magistrates also often refused to fully enforce the legislation, as they would continue to do until 1895. The government acknowledged that the legislation had been largely ineffective and repealed it in 1871, re-enacting its key measures through the *Prevention of Crime Act 1871*.[6]

Despite the new legislation, from 1871 to 1895 the numerous registers of habitual criminals were less useful than had been hoped by the parliament. While the registry was intended to ensure repeat offenders were recognized as such, prior to the 1890s the registry was rarely used by members of the Metropolitan Police Force.[7] Even when it was, few recidivists were identified in this way. There were two principal reasons for this. Its utility was significantly lessened by technical limitations, and the manner in which the registers were compiled mitigated against their usefulness. The definition of crime in the *Prevention of Crime Act 1871*, like that in the 1869 act, meant that vast numbers of offenders who had only committed misdemeanours, and who could not reasonably be

---

[5] 198 *Parl. Deb.*, HC (3rd ser.), col. 1278–82 (4 Aug. 1869).
[6] The Earl of Kimberley (Liberal), 205 *Parliamentary Debates*, HL (3rd ser.), col. 1679–83 (25 Apr. 1871).
[7] Godfrey Lushington, Home Office clerk, Memorandum: 'Registry of Criminals', Jan. 1875, TNA, MEPO 6/90/2, pp. 8, 10.

termed habitual criminals or thought of as members of a criminal class, were registered. This made the registers very bulky and difficult to search. Thus, the many registers of habitual criminals remained little used until 1889, when a further change was made to their composition ensuring that more criminals believed by the police to be habituated to crime were listed.[8]

Police supervision was, if anything, even less effective in London than registration. The capital's police magistrates ensured that this was the case. Before convicting an individual under supervision of failing to report themselves to their local police station, magistrates insisted that the commissioner of the Metropolitan Police Force had to personally provide testimony.[9] As a result of this unique interpretation of the reporting provisions of the 1871 act, not one conviction for failing to report was secured in London before 1880. This significant problem was rectified through the *Prevention of Crime Act 1879*. Yet it is likely that, even after this time, most of those who experienced supervision in London were not carefully watched. Following the formation of the CSO in 1880 the emphasis of supervision changed from deterrence to rehabilitation.[10] Therefore, staff at the CSO spent far more time and energy trying to secure employment for those under supervision than they did in watching them. In addition, members of the Metropolitan Police Force were consistently reminded of the importance of forging good relations with members of London's working class and not carrying out heavy-handed surveillance.[11] Because of these factors police supervision in London never achieved anything like its oppressive potential.

The habitual criminals' legislation also failed to ensure longer sentences for recidivists. Instead, between 1871 and 1895 the sentences passed upon London's repeat offenders became significantly more lenient.[12] Once again, the police magistrates undermined the intentions of the parliament. To an even greater extent than the Metropolitan Police Force, London's police magistrates were mindful of not alienating members of the working class. Perhaps not surprisingly,

---

[8] *Report of the Commissioner of Police of the Metropolis: For the Year 1890*, [C 6472] HC 1891, xlii, p. 6.
[9] Douglas Labalmondiere, assistant commissioner of the Metropolitan Police Force, to the Home Office, 6 May 1872, TNA, HO 45/9320/16629A.
[10] James Monro, 'A Report of the History of the Department of the Metropolitan Police known as the Convict Supervision Office: Detailing System, and Showing Results and Effects Generally on the Habitual Criminal Population', 1886, TNA, HO 144/184/A45507, pp. 8–9.
[11] *Prisons Committee: Report from the Departmental Committee on Prisons*, [C 7702] HC 1895, lvi, p. 393.
[12] *Judicial Statistics, England and Wales, 1894. Part I – Criminal Statistics*, [C 8072] HC 1896, xciv, p. 18; V. A. C. Gatrell, 'The Decline of Theft and Violence in Victorian and Edwardian England', in V. A. C. Gatrell, Bruce Lenman and G. Parker (eds.), *Crime and the Law: The Social History of Crime in Western Europe since 1500*, London: Europa Publications, 1980, p. 368.

therefore, magistrates acted to mitigate the severity of the habitual criminals' legislation, and other laws, in numerous ways.[13] Further reasons for the failure of the acts to increase the severity of sentences were ongoing disagreements on the bench concerning the proper punishment of recidivists, the rise of Lombrosian criminology and a declining rate of crime. While the acts had staunch supporters in the SSA, in parliament and in the press, they had equally staunch opponents among many police, magistrates and judges. And, over time, it was the views of the latter group, charged with imposing the legislation on London's working class, that prevailed, rendering the acts largely ineffective.

These findings contradict arguments put forward by leading historians of late nineteenth-century British penal policy. In short, there is a broad consensus that changes in penal policy resulted, first and foremost, from moral panics about crime and that the measures which were enacted as a consequence were readily used in a repressive way by agencies of the state against members of the working class. However, this narrative – which is heavily influenced by theoretical work on moral panics and their effects, and social control interpretations of changing penal policies – is simply incorrect in the case of the Gladstone government's habitual criminals' legislation.

Until the 1980s numerous historians put forward Whig accounts of Britain's changing penal system in the nineteenth century.[14] In such accounts the arguments of Victorian reformers were largely accepted. It was claimed that a move away from the previous solely physical regimes to the use of the penitentiary, in which punishment was tailored to the individual, aiming to change behaviour by a calibrated system of both physical and mental rewards and punishments, was evidence of progress. Then, since the 1980s, many scholars have utilized social control interpretations to re-evaluate the British penal system of the nineteenth century. They have claimed that penal changes did not result from an effort to

---

[13] Ellis and Ellis, solicitors, to Edmund Henderson, commissioner of the Metropolitan Police Force, 11 Nov. 1869, TNA, MEPO 3/88; Adolphus Liddell to Edmund Henderson, 14 Jan. 1870, TNA., MEPO 3/88; Draft circular, 6 May 1870, TNA, HO 12/184/85459A/40; Superintendent of F division to Edmund Henderson, 18 May 1870, TNA, MEPO 3/88; J. B. Manning, governor of London's Pentonville prison, *Report of a Committee Appointed by the Secretary of State to Inquire into the Best Means Available for Identifying Habitual Criminals; with Minutes of Evidence and Appendices*, [C 7263] HC and HL 1894, lxxii, p. 42.

[14] Leon Radzinowicz and Roger Hood, 'Incapacitating the Habitual Criminal: The English Experience', *Michigan Law Review*, vol. 78, no. 8 (Aug. 1980), pp. 1305–89; Martin Wiener, 'The March of Penal Progress?' *Journal of British Studies*, vol. 26, no. 1 (Jan. 1887), pp. 84–95.

punish more humanely, but to punish more effectively.[15] The state, represented in particular by the government, parliament, police forces, magistrates and judges, was unified in its objective of better controlling elements of the working class that were perceived as a threat. While legislative measures were not part of a coherent programme, they nonetheless specifically targeted an identifiable subsection of the working class, the criminal class. The scholars who make this revisionist argument see the *Habitual Criminals Act 1869* and the *Prevention of Crime Act 1871* as key evidence of the state's desire to suppress the criminal class and, more broadly, to discipline what were believed to be the most unruly and least law-abiding elements of the working class.[16]

Revisionist accounts, which now dominate the literature, often claim that the development of the post-transportation penal system was ad hoc, with legislation primarily being introduced in response to public panics about crime, rather than as a result of a plan.[17] Crime reporting in the 1850s and 1860s, and the panics it caused, clearly influenced various governments. Yet penal policy in these decades was not totally ad hoc. Rather, legislative measures were often borrowed from the agendas of Sir Walter Crofton, and then – after 1857 – the SSA.[18] This was particularly so in 1869, when there was no panic about crime. This means that the principal understanding of the reasons for the introduction of the *Habitual Criminals Bill 1869* into parliament is not correct.

Once enacted the habitual criminals' legislation gave the Metropolitan Police Force significant additional powers, as several historians have pointed out.[19]

---

[15] Wiener, 'The March of Penal Progress?' pp. 84, 95; Stefan Petrow, *Policing Morals: The Metropolitan Police and the Home Office 1870–1914*, Oxford: Clarendon Press, 1995, pp. 51, 82; Barry Godfrey, David Cox and Stephen Farrall, *Serious Offenders: An Historical Study of Habitual Criminals*, London: Oxford University Press, 2010, p. xii; Douglas Hay, 'Crime and Justice in Eighteenth and Nineteenth Century England', *Crime and Justice*, vol. 2 (1980), p. 66; Clive Emsley, *Crime and Society in England: 1750–1900*, 2nd ed., London: Longman, 1996, pp. 172–4.

[16] Petrow, *Policing Morals*, pp. 51, 82; Godfrey, Cox and Farrall, *Serious Offenders*, p. xii; Hay, 'Crime and Justice in Eighteenth and Nineteenth Century England', p. 66; Emsley, *Crime and Society in England*, pp. 172–4; Helen Johnston, *Crime in England 1815–1880: Experiencing the Criminal Justice System*, Abingdon: Routledge, 2015, p. 36.

[17] Peter Bartrip, 'Public Opinion and Law Enforcement: The Ticket-of-Leave Scares in Mid-Victorian Britain', in Victor Bailey (ed.), *Policing and Punishment in Nineteenth Century Britain*, London: Croom Helm, 1981, p. 174; W. G. Runciman, *Very Different, but Much the Same: The Evolution of English Society since 1714*, Oxford: Oxford University Press, 2015, p. 69; Pete King, 'Moral Panics and Violent Street Crime 1750–2000: A Comparative Perspective', in Barry Godfrey, Clive Emsley and Graeme Dunstall (eds.), *Comparative Histories of Crime*, Cullompton: Willan, 2003, p. 57; Drew D. Gray, *London's Shadows: The Dark Side of the Victorian City*, London: Continuum, 2010, p. 57.

[18] The Earl of Carlisle, 'Address on the Punishment and Reformation of Criminals', in *Transactions of the National Association for the Promotion of Social Science 1858*, London: John W. Parker and Son, 1859, pp. 70, 72.

[19] Petrow, *Policing Morals*, p. 51; Martin Wiener, *Reconstructing the Criminal: Culture, Law and Policy in England, 1830–1914*, Cambridge: Cambridge University Press, 1990, p. 149; Godfrey, Cox and Farrall, *Serious Offenders*, p. 205.

Conclusion   173

The dominant position in the relevant literature is that, despite some defects, the acts of 1869 and 1871 were oppressive instruments of control that enabled the monitoring and even creation of a criminal class. Numerous historians have shown, quite correctly, that registration had the capacity to label individuals as criminal in the eyes of the police, magistrates and judges.[20] They have also claimed that contemporaries were right to be troubled about police supervision, for it infringed the rights of members of the working class. Supervision was used in an oppressive way that endangered employment and, therefore, rehabilitation.[21] Finally, several historians have argued that longer sentences for repeat offenders resulted from the implementation of the acts of 1869 and 1871.[22] However, due to a range of factors – including the refusal of both police magistrates and the Metropolitan Police Force to strictly enforce the legislation – the impact of the acts upon habitual criminals in London was much more limited than its sponsors had hoped and than many historians claim. The theoretical frameworks of moral panic and social control have been very useful in explaining the reasons for, and impact of, many actions of the state.[23] Yet they are insufficient to explain the genesis and outcomes of the habitual criminals' acts of 1869 and 1871. In fact, the utilization of these frameworks has led to conclusions that are incorrect.

The evidence presented here not only has implications for the study of the state's efforts to curtail the activities of repeat offenders in the UK in the mid- and late Victorian period. Several scholars who incorrectly claim that the habitual criminals' legislation of Gladstone's first government had a significant negative impact on many members of the working class also argue, more generally, that the outcome of increased police power during the nineteenth century was 'nightmarish' for the poor.[24] For example, V. A. C. Gatrell has said that, primarily because of the expanded scope of police action, the mid- and late Victorian state came very close to the 'total regulation' of working-class lives.[25] And Stefan

---

[20] Petrow, *Policing Morals*, p. 51; Wiener, *Reconstructing the Criminal*, p. 149; Godfrey, Cox and Farrall, *Serious Offenders*, p. 205.
[21] Johnston, *Crime in England*, p. 36; Barbara Weinberger, 'The Criminal Class and the Ecology of Crime', *Historical Social Research*, vol. 15, no. 4 (1990), p. 129; Emsley, *Crime and Society in England*, p. 174; Wiener, *Reconstructing the Criminal*, p. 149; Godfrey, Cox and Farrall, *Serious Offenders*, p. 205; Petrow, *Policing Morals*, p. 151; Jennifer Davis, 'From "Rookeries" to "Communities": Race, Poverty and Policing in London, 1850–1985', *History Workshop*, no. 27 (Spring 1989), pp. 68, 71.
[22] Godfrey, Cox and Farrall, *Serious Offenders*, pp. 161–77; Petrow, *Policing Morals*, p. 51; Johnston, *Crime in England*, p. 36.
[23] For example see Stanley Cohen, *Folk Devils and Moral Panics: The Creation of the Mods and Rockers*, 3rd ed., London: Routledge, 2002 (first published in 1972), pp. 1–7; A. P. Donajgrodzki (ed.), *Social Control in Nineteenth Century Britain*, London: Croom Helm, 1977, p. 9.
[24] Petrow, *Policing Morals*, pp. 294–5.
[25] Gatrell, 'The Decline of Theft and Violence in Victorian and Edwardian England', pp. 244–5.

Petrow discusses legislation in four areas – habitual criminals, prostitution, gambling and drinking – that undoubtedly greatly enhanced the powers of the police.[26] The police, Petrow implausibly argues, were in fact 'all powerful'.[27] Helen Johnston has, very recently, carried out some further research on these topics, which primarily focuses on the provinces. Like Petrow, she claims that the police and the Home Office shared a 'goal' to 'remove or limit the possibilities of temptation to crime or immorality by regulating the "purveyors of immoral behaviour"'. She borrowed the latter expression from Petrow and specifically referred to criminals released on licence, alcohol licencing, prostitution and bookmakers.[28] Various other scholars have noted the increased legislative mechanisms through which the police had the potential to exert greater control over the working class.[29] They argue that the police used these mechanisms, often with the cooperation of magistrates and judges, to ruthlessly suppress numerous working-class activities in an effort to alter the morals of the poor, imposing the middle-class norms of respectability.[30] However, as Dany Lacombe has noted, the state 'does not have this unity'.[31] The ineffectiveness of the habitual criminals' legislation of 1869 and 1871 in London raises serious doubts about the accuracy of the prevailing consensus in the literature concerning nineteenth-century British penal policy: that legislative attempts to control the working class were vigorously enforced by the police and the courts, resulting in great hardship for elements among the working class. These doubts invite further research. Studies of the impact of the legislation in other parts of Britain will also help to illuminate whether the actions of London's police and magistracy were unusual. Additionally, given the reluctance of members of the Metropolitan Police Force and London's police magistrates to fully enforce the acts of 1869 and 1871, it is likely that they also acted to mitigate the severity of other legislation. Other efforts to control sections of the working class in London are, therefore, ready

---

[26] Petrow, *Policing Morals*, pp. 294–5.
[27] Ibid., p. 299.
[28] Ibid., p. 296; Johnston, *Crime in England*, p. 152.
[29] Wiener, *Reconstructing the Criminal*, p. 381; Hay, 'Crime and Justice in Eighteenth and Nineteenth Century England', p. 58.
[30] Hay, 'Crime and Justice in Eighteenth and Nineteenth Century England', p. 58; Wiener, 'The March of Penal Progress?' p. 47; Gatrell, 'The Decline of Theft and Violence in Victorian and Edwardian England', p. 255; Wiener, *Reconstructing the Criminal*, p. 381; Petrow, *Policing Morals*, pp. 294–5; Sean McConville, 'The Victorian Prison: England, 1865–1965', in Norval Morris and David J. Rothman (eds.), *The Oxford History of the Prison*, Oxford: Oxford University Press, 1995, p. 165; Miles Ogborn, 'Discipline, Government and Law: Separate Confinement in the Prisons of England and Wales, 1830–1877', *Transactions of the Institute of British Geographers*, New Series, vol. 20, no. 3 (1995), pp. 306–7.
[31] Dany Lacombe, 'Reforming Foucault: A Critique of the Social Control Thesis', *British Journal of Sociology*, vol. 47, no. 2 (Jun. 1996), p. 340.

for re-evaluation. A re-assessment of the impact of government intervention in the three policy areas which are identified by Petrow, and also discussed by Johnston, would be an excellent place to start.[32] Given the errors in their analysis of habitual criminals' legislation, it is entirely possible that they are also wrong concerning the outcome of laws regarding prostitution, gambling and drink. However, this reappraisal will have to be left to other scholars.

---

[32] Petrow, *Policing Morals*, pp. 294–9; Johnston, *Crime in England*, p. 152.

Bibliography

Primary Sources

Unpublished

The National Archives, London

Home Office Papers
Old Criminal Papers, 1849–71
Registered Papers, Criminal, 1871–2, 1886–7
Circulars, 6 Apr. 1871–15 Apr. 1875
Prisons Staff and Office Questions: Register of Habitual Criminals, 1874–85
Report on the Working of the Prevention of Crimes Act by the Convict Supervision Office, 1886
Report on Anthropometrical System of Registration of Prisoners for Identification and Introduction in England, 1887–1907

Home Office and Prison Commission Papers
A copy of the Distributed National Alphabetical Register of Habitual Criminals in England and Wales, 1869–76

Metropolitan Police Papers
Extracts from Police Orders, 1 Feb. 1842–28 Feb. 1854
Habitual Criminals Registers and Miscellaneous Papers, 1853–74
Police Orders, 1 Sept. 1857–31 Dec. 1858, 1865, 1872
Habitual Criminals Act, 1870, and Prevention of Crimes Act, 1871: Correspondence, 1869–71

The Gloucesterchire Archives
The Papers of Thomas Barwick Lloyd Baker

Published

Parliamentary Papers

First Report of the Commissioners Appointed to Inquire as to the Best Means of Establishing an Efficient Constabulary Force in the Counties of England and Wales, [C 169] H.C. 1839, xix
Tenth Report of the Inspectors Appointed under the Provisions of the Acts 5 & 6 Will. IV c. 38, to Visit Different Prisons of Great Britain, IV. Scotland, Northumberland, and Durham, [C 688] H.C. and H.L. 1845, xxiv

Report from the Select Committee on Newspaper Stamps: Together with the Proceedings of the Committee, Minutes of Evidence, Appendix, and Index, [C 558] H.C. 1851, xvii

First Report from the Select Committee of the House of Commons on Transportation; Together with the Minutes of Evidence, and Appendix, [C 244] H.C. 1856, xvii

Second Report from the Select Committee of the House of Commons on Transportation; Together with the Minutes of Evidence, and Appendix, [C 296] H.C. 1856, xvii

Third Report from the Select Committee of the House of Commons on Transportation; Together with the Minutes of Evidence, and Appendix, [C 355] H.C. 1856, xvii

Fourth Report of the Directors of Convict Prisons in Ireland, [C 2376] H.C. 1857, xxx

General Report on the Convict Prisons, with Observations on Several Questions Connected with Management and Disposal of Convicts, Tickets-of-Leave, Supervision of the Police, Irish System, Etc., 1860–61, [C 3055] H.C. and H.L. 1862, xxv

Report of the Commissioners Appointed to Inquire into the Operation of the Acts Relating to Transportation and Penal Servitude. Vol. 2. Minutes of Evidence, [C 3190] H.C. 1863, xxi

Report from the Select Committee of the House of Lords, on the Present State of Discipline in Gaols and Houses of Correction; Together with the Proceedings of the Committee, Minutes of Evidence, Appendix and Index, [C 499] H.C. 1863, ix

Correspondence between the Secretary of State for the Home Department and the Directors of Convict Prisons, on the Subject of the Recommendations of the Royal Commission on the Penal Servitude Acts, [C 61] H.C. 1864, xlix

Reports of the Commissioner of Police of the Metropolis, H.C. 1868–95

Judicial Statistics, England and Wales. Part I – Criminal Statistics, H.C. 1868–97

Memorandum Respecting the Decrease in Crime in England and Wales, Especially in the Crimes Affected by the Habitual Criminals Act, 1869, and the Prevention of Crime Act, 1871, [C 665] H.C. and H.L., 1872, i

Report from the Select Committee on Pawnbrokers Bill; Together with the Proceedings of the Committee and Minutes of Evidence, [C 288] H.C. 1872, xii

Report of the Commissioners Appointed to Inquire into the Working of the Penal Servitude Acts. Vol. I – Commissions and Report, [C 2368] H.C. and H.L. 1878–9, xxxvii

Report of a Committee Appointed by the Secretary of State to Inquire into the Best Means Available for Identifying Habitual Criminals; with Minutes of Evidence and Appendices, [C 7263] H.C. and H.L. 1894, lxxii

Prisons Committee: Report from the Departmental Committee on Prisons, [C 7702] H.C. 1895, lvi

Statutes

Penal Servitude Act, 16 & 17 Vict., c. 99, 1853
Penal Servitude Act, 27 & 28 Vict., c. 47, 1864
Habitual Criminals Act, 32 & 33 Vict., c. 99, 1869
Prevention of Crime Act, 34 & 35 Vict., c. 112, 1871

Newspapers and Periodicals

These newspapers and periodicals were published in London unless otherwise stated.
All the Year Round
Daily News
Daily Star
Era
Express
Hansard
Illustrated London News
Law Times
Leicester Chronicle (Leicester)
Lloyd's Weekly Newspaper
Morning Post
Police Gazette
Public Opinion
Railway Times and Joint-Stock Chronicle
Standard
Times
Transactions of the National Association for the Promotion of Social Science
West London Observer

Contemporary Books and Articles

Anderson, Robert, 'Morality by Act of Parliament', *Contemporary Review*, vol. 59 (1891), pp. 77–88.

Anonymous, *Five Years' Penal Servitude by One Who Has Endured It*, London: Richard Bentley and Son, 1877.

Anonymous, *Convict Life, or, Revelations Concerning Convicts and Convict Prisons, by a Ticket-of-Leave Man*, London: Wyman, 1879.

Baker, Thomas and Barwick, Lloyd, *War with Crime: Being a Selection of Reprinted Papers on Crime, Reformatories, Etc.*, London: Longmans, 1889.

Bidwell, George, *Forging His Chains: The Autobiography of George Bidwell*, Hartford: S.S. Scranton, 1888.

Booth, Charles, *Life and Labour of the People of London*, vol. 17, London: Macmillan, 1902.

Carpenter, Mary, *Our Convicts*, vol. 1, London: Longman, Green, Longman, Roberts and Green, 1864.

Clarkson, Charles and Richardson, J. Hall, *Police!*, New York and London: Garland Publishing, 1984 (first published 1889).

Colquhoun, Patrick, *A Treatise on the Police of the Metropolis*, London: Patterson Smith, 1795.
Cox, Edward, *The Principles of Punishment: As Applied in the Administration of Criminal Law, by Judges and Magistrates*, London: Law Times Office, 1877.
Davitt, Michael, *The Prison Life of Michael Davitt as Related by Himself*, London: n.p., 1878, pp. 1–40.
Davitt, Michael, *Leaves from a Prison Diary, or, Lectures to a 'Solitary' Audience*, vol. 1, London: Chapman and Hall, 1885.
Dickens, Charles, 'Spy Police', *Household Words*, vol. 1 (21 Sept. 1850), pp. 611–4.
Du Cane, Sir Edmund, *The Punishment and Prevention of Crime*, London: Macmillan, 1885.
Grant, J., *The Newspaper Press*, vol. 2, London: Tinsley Brothers, 1871.
Greenwood, James, *The Seven Curses of London*, London: Stanley Rivers and Co., 1869.
Halkett, Samuel and Laing, John, *Dictionary of Anonymous and Pseudonymous Literature of Great Britain: Including the Works of Foreigners Written in, or Translated into the English Language*, vol. 4, Edinburgh: n.p., 1888.
Hardaker, A., *A Brief History of Pawnbroking: With Full Narrative of How the Act of 1872 Was Fought for and Obtained and the Stolen Goods Bill Opposed and Defeated*, London: Jackson, Ruston and Keeson, 1892.
Harris, Richard (ed.), *The Reminiscences of Sir Henry Hawkins (Baron Brampton)*, London and New York: Thomas Nelson & Sons, 1904.
Hill, Matthew Davenport, *Draft Report on the Principles of Punishment: Presented to the Committee on Criminal Law Appointed by the Law Amendment Society, in December, 1846*, London: William Clowes and Sons, 1847.
Hill, Matthew Davenport, *Two Charges: Delivered by the Recorder, to the Grand Juries of Birmingham, at the Michaelmas Quarter Sessions for the Years 1850 & 1851*, Bristol: n.p., 1851.
Hill, Matthew Davenport, *Suggestions for the Repression of Crime: Contained in Charges Delivered to Grand Juries of Birmingham; Supported by Additional Facts and Arguments*, London: John W. Parker and Son, 1857.
Hill, Matthew Davenport, *Papers on the Penal Servitude Acts: And on the Regulations of the Home Department for Carrying Them into Execution*, London: Longman, Green, Longman, Roberts and Green, 1864.
Holland, H. W., 'Professional Thieves', *The Cornhill Magazine*, vol. 6, no. 35 (Nov. 1862), pp. 640–53.
Jebb, Joshua, 'Reports of the Directors of the Convict Prisons on the Discipline and Management of Pentonville, Millbank, and Parkhurst Prisons, and of Portland, Portsmouth, Dartmoor, Chatham, and Brixton Prisons, with Fulham Refuge and the Invalid Prison at Woking, for the Year 1860. With Memorandum by Sir Joshua Jebb, K.C.B., Chairman, & c.', *Justice of the Peace, and County, Borough, Poor Law Union, and Parish Law Recorder*, vol. 26, no. 11 (15 Mar. 1862), pp. 170–1.
Jeyes, S. H., *The Life of Sir Howard Vincent*, London: George Allen, 1912.

Letters of the Rt. Hon. Henry Austin Bruce, G.C.B., Lord Aberdare of Duffryn, vol. 1, Oxford: Horace Hart, 1902.

Lombroso, Cesare, *Criminal Man*, Mary Gibson, Mary and Rafter, Nicole Hahn (trans. and ed.), London: Duke University Press, 2006 (first published 1876).

Martineau, Harriet, 'Life in the Criminal Class', *The Edinburgh Review*, vol. 122, no. 250 (Oct. 1865), pp. 337–71.

Mayhew, Henry and Binny, John, *The Criminal Prisons of London: And Scenes of Prison Life*, London: Griffin, Bohn, and Co., 1862.

Mineka, Francis E. and Lindley, Dwight N. (eds.), *The Later Letters of John Stuart Mill 1849–1873*, vol. 15, Toronto: University of Toronto Press, 1972.

Morrison, Arthur, *Child of the Jago*, 3rd ed., Woodbridge: The Boydell Press, 1982 (first published 1896).

Pike, Luke, *A History of Crime in England*, vol. 2, New Jersey: Patterson Smith, 1968 (first published 1876).

Plowden, Alfred, *Grain or Chaff?: The Autobiography of a Police Magistrate*, London: T.F. Unwin, 1903.

Quennell, Peter (ed.), *London's Underworld: Being Selections from 'Those That Will Not Work', the Fourth Volume of 'London Labour and the London Poor' by Henry Mayhew*, vol. 7, London: Hamlyn, 1969.

Quinton, R. F., *Crime and Criminals: 1876–1910*, London: Garland Publishing, 1984 (first published 1910).

Reeve, H., 'The Newspaper Press', *Edinburgh Review*, vol. 102 (Oct. 1855), pp. 470–98.

Solly, Henry, *A Few Thoughts on How to Deal with the Unemployed Poor of London, and with Its 'Roughs' and Criminal Classes*, n.p.: Society of Arts, 1868.

The Transportation of Criminals: Being a Report of a Discussion at a Special Meeting of the Association Held at Burlington House, on the 17th February 1863, London: Emily Faithfull, 1863.

Vincent, Howard, 'Discharged Prisoners: How to Aid Them', *Contemporary Review*, vol. 43 (Mar. 1883), pp. 325–31.

Waddy, H. T., *The Police Court and Its Work*, London: Butterworth and Co., 1925.

Wensley, Frederick, *Forty Years of Scotland Yard: The Record of a Lifetime's Service in the Criminal Investigation Department*, New York: Garden City Publishing Co., 1930.

Secondary Sources

Books and Articles

Ascoli, David, *The Queen's Peace: The Origins and Development of the Metropolitan Police, 1829–1979*, London: Hamish Hamilton, 1979.

Bailey, Victor, Review of V. A. C. Gatrell, Bruce Lehman and Geoffrey Parker (eds.), *Crime and the Law: The Social History of Crime in Western Europe since 1500*, London: Europa Publications, 1980, *Social History*, vol. 7, no. 3 (Oct. 1982), p. 349.

Bailey, Victor, *Policing and Punishment in Nineteenth Century Britain*, London: Croom Helm, 1981.

Banks, Stephen, *Informal Justice in England and Wales, 1760–1914: The Courts and Popular Opinion*, Woodbridge: The Boydell Press, 2014.

Barker, Hannah, *Newspapers, Politics, and English Society, 1695–1855*, New York: Routledge, 2000.

Bartrip, Peter, 'Public Opinion and Law Enforcement: The Ticket-of-Leave Scares in Mid-Victorian Britain', in Victor Bailey (ed.), *Policing and Punishment in Nineteenth Century Britain*, London: Croom Helm, 1981, pp. 150–81.

Bartrip, Peter, 'Hill, Matthew Davenport (1792–1872)', in H. C. G. Matthew and Brian Harrison (eds.), *Oxford Dictionary of National Biography*, Oxford: Oxford University Press, 2004; online ed., Lawrence Goldman (ed.), http://www.oxforddnb.com/view/article/13286.

Beattie, J. M., *Crime and the Courts in England, 1660–1800*, Oxford: Clarendon Press, 1986.

Beattie, J. M., *The First English Detectives: The Bow Street Runners and the Policing of London, 1750–1840*, Oxford: Oxford University Press, 2012.

Beier, A. L., 'Identity, Language, and Resistance in the Making of the Victorian "Criminal Class": Mayhew's Convict Revisited', *The Journal of British Studies*, vol. 44, no. 3 (Jul. 2005), pp. 499–515.

Bell, A., *Literature and Crime in Augustan England*, London: Routledge, 1991.

Bentley, David, *English Criminal Justice in the Nineteenth Century*, London and Rio Grande: The Hambledon Press, 1988.

Brewster, J., 'The Wilkites and the law, 1763–1774: A Study of Radical Notions of Governance', in J. Brewster and J. Styles (eds.), *An Ungovernable People: The English and Their Law in the Seventeenth and Eighteenth Century*, London: Hutchinson, 1980, pp. 128–71.

Briggs, John, Harrison, Christopher, McInnes, Angus and Vincent, David, *Crime and Punishment in England: An Introductory History*, London: University College London Press, 1996.

Carroll-Burke, Patrick, *Colonial Discipline: The Making of the Irish Convict System*, Dublin: Four Courts Press, 2000.

Cohen, Stanley, *Folk Devils and Moral Panics: The Creation of the Mods and Rockers*, 3rd ed., London: Routledge, 2002 (first published in 1972).

Craven, Cicely, 'The Progress of English Criminology', *The Journal of Criminal Law and Criminology*, vol. 24, no. 1 (May–Jun. 1933), pp. 230–47.

Crone, Rosalind, *Violent Victorians: Popular Entertainment in Nineteenth-Century London*, Manchester: Manchester University Press, 2012.

Davis, Jennifer, 'The London Garotting Panic of 1862: A Moral Panic and the Creation of a Criminal Class in Mid-Victorian England', in V. A. C. Gatrell, Bruce Lenman and G. Parker (eds.), *Crime and the Law: The Social History of Crime in Western Europe since 1500*, London: Europa Publications, 1980, pp. 190–213.

Davis, Jennifer, 'A Poor Man's System of Justice: The London Police Courts in the Second Half of the Nineteenth Century', *The Historical Journal*, vol. 27, no. 2 (Jun. 1984), pp. 309–35.

Davis, Jennifer, 'From "Rookeries" to "Communities": Race, Poverty and Policing in London, 1850–1985', *History Workshop*, no. 27 (Spring 1989), pp. 66–89.

DeLacy, Margaret, review of Janet Semple, *Bentham's Penitentiary: A Study of the Panoptic Penitentiary*, Oxford: Clarendon Press, 1993, *The American Historical Review*, vol. 99, no. 5 (Dec. 1994), pp. 1690–1.

Donajgrodzki, A. P. (ed.), *Social Control in Nineteenth Century Britain*, London: Croom Helm, 1977.

Duman, D., *The Judicial Bench in England 1727–1875: The Reshaping of a Professional Elite*, London: Royal Historical Society, 1982.

Emsley, Clive, *Crime and Society in England, 1750–1900*, 2nd ed., London: Longman, 1996.

Emsley, Clive, 'Jebb, Sir Joshua (1793–1863)', in H. C. G. Matthew and Brian Harrison (eds.), *Oxford Dictionary of National Biography*, Oxford: Oxford University Press, 2004; online ed., Lawrence Goldman (ed.), http://www.oxforddnb.com/view/article/14683.

Emsley, Clive, *Hard Men: The English and Violence since 1750*, London: Hambleton and London, 2005.

Foucault, Michel, *Discipline and Punish: The Birth of the Prison*, Alan Sheridan (trans.), London: Allen Lane, 1977 (first published 1975).

Garland, David, *Punishment and Welfare*, London: Gower, 1985.

Garland, David, 'Foucault's "Discipline and Punish" – an Exposition and Critique', *American Bar Foundation Journal*, vol. 11, no. 4 (Autumn 1986), pp. 870–85.

Gascoigne, John, *The Enlightenment and the Origins of European Australia*, Cambridge: Cambridge University Press, 2002.

Gatrell, V. A. C., 'The Decline of Theft and Violence in Victorian and Edwardian England', in V. A. C. Gatrell, Bruce Lehman, and Geoffrey Parker (eds.), *Crime and the Law: The Social History of Crime in Western Europe since 1500*, London: Europa Publications, 1980, pp. 238–70.

Gatrell, V. A. C., *The Hanging Tree: Execution and the People of England, 1770–1868*, Oxford and New York: Oxford University Press, 1994.

Gelb, Karen, *Myths and Misconceptions: Public Opinion versus Public Judgment about Sentencing*, Melbourne: Sentencing Advisory Council, 2016.

Gilmartin, Kevin, *Print Politics: The Press and Radical Opposition in Early Nineteenth-Century England*, Cambridge: Cambridge University Press, 1996.

Godfrey, Emelyne, 'Stranglehold on Victorian Society', *History Today*, vol. 59, no. 7 (Jul. 2009), pp. 54–9.

Godfrey, Barry, Cox, David and Farrall, Stephen, 'Persistent Offenders in the North West of England, 1880–1940: Some Critical Research Questions', *Crimes and Misdemeanours*, vol. 1, no. 1 (2007), pp. 69–89.

Godfrey, Barry, Cox, David and Farrall, Stephen, *Serious Offenders: An Historical Study of Habitual Criminals*, London: Oxford University Press, 2010.

Goldman, Lawrence, 'The Social Science Association, 1857–1886: A Context for Mid-Victorian Liberalism', *The English Historical Review*, vol. 101, no. 398 (Jan. 1986), pp. 95–134.

Goldman, Lawrence, *Science, Reform and Politics in Victorian Britain: The Social Science Association 1857–1886*, London: Cambridge University Press, 2002.

Gray, Drew D., *Crime, Prosecution and Social Relations: The Summary Courts of the City of London in the Late Eighteenth Century*, Basingstoke: Palgrave Macmillan, 2009.

Gray, Drew D., *London's Shadows: The Dark Side of the Victorian City*, London: Continuum, 2010.

Green, D. and Parton, A., 'Slums and Slum Life in Victorian England: London and Birmingham at Mid-Century', in M. Gaskell (ed.), *Slums*, Leicester: Leicester University Press, 1990, pp. 17–91.

Hay, Douglas, 'Crime and Justice in Eighteenth and Nineteenth Century England', *Crime and Justice*, vol. 2 (1980), pp. 45–84.

Harding, Christopher, '"The Inevitable End of a Discredited System"? The Origins of the Gladstone Committee Report on Prisons, 1895', *The Historical Journal*, vol. 31, no. 3 (Sept. 1988), pp. 591–608.

Ignatieff, Michael, *A Just Measure of Pain: The Penitentiary in the Industrial Revolution, 1750–1850*, London: Macmillan, 1978.

Inwood, Stephen, 'Policing London's Morals: The Metropolitan Police and Popular Culture, 1829–1850', *London Journal*, vol. 15, no. 2 (1990), pp. 129–46.

Johnston, Helen, 'Victorian Prison', in Yvonne Jewkes and Jamie Bennett (eds.), *Dictionary of Prisons and Punishment*, Cullompton: Willan, 2008, p. 306.

Johnston, Helen, *Crime in England 1815–1880: Experiencing the Criminal Justice System*, Abingdon: Routledge, 2015.

Jones, D. J. V., 'The New Police, Crime and People in England and Wales, 1829–1888', *Transactions of the Royal Historical Society*, 5th series, vol. 33 (1983), pp. 151–68.

Jones, Gareth Stedman, *Outcast London: A Study in the Relationship between the Classes in Victorian Society*, Oxford: Clarendon Press, 1971.

King, Pete, 'Moral Panics and Violent Street Crime, 1750–2000: A Comparative Perspective', in Barry Godfrey, Clive Emsley and Graeme Dunstall (eds.), *Comparative Histories of Crime*, Cullompton: Willan, 2003, pp. 53–71.

Krinsky, Charles (ed.), *The Ashgate Research Companion to Moral Panics*, Farnham and Burlington: Ashgate Publishing, 2003.

MacDonagh, Oliver, 'The Nineteenth Century Revolution in Government: A Reappraisal', *The Historical Journal*, vol. 1, no. 1 (Mar. 1958), pp. 52–67.

MacDonagh, Oliver, *Early Victorian Government: 1830–1870*, London: Weidenfeld and Nicholson, 1977.

MacDonagh, Oliver, 'The Economy and Society, 1830–45', in W. E. Vaughan (ed.), *A New History of Ireland*, vol. 5, *Ireland under the Union, I: 1801–1870*, Oxford: Clarendon Press, 1989, pp. 218–41.

Manchester, A. H., *A Modern Legal History of England and Wales, 1750–1950*, London: Butterworth, 1980.

Mays, G. Larry and Winfrey, L. Thomas Jnr., *Essential of Corrections*, 4th ed., Belmont: Wadsworth, 2009.

McConville, Sean, *English Local Prisons 1860–1900: Next Only to Death*, London: Routledge, 1995.

McConville, Sean, 'The Victorian Prison: England, 1865–1965', in Norval Morris and David J. Rothman (eds.), *The Oxford History of the Prison: The Practice of Punishment in Western Society*, New York: Oxford University Press, 1995, pp. 131–67.

McDonald, Lynn, 'Theory and Evidence of Rising Crime in the Nineteenth Century', *The British Journal of Sociology*, vol. 33, no. 3 (Sept. 1982), pp. 404–20.

McGowen, Randall, 'Civilising Punishment: The End of the Public Execution in England', *The Journal of British Studies*, vol. 33, no. 3 (Jul. 1994), pp. 257–82.

Mee, Jon, *The Cambridge Introduction to Charles Dickens*, Cambridge: Cambridge University Press, 2010.

Melling, Michael, 'Cleaning House in a Suddenly Closed Society: The Genesis, Brief Life and Ultimate Death of the Habitual Criminals Act, 1869', *Osgoode Hall Law Journal*, vol. 21, no. 2 (Sept. 1983), pp. 315–62.

Murdoch, Lydia, *Imagined Orphans: Poor Families, Child Welfare, and Contested Citizenship in London*, New Jersey, and London: Rutgers University Press, 2006.

Nead, Lydia, *Victorian Babylon: People, Streets and Images in Nineteenth-Century London*, New Haven and London: Yale University Press, 2000.

Nicholas, Stephen and Shergold, Peter R., 'Unshackling the Past', in Stephen Nicholas (ed.), *Convict Workers: Reinterpreting Australia's Past*, Cambridge and Sydney: Cambridge University Press, 1988, pp. 3–13.

Pavlich, George, 'The Emergence of Habitual Criminals in 19th Century Britain: Implications for Criminology', *Journal of Theoretical and Philosophical Criminology*, vol. 2, no. 1 (2010), pp. 1–62.

Perkin, Harold, *The Origins of Modern English Society, 1780–1880*, London: Routledge, 1969.

Peters, R. H., 'Political Interference with Police: Is It Something New?' *Police Journal*, vol. 64, no. 2 (Apr. 1991), pp. 96–103.

Petrow, Stefan, *Policing Morals: The Metropolitan Police and the Home Office 1870–1914*, Oxford: Clarendon Press, 1994.

Philips, D., 'A New Engine of Power and Authority: The Institutionalisation of Law Enforcement in England 1780–1830', in V. A. C. Gatrell, Bruce Lehman, and Geoffrey Parker (eds.), *Crime and the Law: The Social History of Crime in Western Europe since 1500*, London: Europa Publications, 1980, pp. 155–89.

Pick, Daniel, *Faces of Degeneration: A European Disorder, c. 1848–c. 1918*, Cambridge: Cambridge University Press, 1989.

Porter, Bernard, *The Origins of the Vigilant State: The London Metropolitan Police Special Branch before the First World War*, London: Weidenfeld and Nicolson, 1987.

Pratt, John, *Governing the Dangerous: Dangerousness, Law and Social Change*, Sydney: Federation Press, 1997.

Priestley, Philip, *Victorian Prison Lives*, London: Methuen, 1985.

Radzinowicz, Leon and Hood, Roger, 'Judicial Discretion and Sentencing Standards: Victorian Attempts to Solve a Perennial Problem', *University of Pennsylvania Law Review*, vol. 127, no. 5 (1978–1979), pp. 1288–349.

Radzinowicz, Leon and Hood, Roger, 'Incapacitating the Habitual Criminal: The English Experience', *Michigan Law Review*, vol. 78, no. 8 (Aug. 1980), pp. 1305–89.

Radzinowicz, Leon and Hood, Roger, *A History of the English Criminal Law and Its Administration from 1750*, vol. 5. *The Emergence of Penal Policy*, London: Stevens and Sons, 1990.

Runciman, W. G., *Different, but Much the Same: The Evolution of English Society since 1714*, Oxford: Oxford University Press, 2015.

Samuel, Raphael, *East End Underworld: The Life of Arthur Harding*, London: Routledge and Kegan Paul, 1981.

Shannon, Richard, *The Age of Disraeli, 1868–1881: The Rise of Tory Democracy*, London and New York: Longman, 1992.

Shannon, Richard, *Gladstone: 1865–1898*, vol. 2, Chapel Hill: North Carolina University Press, 1999.

Shoemaker, Robert B., *The London Mob: Violence and Disorder in Eighteenth Century England*, London: Hambledon, 2004.

Silver, Allan, 'The Demand for Order in a Civil Society: A Review of Some Themes in the History of Urban Crime, Police and Riot', in David Bordua (ed.), *The Police: Six Sociological Essays*, New York: John Wiley and Sons, 1967, pp. 1–24.

Sindall, R., 'The London Garotting Panics of 1856 and 1862', *Social History*, vol. 12, no. 3 (Oct. 1987), pp. 351–9.

Sindall, R., *Street Violence in the Nineteenth Century: Media Panic or Real Danger?* Leicester: Leicester University Press, 1990.

Smith, Phillip, *Policing Victorian London*, London: Greenwood Press, 1985.

Stevenson, S. J., 'The "Habitual Criminal" in Nineteenth-Century England: Some Observations on the Figures', *Urban History*, vol. 13 (May 1986), pp. 37–60.

Storch, Robert D., 'The Plague of Blue Locusts', *International Review of Social History*, vol. 20, no. 1 (Apr. 1975), pp. 61–90.

Storch, Robert D., 'The Policeman as Domestic Missionary: Urban Discipline and Popular Culture in Northern England, 1850–1880', *Journal of Social History*, vol. 9, no. 4 (1976), 481–509.

Taylor, David, 'Beyond the Bounds of Respectable Society', in Julia Rowbotham and Kim Stevenson (eds.), *Criminal Conversations: Victorian Crimes, Social Panic and Moral Outrage*, Columbus: Ohio State University Press, 2005, pp. 3–22.

Taylor, Howard, 'Rationing Crime: The Political Economy of Criminal Statistics since the 1850s', *The Economic History Review*, vol. 51, no. 3 (Aug. 1998), pp. 569–90.

Tebbut, Melanie, *Making Ends Meet: Pawnbroking and Working-Class Credit*, New York: St. Martin's Press, 1983.

Thomas, Donald, *The Victorian Underworld*, London: Hodder & Stoughton, 1998.

Thomas, D. A., *Constraints on Judgement: The Search for Structured Discretion in Sentencing, 1860–1910*, Cambridge: Institute of Criminology Occasional Series No. 4, 1979.

Tobias, J. J., *Crime and Industrial Society in the Nineteenth Century*, London: B. T. Batsford, 1967.

Tomkins, Alannah, 'Pawnbroking and the Survival Strategies of the Urban Poor in 1770s York', in Steven King and Alannah Tomkins (eds.), *The Poor in England 1700–1850: An Economy of Makeshifts*, Manchester: Manchester University Press, 2003, pp. 166–82.

Walkowitz, Judith R., *Prostitution and Victorian Society: Women, Class, and the State*, Cambridge and New York: Cambridge University Press, 1988 (first published 1980).

Weinberger, Barbara, 'The Criminal Class and the Ecology of Crime', *Historical Social Research*, vol. 15, no. 4 (1990), pp. 121–39.

Welshman, John, *Underclass: A History of the Excluded since 1880*, London: Hambledon Continuum, 2006.

Wiener, Martin, review of A. P. Donajgrodzki (ed.), *Social Control in Nineteenth Century Britain*, London: Croom Helm, 1977, *Journal of Social History*, vol. 12, no. 2 (Winter 1978), pp. 314–21.

Wiener, Martin, 'The March of Penal Progress?', *Journal of British Studies*, vol. 26, no. 1 (Jan. 1987), pp. 83–96.

Wiener, Martin, *Reconstructing the Criminal: Culture, Law and Policy in England, 1830–1914*, Cambridge: Cambridge University Press, 1990.

Wiener, Martin, 'Judges v. Jurors: Courtroom Tension in Murder Trials and the Law of Criminal Responsibility in Nineteenth-Century England', *Law and History Review*, vol. 17, no. 3 (Aug. 1999), pp. 467–506.

Wiener, Martin, *Men of Blood: Violence, Manliness and Criminal Justice in Victorian England*, Cambridge and New York: Cambridge University Press, 2004.

Wong, Yue-Chim Richard, 'An Economic Analysis of the Crime Rate in England and Wales, 1857–1892', *Economica*, vol. 62, no. 246 (May 1995), pp. 235–47.

Theses

Davis, Jennifer, 'Law Breaking and Law Enforcement: The Creation of a Criminal Class in Mid-Victorian London', unpublished Ph.D. thesis, Boston College, 1984.

Lees, L., 'Social Change and Social Stability among the London Irish, 1830–1870', unpublished doctoral thesis, Harvard University, 1969.

Stanford, Terence, 'The Metropolitan Police 1850–1914: Targeting, Harassment and the Creation of a Criminal Class', unpublished doctoral thesis, University of Huddersfield, 2007.

Stevenson, S. J., 'The 'Criminal Class' in the Mid-Victorian City: A Study of Policy Conducted with Special Reference to Those Made Subject to the Provisions of 34 & 35 Vict., c.112 (1871) in Birmingham and East London in the Early Years of Registration and Supervision', unpublished doctoral thesis, University of Oxford, 1983.

Tomlinson, Heather, 'Victorian Prisons: Administration and Architecture, 1835–1877', unpublished doctoral thesis, University of London, 1975.

Index

Acts of Parliament *see under the name of individual acts*
Adderley, Sir Charles 67
alias 47, 103
Anthropology 102–3
assizes 125, 143
Australia 2–3, 21–2, 25, 30–1, 33, 38, 43, 58–9

Bailey, Victor 9, 30
Bayley, Adrian 167
Beier, A. L. 14
Bentham, Jeremy 32
Binny, John 21
Bodkin, William 150–1
Booth, Charles 107
Bow Street Runners 36
Browne, Thomas Murray 156
Brougham, Lord 5, 40–1
Bruce, H. A. 25, 53–5, 58, 67–9, 71–2, 83–4, 169
burglary 76, 142

Carnarvon, The Earl of 47, 49, 53, 64, 66, 77–8, 82–3, 116
Carpenter, Mary 22–3
Central Criminal Court 47, 79, 142–3, 146, 150, 152, 163–4
Chambers, Thomas 150, 152, 163
charities 96, 124, 135
Charley, William Thomas 163
children 127
Cleveland, the Duke of 64, 140
clubs 3
Commissions of Inquiry, into
  the Best Means Available for Identifying Habitual Criminals, 1895 88–91, 99, 103–5, 108–9, 111, 116, 148–9, 158, 164, 171
  the Operation of the Acts Relating to Transportation and Penal Servitude, 1863 39, 42, 46–8, 89, 108, 128, 136, 139, 142–3, 145
  the working of the Penal Servitude Acts, 1878–9 96
Conservative Party 8, 16, 38, 41, 46–7, 61, 64–5, 67–8, 70–1, 82–3, 85, 89, 94, 116–17, 123, 129, 139, 144–5, 152–3, 163
conspiracy 69, 90, 125, 148
costermongers 82
Cox, David 4, 11–12, 21, 32, 117, 141, 153
Cox, Edward 145, 150
criminology
  Italian school 101, 159
  Lombroso, Cesare 23, 101–2, 106, 159–60, 165
Crofton, Sir Walter 42–3, 46–7, 52–5, 58–9, 69, 78, 87, 89, 131, 156, 172
Cross, Richard A. 71, 123, 145
Curtis, Richard 148

Davitt, Michael 125
detectives 12, 89, 98
Disraeli, Benjamin 8, 94–5
Du Cane, Sir Edmund 92, 95, 103–4
Duce, Henry 151

East End of London 110, 121, 133
Edlin, Peter 150, 161–2
Erle, Sir William 38, 143

Farrall, Stephen 4, 11–12, 21, 32, 117, 141, 153
felony 50, 55, 64, 68, 75, 140, 143, 145, 153, 159
Fielding, Henry 36
fingerprints 4, 88

Fletcher, John Dunnington 161–2
Foucault, Michel 8, 33
France 1
free will 24
Fulton, Forrest 163

Garotte 3, 5, 37, 44–5, 48, 56–7
Gatrell, V. A. C. 9–10, 159–61, 173
Gladstone, William 1, 6–7, 10, 12–13, 26, 51, 53–5, 60, 62, 72–3, 86–7, 90, 105, 110, 112, 114–15, 120, 137–9, 141, 149, 154, 157, 164–5, 168, 171, 173
Godfrey, Barry 4, 11–12, 21, 32, 117, 141, 153
Goldman, Lawrence 6, 30, 41, 50, 55–7
Gurney, Russell 76, 150, 152

Hall, Charles 163
Harding, Arthur 121, 127, 133, 162
Hastings, George 40, 50, 87
Hawkins, Sir Henry 150, 161
Hay, Douglas 9
Henry, Sir Thomas 77, 91, 120, 148
Herschell, Lord 154
Hill, Frederic 53–4
Hill, Matthew Davenport 35–6, 38–9, 42–4, 49–52, 54, 59, 68–9
Home Office 26, 36, 39, 46, 50, 54, 56, 70, 72–5, 77, 91, 93–5, 97, 102, 104, 107–9, 111–13, 122, 130, 134, 142, 148, 153–5, 159–60, 174
    Criminal Department 93, 107
    Everest, George 108
    Garcia, Colonel 155
    Grace, Mr 104–5, 107
    Liddell, Adolphus 75, 77, 148
    Lushington, Godfrey 93, 112, 153
    Murdoch, Charles 107
    Waddington, Horatio 46, 142
Hood, Roger 7–8, 10–1, 22, 30, 36, 59, 94, 103, 134, 143, 146
Hopwood, Charles 54–5
housebreaking 69, 90
Hynch, Derryn 167

Inwood, Stephen 14
Ireland *and the Irish* 42–3, 46, 50, 59, 63, 109, 125, 156
Italy 36

Jebb, Sir Joshua 43
Johnston, Helen 12–3, 116–17, 174–5
judicial and magisterial discretion 68, 75, 80, 83, 140, 143, 153–4, 165

Kimberley, the Earl of 1, 22, 25, 55, 63–6, 72, 78, 83

Lacombe, Dany 174
larceny 80, 91, 142, 158
Law Amendment Society 40
Liberal Party 1, 5, 25–6, 30, 41, 43–7, 49, 53–4, 63–5, 67, 69–71, 77, 83, 85, 89, 103, 111, 113, 117, 128–9, 140, 145, 152, 168
Liberty 1, 13, 36, 52–3, 61, 67, 70, 83, 119
Licences 29, 31, 34, 36–9, 42–6, 48–50, 52–3, 55–7, 59, 63–5, 69, 73–4, 83–9, 93, 96, 101, 107, 112–13, 115–19, 121, 123, 126, 129, 131, 133–7, 154, 164, 168, 174
Littler, Ralph 156, 161–2
Loveland, Richard Loveland 161–2
Lush, Sir Robert 146

mandatory minimum sentences 48, 50, 55, 63–4, 67
Manning, J. B. 111, 155
manslaughter 158
Martineau, Harriet 22–4
Mayhew, Henry 20–4
Meagher, Jill 167
Metropolitan Police District 2–3, 10, 14, 71, 79, 118, 121–3, 132
Metropolitan Police Force 2, 6, 9–10, 14–15, 26, 38, 46, 61, 63, 70, 72–3, 75–6, 83, 85, 87, 89–90, 92–4, 96–105, 107–9, 111, 112, 118–21, 124–8, 130–3, 136–8, 143, 146, 149, 154, 157, 160, 169–70, 172–4
    Assistant Commissioner James Monro 98, 125, 130–2, 135
    Assistant Commissioner Robert Anderson 130, 137
    Commissioner Edmund Henderson 52–3, 72–5, 77, 93–4, 105, 121–2, 126–7
    Commissioner Sir Richard Mayne 38, 46, 143

Convict Supervision Office 88, 96,
    100–1, 116, 140
  Chief Inspector Neame 97
  Director Howard Vincent 128–30,
    132
  Divisions: Clapham 92, 120; F 76;
    N 75; Southwark 61, 92; Wandsworth
    120; Whitechapel (or H) 77, 92
  Orders 14, 89, 95, 136
  Police Gazette 83, 97, 122
  relations with working class 13–14,
    127, 137, 170
  Scotland Yard 88, 90, 94–5
Middlesex Sessions 79, 143, 150–1, 156,
  161–4
Mill, John Stuart 40
misdemeanours 69, 79, 90, 92, 113, 143,
  146, 169
Mission Refuge 130
moral panic 5–6, 26, 44–5, 56, 168, 171,
  173
murder 121, 158, 167
Murdoch, Lydia 81

National Reformatory Union 40

Pakington, Sir John 144
penal policy 41, 46–7, 50, 59, 167, 171–2,
  174
Penal Servitude Acts 39, 42, 45–7, 49–50,
  54, 64–5, 70, 83, 96, 124, 127–8,
  145, 153
Petrow, Stefan 9–12, 40, 56, 62, 88, 101,
  110, 113, 117, 140–1
photography 77, 84–5, 87, 89–91, 93,
  97–8, 102, 111, 148
Pilkington, James 3, 44, 46
poverty 25, 152
Prentice, Samuel 161–2
press, the 20, 29, 44, 45, 58, 61, 66, 68, 70,
  73, 78, 132
  All the Year Round 44
  Daily News 3, 18, 57, 71, 75
  Illustrated London News 44
  Lloyd's Weekly Newspaper 57
  Morning Post 57, 71, 92
  Pall Mall Gazette 61, 71
  Standard 18, 37, 57, 144
  Times 3, 5, 14, 18–19, 23, 37, 48, 56–8,
    60, 68, 78, 95, 131, 144, 156, 159, 163

Prevention of Crimes Act, 1879 132, 137,
  140, 164, 170
Prevention of Crimes Amendment Act
  1876 8
prisons
  Brixton Prison 118
  Clerkenwell Prison 135
  Holloway Prison 98–9, 105–6
  Millbank Prison 32, 118
  panopticon 32
  penitentiary 32–4, 145, 153, 171
  Pentonville Prison 32, 111, 155
  Prisons Committee: Report from
    the Departmental Committee on
    Prisons, 1895 127, 155, 170
  Wormwood Scrubs Prison 135
prostitution 17, 20, 33, 174–5
public opinion 14, 20–1, 29, 44

Radzinowicz, Leon 7–8, 10–1, 22, 30, 36,
  59, 94, 103, 134, 143, 146
receivers of stolen goods 64–6, 69, 75, 77,
  84, 158
reformation 34, 42, 52, 67, 129–31, 135,
  156
religion 6, 43
respectability 8, 24, 26, 40, 71, 76, 128
Romilly, Lord 32, 64, 66
rookery 2, 81, 109
Royal Society for the Assistance of
  Discharged Prisoners 96, 124,
  135
Russell, Lord John 41

Select Committees
  on the Pawnbrokers Bill, 1872 66, 76
  on the Present State of Discipline in
    Gaols and Houses of Corrections,
    1862 47, 49, 140
  on Transportation, 1856 21, 37–40, 143
Sheil, John 156
social control 63, 80, 85–6, 119, 165, 171,
  173
Social Science Association 6, 29, 50–5, 58,
  60, 68, 87, 168–9
spying and surveillance, *including popular
  attitudes towards* 13–14, 115, 117,
  119, 133–4
St Giles Christian Mission 135
Standford, Terence 14, 98, 136

Stedman Jones, Gareth 2
Stevenson, S. J. 14–5, 82, 109–13

Taylor, Howard 14
ticket-of-leave 31, 37, 42, 46, 48–9, 59, 118, 126
Tory Party 41, 47, 64
transportation 2–3, 17–18, 21–2, 25, 30–4, 38–40, 42–3, 53, 57–9, 62–3, 67, 70–1, 139, 141–3, 168, 172

Vigilance Association for the Defence of Personal Rights 40
violence 3, 25, 44, 46, 144, 152, 160

Whig Party 20, 32, 34
whiggism 7, 10
Wiener, Martin 4, 8–9, 32, 50, 134, 165
women 7, 40–2, 68, 115, 118, 129, 156
Woodhouse, William 149

www.ingramcontent.com/pod-product-compliance
Lightning Source LLC
Chambersburg PA
CBHW070638300426

44111CB00013B/2160